Shiny Side Up

From First Ride to Fast Rider

Andrew Goodman

www.shiny-side-up.net

We recognise that some words, model names, and designations mentioned in this book are the property of the trademark holder. We use them only for identification purposes.

WARNING: Riding motorcycles is inherently dangerous and can result in serious injury or death. The author and the publisher disclaim any liability incurred in connection with the use of the techniques and concepts described in this book. Ride within your personal limits. Always wear a helmet and protective riding gear, and observe the speed limit.

Copy Editor: Michael Scott

Cover Photo: Dave Kneen

Cover Design: Dejan Jovanovic

.

ISBN: 978-1-9161574-1-5

Dedicated with Love to Tansy, Georgiana and Mabel.

CONTENTS

PREFACE

You live more in five minutes on a bike like that,
going flat out, than some people in a lifetime.

-   Burt Munro

My first ride on a motorcycle was back in the 1990s. I was offered a pillion ride to university by my classmate, John[1] . What followed was an eye-watering blur of speed and adrenaline. Perched on the tiny back seat of his lime green Kawasaki ZXR400, I clung on for dear life. Sixty intense seconds later, having broken countless traffic laws, I dismounted, legs wobbling and stepped into the lecture theatre.

I spent that lecture revisiting the thrill I had just experienced. Something was born in me that day. A seed was planted. That seed took a while to germinate, and it was several years before I got my own licence and a bike of my own, but once the idea was born in me, I knew somehow, someway I was going to learn to ride. And so I did.

Twenty-odd years later and I'm older, and wiser, with a few more grey hairs. My lifestyle has changed a great deal – but I still love riding motorcycles as much as I ever have.

Throughout those years, my relationship with motorcycles has remained fresh, exciting, and adventurous. My two wheeled adventure has been deeply personal. Yours will be too; taking you down the fun avenues that you choose to explore. You will discover new friends along the way, and some of your old friends will move away. As you test yourself both mentally and physically, you will learn from the consequences of your actions, and eventually come to trust your supreme judgement above all others.

---

[1] John went on to become a Health and Safety Consultant

Becoming a biker will increase your mental fortitude.

Through riding, you will come to learn who you are, what you are made of, and why motorcycling matters more than ever in the 21st Century, and why it should be celebrated for the wondrous activity that it is.

This book has been many years in the making. The idea came to me after a particularly emphatic ride. I returned in such appreciation that I felt a very strong urge to share my enthusiasm for a hobby which has given me so much over the years with as many people as possible, that others might also have as much fun.

I started writing down what I had learned; how I approach the activities in the best frame of mind to extract the best results out of them. This is what I want for you, and this is why I have written this book; that others might choose to embark on the lifelong journey. I want you to get into motorbikes as deeply and as richly as you choose, to experience the thrill of life on two wheels, to live the full rich life you came here to live. Motorcycles are awesome. You're going to have so much fun.

I hope you enjoy reading the book as much as I have enjoyed writing it.

Andrew
April 2019

HOW TO GET THE MOST FROM THIS BOOK

It is not my intention that this book tells you what to do. If you were going on holiday, and I gave you an itinerary of where you would go and what you would see, it would take all the fun out of your trip. You might even ponder the point of going in the first place, if you knew what was going to happen before you got there.

Your life is an adventure, but only you can decide how much fun and excitement you will have along the way, and how things will play out. It is my intention to make you aware of the fundamentals of being a motorcycle owner and rider; the ground rules if you will, so that you can find your feet, discover your own path, and ride with a greater level of confidence and success from the get-go. It all starts and ends with you; your bike, your skills and most important of all, your attitude.

Who will find this Book Useful?

I would consider this book essential reading for anyone who wants to get onto two wheels: whether you are a teenager and brand new to motorbikes; or wanting to refresh your skills after a few years away; or find yourself looking for an exciting, fresh new hobby in your retirement. You may have been shaken up by a recent crash, and feel there are more questions than there are answers to those questions. If so this book will help you answer those questions. This book holds something valuable for everyone.

It is said that we don't really learn much from reading books. We learn most effectively through doing things and living our lives. I agree with this view, but the fact remains that books are condensed wisdom, and immensely useful at pointing out what we have experienced, after the fact, to help us process and make better sense of life, which can help us to consolidate our learning experience.

With this in mind, regard this book as an accompaniment to your riding progression, and refer to it as often as you see fit. It will give you many insights into your riding experiences as you grow in confidence, make your own mistakes and learn from them.

It will take a while for this material to sink in. Don't worry if it doesn't mean much to you on the first reading. I have laid out this book in a logical order, and while I recommend reading it in its entirety, you can delve into the book wherever you see value.

Chapters can be read in isolation and treated as reference material prior to the following activities: buying a motorcycle; attending a track day; touring; servicing your bike at home; or starting to commute by motorcycle.

I am a Chartered Mechanical Engineer by profession. As I come from a technical background, I have explained the physics behind some technical elements of motorcycle dynamics.

I have kept the mathematical equations to a minimum and only included 'techno-babble' where I feel it adds value or clarity. This material should be accessible to anyone with a basic grasp of physics, and an interest in motorcycles. And if you're reading this, that means you!

In this book I will share with you what I've discovered about motorbikes from years of buying, riding, crashing and fixing them largely thanks to my constantly questioning mind. I will also share some of the simple concepts that I use to have fun and stay safe out on the roads.

I hope to show you a way of seeing the world from behind the handlebars where you are steering your bike on a course and speed that feels comfortable to you, and where you needn't fear anything to do with motorcycles, where the edge is as sharp or as blunt as you like it to be, so that motorcycles can become a real joy in your life right from the very beginning. I hope that your foray into the sport becomes a life-long passion, which will provide you with decades of enjoyment and personal growth.

How this Book is Laid Out

Besides the usual tips and tricks, this book delves into the significance of rider attitude, the importance of effective focus, and specific techniques to use your *rider instinct* to steer you clear of potential trouble. If you take anything away from this book, I hope it is this: Your frame of mind and mental attitude towards riding motorcycles is key. If every time you ride, you are in a good mood, you're very unlikely to have any mishaps whatsoever[2].

I cover the technology of motorcycle engines, the types of motorcycle available, and how to track down and buy the right bike at the right price.

Once you have bought yourself a bike, I will cover setting it up and

---

[2] While I have no evidence to back up this claim, I have found it to be the case in my own personal experience, and my observations of others'

customising it to suit you, as well as how to perform routine maintenance tasks that will help you get to know your motorcycle properly.

The chapter on motorcycle rider equipment will help you find the most appropriate gear, and we will discuss grip in detail; how tyres work, and finding the right tyres for your bike.

There are chapters on how to approach the different riding environments, from commuting, track day riding and touring, to riding in winter and other adverse weather conditions.

Along with the technical sections, I have included a great deal of my own personal opinion on the various subjects covered. I make no apologies for being opinionated. It is not possible for anyone to write an unbiased account of anything. Even if it were possible, it would make pretty dull reading. So remember that this book is only my opinion, it is not fact, so please don't take any of it too seriously.

It is my intention to be deliberately upbeat about motorcycles. A motorcycle ambassador, if you like. I want to encourage as many people as possible to learn to ride, and to develop precise control of their machines and their minds so they can achieve whatever they want out of the sport.

If you want to read a book about the dangers of motorcycles, including graphic pictures of what happens when things go wrong, you will find such things exist also. But you will find such material neither enjoyable nor helpful to your intention to ride and have fun and stay safe.

It's true, of course, bad things do happen to bikers. The most important question is, do you want them to happen to you? If you entertain these kinds of thoughts you will eventually come across the same in your life. Focus on what you want, and you will eventually get there.

My comments on riding technique and personal attitude come out of my personal experience on to wheels; it is a system that works for me. Please do not read this book as a list of instructions that you must follow in order to chart a successful path on two wheels. Please accept the spirit of the words I offer, and where they have taken me, and develop your own confidence in your understanding and your ability.

I am not interested in telling you what to do. Naturally I want you to understand the basics, and to go on to develop your own set of skills and experience; tools which complement your attitude and riding style, and help you to achieve what you want to achieve out of biking.

Whether you want to stand on the top of the podium at the Isle of Man TT, or just feel supremely confident riding to work every day in all seasons. You have supreme guidance at your disposal, and you can learn to apply it to your riding.

This book is based upon my experience of riding in the UK and Europe, but the concepts are just as relevant to the rest of the world; anywhere with a decent level of road infrastructure and reasonable driving standards. Road laws do vary from continent to continent, however, so make sure you are up to speed with local driving laws where you live.

The book is split into three broad sections:

- Section 1: The Basics
- Section 2: You and Your Bike
- Section 3: Riding

If you're ready, let's get started on the basics.

SECTION 1: THE BASICS

1. WHY LEARN TO RIDE?

Unless you try to do something beyond what you
have already mastered, you will never grow...

-   Ralph Waldo Emerson

Once upon a time, when cars had real style, motorway service stations were considered 'haute cuisine' and choosing a car with the best 'crash protection' meant buying the one with the longest bonnet, the world was a simpler, more carefree place to live.

Life was much worse that it is presently, but people had no idea. Back in the 1970s now was great, but it was continually getting better.

Parents threw their children into the back seat of their cars and went on their way. Those same children played merrily in largely empty streets, spoke kindly to strangers, and would happily disappear for hours at a time without fear of upsetting their parents.

Most still lived in something of a bubble; blissful in their ignorance to the dangers of life, with a childlike enthusiasm. Newly liberated adults explored sexuality and sensuality fully. They hitch-hiked into dangerous and unexplored corners of the planet, mainly because they didn't appreciate the dangers they might find when they got there. What they found was adventure, a new perspective, and a sense that the world is full of good-natured people going about the business of living their lives.

Now fast-forward 40 years, and things have changed. All of the baby boomers have grown up. They've had their fun, smoked their pot (and the rest), read the communist manifesto, sobered up (or died of their excesses) and now they're running the show.

The world has changed, information is everywhere, and most of it appears to be bad. If you believe everything the media tells you, you'll probably see the world as a rather scary place with untold danger lurking around every corner.

24 hour news channels reach to the far corners of the world to find what little doom and gloom exists and broadcast it directly into our sitting rooms. We feel guarded, and withdraw a little from the adventure of life. In trying to protect ourselves from dying, we actually forget to live.

Even in a society like this, there are people who are still very clear about who they are, and about what they want to be, do and have. Having taken all of the small print warnings into account, they still choose to participate fully. They sense that they have come to Planet Earth to have a fun time, to live their lives as fully as possible, not to shrink away from any kind of risk and missing out on all of the fun.

They would rather risk their lives exercising their freedom to choose, than to be safe and sound indoors, wrapped up in cotton wool. These pure souls join the military, they become freelance musicians, they skydive, they ride horses, they fly helicopters, they ride motorcycles.

They want to experience life, not just as bystanders, but as full-blown participants. They want to experience the visceral thrill of life, and they are prepared to put up with the consequences.

Bikers fall squarely into this category. Of course people get injured and sometimes killed riding motorcycles, just as there are people who die of stress related heart attacks on the train to work, or by choking on a large mouthful of steak after one too many glasses of red wine.

There are untold ways that people choose to exit life, we're all going to die eventually, the real question is *what do you want to do before you get there?* What separates bikers from the masses is a deeper calling from within, a voice which shouts "I want to live my life and I want to live it fully!"

My own personal call to action came when I was in my early twenties. Even though my parents had always expressed concern and begged me never to go anywhere near motorbikes, I went against their wishes and learned to ride anyway.

I spent my youth attempting to jump my Raleigh Chopper over home-made plywood ramps, but I never gave motorcycles much thought growing up, as my parents had blasted me with such disapproval at the merest mention of the subject.

I also grew up as a sensitive child surrounded by people who made it quite clear that things would work out better for me if I followed their advice. They trained me well, and for a while it worked out well for them, but not so well for me.

I became very good at being an obedient son who put others' wishes ahead of my own. I reached a place where my own desires didn't matter anymore. I took all of my cues from the outside world. I was obsessed with what other people thought of me, and I had no real sense of who I was, or what I wanted out of life.

As I started my career, and forged my own path in life, I was earning my own money, living away from home, and making my own decisions. It slowly dawned on me that I was responsible for my life, and that nobody else was going to help any longer. I was on my own, and if I was going to start to build up a sense of self-confidence, I was going to have to start making my own choices in life, and learning from the consequences of those choices. I also realised that I could choose whatever I wanted, and I answered to nobody else.

Living in the South-East of England in the early 2000s, commuting by car to work was starting to take its toll on my health. Every morning I awoke at 5am to beat the traffic, only to end up sitting in endless traffic jams on the London orbital. On the way home from work I would struggle to stay awake at the wheel.

One day, sitting in stationary traffic on the M25 between Leatherhead and Guildford, a motorcycle filtered past at speed nearly clipping my wing mirror. It was bright blue, shiny and beautiful and in that moment I thought, "How I would love to be that person moving through the traffic jam".

I made a decision, then and there, that I was going to learn to ride and get myself a motorbike. As soon as the decision was made, things started to fall into place. Before long I was obsessed and couldn't get the idea out of my head. I devoured all the motorcycle reading material I could get my hands on.

Learning about motorcycles was such fun and a total breath of fresh air to me. It was a completely new subject. I knew nobody else who rode motorcycles. The subject was exciting and felt good to think about. I didn't understand at the time, but what I sensed in my gut was the excitement and satisfaction that lay ahead. Looking back on nearly 20 years on two wheels, I can see why I was excited about the prospect of leaning to ride.

If you're just starting out, or even if you're considering getting a bike, let me tell you, you're in for a treat. If you have decided that you want to learn to ride, you've really got no choice but to do it, or you will never be truly happy. In life we must follow our dreams or face the misery of unfulfilled desires.

Think of your relationship with motorcycles as just that, a long-term, good-feeling relationship that will get deeper and more satisfying as it develops. There's no rush, you will end up where you want to be, eventually. Stop rushing, and start enjoying the journey! Set aside some cash, and start dreaming.

The early days of biking are wonderful; so full of sensation that they stick with you forever. Like falling in love with someone who you know is very special to you, your senses are heightened. You feel immense appreciation, you feel excited about what is to come.

There are many highlights; the smell of a bike's exhaust fumes; the aroma of a new helmet; researching and buying your first leather jacket and jeans; your first ride on a full-size bike (when you realise what all the fuss is about); the day you hand over a pile of cash and ride off on your first motorbike; the feeling of freedom that accompanies riding; even the first time you come off your bike and realise that it's not the end of the world. These events will stay with you for life, and you will revisit them fondly for many years to come, because they have made you who you are.

Motorbikes represent personal freedom; freedom to choose in a world which seems determined to legislate and control our every action. Motorcycles represent adventure and excitement; when you're out in the elements, drawing in deep breaths of fresh air, feeling the cold on your chest and the warmth of the sun on your back, you are connected to life at a level that few have experienced or ever will.

Many people don't understand motorbikes, and they have no desire to either. More fool them. From their position of ignorance, they may try to warn you of the dangers. Many have their reasons; some of them wanted to ride but never grew the balls to go and do it, others have seen friends and loved ones killed and seriously injured.

Even so, the simple fact is that your life is far more likely to be claimed by cancer, heart disease or obesity-related illness than a road traffic accident. The highest cause of death for men younger than 40 is suicide.

Life is Risky

We live in strange times. Decades of collectivism and the gradual yet incessant growth of the state have left Western societies looking outside of themselves for guidance. Self-responsibility is in short supply.

Governments now perform as many functions as they can persuade the people to outsource to them; from welfare to public services to safety watchdogs. As governments take on more responsibility, individuals are left with less. People blame everybody but themselves for their lot in life; their poverty, their obesity and all manner of failures are apparently the fault of someone else.

In response to a general lack of backbone, governments have stepped in. Their aim is to reduce the risk of harm. In so doing they hamper society's freedom. Instead of being allowed out into the world to live the exciting, adventurous pioneering lives they dreamed of as children, all activities that carry risk are banned or at best heavily discouraged.

People either accept the restrictions to their freedom and in their depression eat, drink and drug themselves to numb the pain of their unfulfilled lives, or they rebel and take matters into their own hands.

The number of individuals killed on UK roads may be lower than at any time in the past, but I guarantee that people are still dying every year; they are just finding different ways to do it.

Medicine is at its most evolved state. One might imagine that by the early 21st Century, that medicine would have found cures to all of the world's diseases, and yet the number of diseases grows year on year. When you consider what dis-ease is, and where it originates, it all makes perfect sense.

Unhappy people get sick. They exist in states of worry, guilt, fear, anger and depression, and their negative frame of mind eventually takes its toll on their mind and body; their emotional dis-ease eventually shows up as physical disease.

The doctors, by the way, are unlikely to make this correlation because happy people don't go to the doctor very often, and so don't tend to show up in their study groups or statistics. You are far more likely to live a long happy healthy life by pleasing yourself, and doing things that you want to do, and never mind what anyone else thinks about it.

You are the only person who can create a satisfying life for yourself. Well-meaning onlookers may care greatly about you, but they are busy enough running their own lives to give you any serious attention, and this is a good thing. Everybody needs to learn how to follow their own internal guidance; what a good idea feels like, and what a bad idea feels like. They only learn which is which, by making decisions and seeing how they turn out.

I didn't know it then, but my rebellion, which brought me closer to motorcycles, was only the very beginning of my journey to understanding who I was, and what I wanted out of life. I am still on that path, but I'm glad I made the decision to start doing what I wanted, rather than following other people's ideas of what my life should be.

Life is about quality, not quantity. Is living 25 years of the most exciting, far-out, explorative, adventurous life worse than hanging on for dear life until 100, hiding away from the world in fear and worry? There's no right or wrong way, but I know which I would rather choose.

For everyone killed and seriously injured on the roads, there are many more who never have any issues. In my opinion, people die when they are ready to; either when things aren't working out the way they expected, and it's not likely that they are going to find their path back to their dreams, or they have lived all of the life they want to live, done all they came here to do, and their work here is done. Life is very deliberate; both the means and location of entry, and the means and timing of exit.

I encourage you to see your life a bit like a theme park. There are an infinite number of amusements for you to participate in, to the depth and detail that interests you. You can leave at any time you choose, but as long as you are entertained by whatever you are focusing upon, you will choose to remain. As soon as you have had enough of the amusements for whatever reason, you will decide to leave and find something else to give your attention to. And so it is with life.

In living your life as fully as you choose, engaging with subjects which interest you, you are more likely to be happy and engaged in your life, and therefore more likely to hang around for longer in a happier, healthier state of mind.

My Grandfather Frank is 95 and still driving around. He holidays in Australia every other year and is as sharp as a tack. I asked him the secret of his success. He told me three things:

1. Don't hang around with old people
2. Exercise your body
3. Always have something to look forward to.

On the basis of his recommendations, I think learning to ride could be the perfect way to prolong your life. It keeps the mind and body young, is a form of gentle exercise to keep the body active, and there is always a great deal to look forward to.

What Kinds of People Ride Motorcycles?

Motorcycles are becoming more popular than ever, but they are certainly not mainstream transportation. Not yet anyway. I suspect this will change in the future when driverless cars remove any sense of fun from personal transport and people seek alternatives. Motorbikes still appeal to people who see themselves as different from the crowd.

Riding motorbikes is a physical activity, so motorcycles appeal to more robust individuals than they do to bookworm types. Bikers are more often than not strong, rugged, outdoorsy types, with practical grainy hands.

If you have a good feel for the physical side of life, good hand-eye coordination, a good sense of timing, are good with your hands, play a musical instrument, prefer walking in the countryside to reading books, prefer dancing to watching a film about other people dancing, would rather drive a car in real life than play a driving computer game, motorbikes will be right up your street.

Travelling around on public transport is like being in the armed forces; the rules are stricter, and it doesn't take much thought to get by, as pretty much everything is decided for you, including the timetables and the rules. You will find yourself moving along with all the other 'troops', down well-established paths. The price you pay for this security is a relative lack of freedom to make your own decisions about where you go and when you get there.

If public transport is like being in the army, riding a motorcycle is more like being self-employed; you have much more freedom about how fast you travel, and where you go, but far less security, too. You also need to be able to focus effectively to make a success of it.

Which mode of transport you prefer depends upon your personality, your sense of adventure, and ultimately how independent a soul you are.

There is something hardwired into every human being, before it is talked out them by worrisome parents (who had it talked out of them), about the desire to explore life; to accept the great stability and solid basis of life, and to participate fully, enjoying the excitement of living now, experiencing life in its most evolved state ever.

Motorcycles are just one example of how the present moment represents the culmination of all that went before, it is literally the best that life has ever been, and it's all here for your enjoyment and pleasure. Don't listen to the media, they just want to sell papers. Buy yourself a motorcycle magazine and start dreaming.

Consider the motorcycle as the modern-day horse, and the biker as a modern-day cowboy. Horses and motorcycles are both thrilling and nerve-wracking at first, both require skill and concentration to perform well, and both will punish a rider with a bad attitude, but once you put in the initial effort and crack it, you're on your way.

Some people ride for practicality's sake, others for the adrenaline rush. Some love the thrill of competitive motorsport, and pushing themselves to the edge of their abilities and sometimes beyond. Most bikers enjoy having a fun and engaging hobby which combines travel, internal-combustion engines, speed, excitement and comradeship.

How you choose to participate is up to you. Make your own way and pick and choose the things that most take your fancy.

2. THE LEADING EDGE

Over the last century, since the first inspired person bolted an internal-combustion engine to a bicycle, motorbikes have evolved from the cheapest means of long distance travel into two-wheeled technological marvels.

They encompass the leading edge in automotive technology, and improvements in reliability, lower manufacturing costs, and a growing consumer market have brought down costs, and increased choice.

Motorbikes are accessible to more of the world's population than ever before. Anyone from lorry mechanics to lawyers, scientologists to millionaire playboys can swing a leg over a motorbike, turn the key, thumb the starter button and ride off into the sunset.

Life is about more

The public highways of Britain grow busier, increasingly congested with traffic, as governments seek to raise revenue by penalising the 'crime' of going too fast. Even so, high performance motorcycles prevail, and it's a jolly good thing they do. Motorcycles seem to represent the last bastion of freedom of choice in a world which has gone crazy trying to protect itself from its own stupidity.

Of course, lawmakers know that laws which restrict personal freedom are dangerous things, likely to incite a violent backlash. They know what people inherently understand; that in Britain laws were created to protect the people, but not from themselves. Our common law system came out of real disputes which required resolving, not some intellectual's bright idea about how life could be better.

We have all known, since we were very little, that we are born free; free to live our lives as we choose, so long as we don't harm anyone else in the process. Indeed, unless we feel that we are free, we will never be happy. If we feel that our freedom is being restricted, in any way whatsoever, we tend to lash out, to try to regain a sense of our own power. Laws reducing personal freedom tend to have the opposite effect to that desired. They tend to make people misbehave even more.

We are here on earth to explore life; to advance life, to move things forward, and evolve the leading-edge to a new plane. Bikers don't just want to be moving along the road in a bus driven by someone else, we don't even want to be driving a car, we want to experience the delicious thrill of riding a motorcycle.

Life holds so many wonderful subjects to explore. In the process of exploring each new subject, we gain a fresh perspective on the world, expand our awareness of life, and keep ourselves young at heart. For many bikers, a quiet life is not an option. We have little choice but to blaze our trail, not someone else's, our very own individual path. We do not accept the well-meaning cautionary tales; we want to experience life on the leading edge, we want to be in control of our lives, and never mind the consequences.

When we start out riding, we have a sense of what we are getting ourselves into. But over the years, in practicing the sport that we come to love, we are reminded of a greater truth; that life is about having a fun journey, it is not just a means to an end. In fact, the destination exists purely as our excuse to take that journey in the first place.

Riding motorcycles is as much a metaphor for life as anything I can think of. If we pay attention, it can teach us a great deal about ourselves. Riding is about enjoying the beautiful vistas along the way, and the not so beautiful vistas. Riding is about acknowledging the seasons, the natural contrasts of hot and cold, light and dark, grip and lack of grip, power and vulnerability.

Motorcycles are life affirming as they bring the inherent contrast of the world to our direct immediate attention; rather than placing you in a protective, air-conditioned box where nothing can harm you; they thrust you, naked and vulnerable, into the world. There's no time to check your phone whilst riding a motorcycle; you either focus on the task at hand, or your life will come to an abrupt end.

But biking isn't just a massive hair-blowing-back experience. It's about exploring the world and seeing what it has to show us. It's about getting out there and discovering who we are. It's about being cold and wet, and therefore appreciating the marvel of a modern centrally heated home. It's about bursts of intense focus, and the down time afterwards. It's about pushing ourselves further than we thought we ever could, both mentally and physically, and becoming a more interesting, more rounded person as a result.

The car driver struggles to stay awake at the wheel of his smooth, quiet, electronically steered box; unable to see the road ahead for all of the increased 'crash protection' in his way, and so bored that he would rather play with his phone than drive his car.

The biker meanwhile has no such problems feeling engaged. He is out in the elements, and from his panoramic viewpoint, the smells and sounds of the world assault his senses. He knows that he is alive, he can feel it. He is also acutely aware that he is the master of his own destiny, and that this privilege, this responsibility, is not taken lightly.

When we are alone in the saddle, feeling the exquisite sense of control that only a biker experiences, we are elevated above the mundane details of life. The intense focus required to ride well distracts us from our worrisome thoughts, and allows us to return to a true sense of peace, one we may not have experienced since we first learned to ride a bicycle, but one that we relish returning to again and again.

Views of nature in the great outdoors bring us back to our quiet, centred state of mind, and remind us that life is good, and so are we. Motorcycles elevate the rider to a frame of mind to experience being in the moment. No mental chatter. No worries. Just you, the bike and the road ahead.

We all talk too much. Sometimes it's better to drop the chat, and go for a ride. Motorcycles are easy to appreciate, easy to love. In the saddle, we marvel at the magnificence of the motorcycle; our sense of power and control, and our freedom to go wherever we choose to. We relish the thrill of speed and the forces of accelerating and braking. We wonder at how clever human beings are; managing to create such amazing contraptions from products that we have essentially dug out of the ground.

Own your Life

Our world is moving away from individual responsibility and deeper into a blame culture, as people look to the state to support them in their increasing disempowerment. People even blame the government for failing to protect them from perfectly foreseeable events that they themselves could have prevented with a little effort.

This 'victim' mentality is the mindset of the loser. If you are going to be a successful biker, I would encourage you to steer well clear of this pathetic, groveling, mindset as it will bring your dreams to shipwreck quicker than you can form them.

Ask yourself; "How do winners think, speak and act?" They certainly don't apologise for themselves, nor blame anyone else for their shortcomings. They take full responsibility for their own successes and their own failures.

This is important, because if you are in charge, then you can do something about the situation you are in. The victim meanwhile, is a lost man, going nowhere, as he waits for someone else to give him permission to succeed. Sadly permission will never be granted. Once you have accepted that you are at the whim and mercy of another, you will never succeed at your endeavours.

Your attitude towards biking is paramount. More important even than the bike you ride, the gear you wear, and even your skills and training. By taking responsibility for your life – starting right now – you put yourself in the position where you are in charge of what you can control (your thoughts and your actions), whilst you ignore the things you can't (other people and their opinions, thoughts and actions), and you get on with building your successful career on two wheels.

This is your life, and you are calling the shots, but unless you know that you are, and act accordingly, you won't be very effective at it. You have everything you need to get exactly where you want to go. We will cover the winner's mindset more in Section Three.

3. THE EARLY DAYS

The early days of any new hobby are the stuff that dreams are made of. Whether you are in your teens, or your mid-seventies, if you haven't yet stepped into the world of motorcycles with both feet, you are in for a serious treat. Before we get going, let's make sure we've got the basics down.

The laws regarding licensing requirements for motorcyclists differ from country to country. If you live somewhere where you aren't required to pass a formal proficiency test before taking to the roads, I would still encourage you to find a competent instructor and get some tuition. Motorbikes are powerful tools, which can easily become destructive in the hands of a poorly trained operator, so it pays to know what you're doing.

Test Passed - Licence in Hand

So, you've taken a riding course and got your licence? Great! What's next? If you have passed your motorcycle test, you have reached the minimum standard acceptable to allow you out onto public roads on your own.

That certificate you are holding in your hands doesn't mean that you are a great rider, or even a good one. It means that you have demonstrated, at least for the duration of the test, that you have the potential *not to be a liability to yourself and others*. You are just at the beginning of your journey.

Learning to ride is an incremental process; whether riding down the shops on a sunny day or commuting in the winter in the rain, every outing is an opportunity to build upon your skills.

When you have just passed your test, consider yourself an absolute beginner. Don't sit back and do nothing, buy yourself a motorbike (see chapter 7) and some decent protective gear and a shiny new helmet, and get out on the roads and start riding.

As you consolidate your training, and grow more comfortable in the saddle, questions will naturally arise. As you make mistakes or find yourself out of your comfort zone, don't look to blame others, take responsibility for yourself and ask yourself "what could I have done better?".

You will find the answers come in books, magazines, on the web, and from fellow riders who have been there and done that. Apply the answers which come to your riding technique and your attitude, and gradually build up your confidence and expertise.

Life is learned through experience. There is no substitute for getting out there and riding. Not buying another book, not watching motorbike racing, and not spending money on that gorgeous titanium exhaust you've been lusting after for months. If you want to improve your riding, you need time in the saddle.

Early Worries

It is natural to be apprehensive in the early days of any activity, especially one that has a sharp edge to it, like riding motorbikes. You may feel that you don't know all the rules, that you are an outsider, and out of your comfort zone.

Never fear, bikers are a friendly bunch, and many will be giving you appreciative nods as you pass them by on the road, as well as friendly advice when you stop for a cup of tea and a slice of cake. You will feel part of the club soon enough.

You may also feel a bit nervous about being allowed out on to the roads on your own. We are trained to be goal-oriented and feel comfortable as long as we have something to aim for. We have a test or an exam to pass, but once we have jumped over that particular hurdle, we often feel at a loose end. What next?

The exhilaration of having passed the test is often replaced with a feeling of trepidation as the full impact of what we have done hits home. After the initial exhilaration of personal freedom passes, thoughts of the big bad world, of traffic accidents and increased vulnerability, may start to creep into your mind. You aren't pleasing your instructor anymore, and you don't have their careful, experienced eye to look out for you as you ride. You are in charge now, out there on your own, and responsible for the consequences of your own actions. You also know the consequences can be fatal.

To avoid getting buyer's remorse, tell yourself that you will progress at a rate that you're happy with, and crack on with your apprenticeship. You may not know it, but you are standing at a critical stage, a stage that many would-be bikers never pass. Many gain their licence to ride, but never get round to buying a bike and becoming a biker.

Don't pause for breath. Take the money that you've been saving up (you have been saving up, haven't you?) and buy yourself a second-hand bike.

The best thing you can do in the early days is to set yourself another goal, to progress your rider development. When I started out, I found commuting to work a perfect excuse to keep things moving along in the right direction. After six months of commuting in all weathers, riding felt as natural to me as walking.

When I started out, I deliberately hit the ground running. I had grown tired of sitting in traffic jams. I valued my sleep more than I valued the warmth and comfort of my car, so I sought a more time-efficient way to get to work.

The Direct Access course was booked and passed, and bike licence in hand, I went out and bought myself a little Suzuki SV650 and started riding to work. For the next 18 months I rode my bike to work every day, even when it snowed. I racked up 30,000 miles, before buying myself another bike and covering another 50,000 miles in the next three years.

Those early years laid the foundation for my biking experience, and I was grateful to have the fun of riding daily. I don't mind admitting it was nerve-wracking at first, but I knew I had to do it every day, to train my muscles to react in the correct ways; to master counter-steering, and have each hand and foot doing its own thing. It was invaluable training, a great beginning and end to the working day, and it cemented in the good habits I had learned from my instructor on my training course.

I have had a few spills along the way, but nothing serious, a few scuffed panels on the bike and on my leathers. The falls I did have, and each near miss with a car, caused me to question my riding, and tweak my technique or attitude to the other road users.

As time went on, I improved my road awareness and my ability to focus. As my confidence grew, my road craft improved too, making me not only a better rider, but a better driver too. The most important lessons were learned in situations where I got into trouble. Hindsight following accidents and incidents taught me the importance of getting my head into the right place before setting off for a ride.

The 'Click'

It was a gradual learning process, but after a few months of daily riding I gradually came to trust in my own ability. I had a good handle on the basics and had grown comfortable with machine control. It was as though I could step back from the situation and observe myself riding, rather than being so completely immersed in the experience that I had no awareness of anything outside of the immediate task at hand. I started to breathe more deeply, my shoulders and arms started to relax and I became much more aware of what was going on around me.

Feelings of fear and tension were replaced with a feeling of elation. It was then that I understood what motorcycles are about, and why riding motorbikes is most definitely for me. It's hard to explain to anyone who hasn't experienced it, but the blend of power, control and sensual feedback is sublime.

I also realised that the many other road users out there weren't trying to kill me after all, they were just going about their business, and just didn't consider me their number-one priority. I stopped being my own worst enemy, and found myself gliding effortlessly through traffic in perfect harmony with the other road users.

Give yourself at least six months to get into it. I promise it will be worth it when you do. Ride as often as you can, setting yourself challenges if you need to. The more experience you get, the more quickly you will feel comfortable in the saddle, and the more fun you will have.

4. ENGINE DESIGN

The beating heart of every motorcycle is its engine. Motorcycle engines are exciting, highly tuned pieces of engineering, and even the basic ones can be fun to thrash to the red line. They're all petrol driven, there's not a clattering diesel in sight. If you love an engine operating at full power – and let's be honest who doesn't? – then you're going to love motorcycle engines.

Not all motorcycles are created equal. Like the people who ride them, motorcycles have different characters. Imbued with the spirit of those who created them; some appear to be the creation of Dr. Frankenstein, while others are altogether more docile.

The character of a motorcycle engine invariably affects the way it is ridden. Climb aboard a two-stroke race-replica with a razor-sharp power-band, and you are more likely to ride it aggressively. You have to work the engine hard to keep it in its sweet spot. By contrast, a Harley-Davidson engine has a much more relaxed feel. The slower-revving, heavy-crank, lumpy V-twin produces ample thrust at any speed, and feels more at home cruising along the boulevard.

The Four-Stroke Otto Cycle

Most engines powering motorcycles are four-stroke spark-ignition reciprocating petrol engines following the Otto cycle. There are other engine designs using different cycles (like the two-stroke cycle), but four-stroke is the prevalent automotive design for ease of maintenance, reliability, and acceptable service intervals.

Four-strokes (to-and-fro movements of the piston) complete the cycle: inlet, compression, power and exhaust. The engine may have any number of cylinders, laid out in a variety of ways – in-line, vee, horizontally opposed …

Each cylinder has a piston, moving up and down; plus inlet and exhaust valves, nowadays invariably in a removable cylinder head and usually operated fairly directly by one or two overhead camshafts. The piston is attached to the crankshaft by a connecting rod (con-rod). The crankshaft converts the reciprocating piston movement into rotary motion. Picture a crank handle used to start a vintage car: your upper arm is the piston, your forearm the con-rod.

An internal-combustion engine is essentially a pump, powered from within by controlled explosions of energy-rich fuel. The engine sucks in air and fuel, and pumps out exhaust gases. As a prime mover, we are interested in the power potential, which is left after the internal friction and pumping losses.

The basic four-stroke cycle goes like this:

Inlet Stroke – Suck

The inlet valve opens as the piston is at the top of the cylinder. As the piston moves down it sucks fresh air into the cylinder. Fuel can be mixed with the air by a carburetor, or by fuel injection into the inlet port.

Compression Stroke – Squeeze

As the piston reaches Bottom Dead Centre (BDC), the inlet valve closes. Then the piston rises up the sealed cylinder, compressing its contents.

Power Stroke – Bang

At Top Dead Centre (TDC), the air fuel mixture is ignited by the sparking plug. The explosion within the closed cylinder pushes the piston down with considerable force, acting on the crankshaft and powering your car / bike / boat / lawnmower etc.

Exhaust Stroke – Blow

As the piston rises again, the exhaust valve opens and the engine's rotational inertia expels the burnt fuel gases from the cylinder.

Repeat As Necessary

At the top of the exhaust stroke, the exhaust valve closes and the inlet valve opens, and the four-stroke cycle repeats until fuel, air or spark are absent.

In practical terms, the timing of the actions is advanced, to take account of inertia of the gas flow – the higher the rev ceiling the greater the advance. Physical rotational inertia also influences the engine's behaviour. Engines with lighter crankshafts have less inertia and spin up more rapidly under acceleration, but they are also easier to stall at idle.

More Cylinders = Smoother Power

With a power stroke only once for two crankshaft revolutions ($360 \times 2 = 720$ degrees) for each cylinder, the more cylinders you have working together, firing at different intervals, the smoother the power output will be.

With a conventional in-line four-cylinder engine, you have one power stroke for each half revolution of the crankshaft (720/4), for an eight-cylinder engine you get an average[3] of one power stroke per 90-degree turn of the crankshaft (720/8), and for a 12-cylinder engine one power stroke for every 60 degrees (720/12). The W16 in a Bugatti Veyron (which has two narrow angle V8s side by side, to minimise overall engine length) has on average a power stroke every 45 degrees.

Such a smooth power delivery is expensive to achieve but reduces stresses on the power train when dealing with very high power outputs, and to deliver a smooth and refined engine output worthy of a million-pound car like the Bugatti Veyron.

The more cylinders in an engine, the smoother the power delivery, but also the more complex and expensive the engine is to manufacture and maintain, and the heavier it will be.

While some custom motorcycles and one memorable 500cc Grand Prix Moto-Guzzi have been built with V8 engines, the largest number of cylinders currently available is six, in-line for the BMW K1600, and horizontally opposed on the Honda GL1600 Goldwing. These are large heavy bikes with an emphasis on refinement over performance.

Two-Stroke Cycle

The two-stroke engine is a very clever and compact design, which delivers a power stroke every two-strokes of the piston, or one rotation of the crankshaft. The two-stroke cycle effectively halves the capacity requirement of an engine, as each piston is working twice as hard; broadly speaking the output of a 250cc two-stroke is equivalent to a 500cc four-stroke.

The power stroke incorporates both inlet and exhaust as it approaches BDC, and is followed by the compression stroke, although there is some overlap between the two.

The two-stroke eliminates inlet and exhaust valves by the positioning of inlet and exhaust ports on the cylinder wall. As the piston travels down on the power stroke it exposes the exhaust port first to expel the burnt mixture, a fraction of a second later the piston uncovers the inlet port for fresh fuel-air mixture to enter the cylinder.

The fresh mixture comes from the crankcase. As the piston descends it pressurises the crankcase and forces mixture through side passages (transfer ports) into the cylinder. As the piston rises again, crankcase pressure drops, and fresh mixture is inhaled. Usually the inlet port between carburetor and crankcase has a non-return reed valve to prevent blow-back in the subsequent descent of the piston.

---

[3] Due to different crankshaft and cylinder orientations, some engines have irregular firing intervals.

The two-stroke design is so clever because it uses the piston to do four jobs:

1) Acting as a piston for the explosion to push down on, thereby extracting power from the fuel while simultaneously ...

2) Acting as a pump to push fresh mixture up into the cylinder.

3) It acts as the inlet valve and ...

4) As the exhaust valve.

This makes the design small, simple and light, with few moving parts, no power-sapping valve train, and with a high power-to-weight ratio and high specific power output due to low internal losses.

Because of the multi-tasking, the two-stroke is a more fragile design than a four-stroke engine, and has much shorter service intervals. At the same time, some unburnt fuel is inevitably lost in the cycle, while lubricating oil for the crankshaft bearings also ends up in the combustion process, leading to exhaust pollution issues. But when a compact powerful engine is required, the two-stroke design is hard to beat.

It's somewhat difficult to describe this clever design on paper. Check out one of the many animations online for a dynamic visualisation.

Torque and Power

Without getting into too much technical detail, it is worth discussing the two terms which crop up when discussing engines; Torque and Power.

Torque is force applied over a distance. If you have ever used a longer lever to give yourself the extra force required to undo a stiff nut or bolt, you will have experienced the benefit of torque.

Torque is applied force (your weight) multiplied by the distance (the lever length). A greater force, or a longer lever, will both increase torque. In the example of undoing a stiff nut, your body weight or arm strength may be limited, but by doubling the length of the lever, you can double its turning effect. Hence the benefit of a breaker bar; it seems effortless when compared to the poor leverage of a shorter socket wrench.

Engines produce torque from the explosions in their cylinders. Generally speaking, the bigger the cylinder, the greater the torque, although the stroke of the engine does come into it, which we will discuss in a minute.

In real terms, torque is that instant 'drive', or 'punch' that an engine produces, the moment you twist the throttle. Big cylinders have big bangs, and hence big torque, smaller cylinders have smaller bangs hence small torque.

Power is torque multiplied by the engine's rotational speed. The faster you can get an engine to spin, the more power it will produce.

If Torque is the size of the bang, then Power is a function of the number of bangs per second, basically increasing as revs rise, until gas flow and / or internal friction call a halt.

If you think of the difference between a heavyweight and a featherweight boxer; a heavyweight boxer delivers big, heavy blows, while a featherweight has much smaller, lighter blows, but as his arms and gloves are lighter, he will tend to deliver them at a faster rate (more punches per second). The heavyweight is a bigger hitter but can't match the punch rate of the lighter fighter. The work done by both may be the same overall, but is delivered in different ways.

Ideally we'd like to have big bangs and high engine speed, for big torque and big power. Due to the limitations of the materials used in engine manufacture, and to stop pistons flying off the end of connecting rods, there is an effective limit to the speed that they can move.

Designers raise the rev ceiling by lightening pistons to reduce their inertia, and using connecting rods made of strong forged alloys, or even titanium. They also make engine designs oversquare (short-stroke), where the length of the piston's stroke is less than its bore).

Oversquare engines reduce loads on the connecting rods, reduce the friction of piston rings (as they don't travel as far for each stroke), and increase the area of the piston that the exploding gases are pushing upon.

'Oversquare' Engines

The cylinder bore is the piston diameter, while the stroke is the distance the piston travels as it moves up and down in the cylinder. Where bore and stroke are the same, the engine is called 'square'.

A long-stroke, or 'undersquare', engine has a longer stroke than bore.

The length of the stroke is related to the circumference defined by the offset crankpin (big end) as the crank spins. The larger the offset the longer the stroke. The advantage of a longer stroke is that the piston exerts more leverage at the crankshaft, which equates to more torque.

The same is true in reverse; the shorter the piston stroke, the smaller the circumference of the crank and the shorter the lever effect on the crankshaft. Most high-compression turbo-diesel engines are long stroke designs, producing lots of torque, but with a relatively low rev limit.

A short-stroke, 'oversquare' engine design has a bigger bore than stroke. As the piston travels a shorter distance for each turn of the crankshaft, the piston speed is lower than in a long stroke engine. The piston has a smaller distance to travel in the same time. (*Speed = Distance / Time*).

Piston speed is a theoretical maximum (constrained by friction, and connecting rod material strength), so the 'oversquare' design allows a higher engine speed for a given piston mass, and hence more power, without resorting to extremely exotic materials.

Most modern sports bike engines have gone the way of the short stroke in the quest for more power from a given capacity. As with all things, the torque / power design of an engine is always a compromise, based upon the requirements of the machine.

In the 1990s Yamaha and Suzuki made racy small-capacity bikes; 250cc four-cylinder screamers. The FZR250R and GSX-R250 had 16,500 rpm redlines. They didn't produce much torque but the stratospheric engine speed gave them a respectable 45-odd horsepower and a top speed of 120mph. This was achievable because of the tiny size of the pistons. Consider that in a four-cylinder 250, each cylinder is 62.5cc, that's about the same volume as a double shot glass.

If you like to work your engines hard, keeping them 'on the boil', then you will love the high-revving nature of a lightweight four-cylinder sports bike (250cc, 400cc and 600cc). If you prefer more low-down shove, using the engine in the low to medium rev range, then a 750cc or 1000cc engine will be more to your liking.

Yamaha Cross-Plane Crankshaft Engine

In 2009, Yamaha introduced into their flagship sports bike YZF-R1, technology plucked straight off Valentino Rossi's MotoGP bike. The idea was a simple one, and the results spoke for themselves; shortly after its introduction, the cross-plane crankshaft R1 was the bike to beat on race tracks the world over.

The cross-plane crankshaft benefits the rider because it eliminates rotational inertia. Something Honda had already been enjoying with their V4 configuration engines, and Ducati and Honda with their V-twins.

Why Rotational Inertia is a Problem

In a traditional in-line four-cylinder engine, the two outside cylinders move up and down together, likewise the two middle cylinders. They are 180 degrees out of sync: as the middle pair of cylinders are moving up, the outer pair are moving down and vice versa.

If we go back to our description of the internal-combustion engine as a self-powered pump, it is the inertia of the spinning crankshaft, refreshed by power strokes, that drives the engine, valve train and ultimately the rear tyre.

Let's isolate a single piston as it moves up and down. Attached by the connecting rod to the crankshaft, it both drives the crank and is driven by it.

The law of conservation of energy says that it can be neither created nor destroyed, it just changes form. Accepting that there are some friction losses inherent in any engine, the movement of the pistons, crankshaft, transmission and rear wheel are linked.

Ignoring the combustion forces for a second and focusing purely on the motion of the engine, consider the piston's velocity in the plane of travel. When the piston is either at the top or the bottom of its stroke, it is stationary. In between, it is accelerated and decelerated by the crank.

The work done by the crank on the piston varies depending on where it is in the cycle. When it is accelerating the piston, the crank is doing work. When it is decelerating the piston, the crank is having work done on it by the piston. When the piston is stationary, the crank is doing very little work.

As energy is neither created nor destroyed, when the piston is stationary, its energy is transferred to the crankshaft and ultimately the rear tyre's contact patch, speeding them up fractionally. When it is accelerated from zero to its maximum velocity energy is transferred from the crankshaft to the piston, slowing the crankshaft and rear tyre down fractionally.

This speeding up and slowing down effect happens many times every second, and causes a pulsing effect on the crankshaft called 'inertial torque'. All four pistons are accelerated to maximum speed, then decelerated to zero simultaneously twice for every single rotation of the crankshaft.

Inertial torque is totally independent of any combustion forces from the power strokes; it is purely associated with the motion of each piston. In the in-line-four configuration, with all four pistons in plane, the inertial torque effect is multiplied by four.

It interferes with smooth delivery of power to the rear tyre. It is like having some background noise affecting your ability to hear a good quality hi-fi. Inertial torque affects the sensation the rider feels at the throttle and what this translates to at the rear tyre.

The faster the engine's speed the more this inertial torque disrupts the drive from the engine to the rear tyre. This is why a big four becomes progressively less 'talkative' to the rider at higher engine speeds, and why modern 1000cc superbikes come fitted with a raft of electronics to keep things in check.

Anyway, back to our Yamaha engineers. To 'iron out' the effect of these inertia forces, Yamaha separated the pistons on the crank by 90 degrees; one is at 360, one at 90, one at 180 and one at 270 degrees. By separating the pairs of crank throws by 90 degrees, as one pair of pistons is speeding up the other is slowing down, which cancels out this inertial torque.

You may have noticed that this is effectively the same as a 90-degree V-4, but in a more compact in-line-four design. In the 90-degree Honda V4 design, instead of using a cross-plane crank, a flat-plane crank is employed to the same effect, eliminating inertial torque and delivering a 'pure' power delivery.

When it was released, many bike journalists commented that the cross-plane crankshaft Yamaha was a design that the rider could really use to drive confidently out of corners without the usual trepidation of a 1000cc 'screamer' engine's power delivery.

The traditional 1000cc approach was; get it stopped, get it turned, stand it up as quickly as possible and use the power to fire it down the straight. Such was the improved feel and feedback from the cross-plane crank design, and so great was rider confidence in the throttle that the new R1 proved far less intimidating to ride, as its trophy cabinet demonstrated.

The strange thing about the cross-plane crank is that it sounds and feels less smooth than a flat-plane in-line four at idle. This is because of the irregular firing order. But when you start to spin the engine fast, a cross plane crankshaft engine is far better balanced and delivers a far smoother result, even though the sound is less of a scream and more of a wail!

Engine Configurations

The motors which turned a bi-cycle into a motor-cycle come in many shapes and sizes. Which one matches your needs?

Single

Single-cylinder engines are cheap to manufacture, lightweight and with a good power to weight ratio. They are generally small-capacity engines (up to around 700cc), due to the excessive vibrations caused by larger pistons above that capacity. They have a 'punchy' power delivery, are typically found in smaller, lighter machines where low weight or low cost is desirable.

Two-stroke and four-stroke singles are available, although two-strokes seem to be favoured in off-road machines and 50cc scooters; singles are found in scooters, off-road bikes, and small capacity trail-bikes. They are also used in lawnmowers, go-karts, chainsaws, strimmers, and leaf blowers. In fact anywhere a compact petrol-driven engine is required, you will likely find a two-stroke single.

Twin

There are three orientations of twin cylinder motorcycle engine.

V-Twin, also called L-twin (as seen in Suzuki TL and SV, Ducati twins, Aprilia, Moto Guzzi, Honda VTR1000, KTM)

Moto-Guzzi mounts its engine longitudinally, which works well with a shaft-drive power off-take (much like the shaft-driven BMW flat twin). The other manufacturers have transverse crankshaft orientation, with the vees set at various included angles between 45 and 90 degrees, and varying amounts of primary balance and additional balancing shafts to smooth things out.

While a 90-degree engine should have better balance, fitting such a long engine into a small motorcycle can cause packaging and weight-distribution issues (see Suzuki's TL1000R and its infamous rotary damper). Honda adopted side-mounted radiators to allow its VTR (and VFR) engine to be moved further forward, putting more weight on the front end.

The 90-degree V-twin is favoured for its mechanical balance, making it relatively smooth for a twin. It differs from other engine designs in that the offset of the cylinders means that pistons can share the same crankpin (they are joined to the crankshaft at the same point). This makes the engine much smoother and more compact than if the crankpins were offset, which introduces a side-to-side rocking force.

V-twin cylinders have an uneven firing interval due to the 90-degree separation; even-firing is only possible on a flat twin and parallel twin.

On a 90-degree V-Twin, the second cylinder fires 270 degrees (three quarters of a turn) after the first, producing some imbalance from firing inertia, and then the first fires 450 degrees (one and a quarter turns) later.

Parallel twin (e.g. BMW's Rotax 800, Kawasaki ER, Honda CB500, Triumph Bonneville, and Yamaha Super Tenere and MT-07)

The parallel twin is composed of twin upright parallel cylinders alongside one another. In terms of mechanical balance, this is much like a single, but cylinders take it in turns to fire, so the firing force is half as much as with a single and each piston and connecting rod only has half the weight, so a higher rev limit is achievable for a given capacity.

Like singles, parallel twins are generally of smaller capacity, because the greater the mass moving up and down the more significant the vibration, especially at higher engine speeds. Many parallel twins use balance shafts or counterweights on the crankshaft to help reduce vibrations; when the cylinders move up the counterweight moves down and vice-versa (see BMW's Rotax 800 parallel twin for an example of a 360-degree parallel twin).

Parallel twins can fire evenly 360 degrees apart when both cylinders move up and down together, but often crankpins are offset by 180 degrees (one piston goes up while the other goes down) or 270 degrees (cylinder two fires three quarters of a turn later) for a smoother engine.

A 360-degree firing interval gives good torque (BMW's F800) but far greater vibration and has a lower rev limit. The 270-degree offset (Yamaha MT and Super Tenere) is effectively a cross-plane crank engine, smoothing out the vibrations substantially (both pistons aren't moving up and down together) and effectively mimicking the firing sequence of a 90-degree V-Twin, albeit in a simpler more compact design. The classic Triumph Bonneville engine of the mid-20th century, with its iconic sound, is a 360-degree parallel twin.

Horizontally opposed twin, aka 'boxer' twin (traditional BMW models with shaft drive)

Smooth, with primary balance, an even 360-degree firing sequence and a low centre of gravity, the boxer pistons' outward-inward motions cancel each other out. As a result of this balance, this engine configuration can be used up to large cylinder capacities effectively without balance shafts

(BMW's 1200cc boxer twin), though the cylinder heads need to be protected in the event of the bike falling on its side, so manufacturers fit heavy duty rocker covers or crash bars.

There is a rocking couple caused by the required offset of the cylinders on the crankshaft. BMW has been producing this venerable design since 1923. This is effectively half a Subaru flat-four, or one third of a Porsche flat-six.

Triple

(Many Triumph models, BMW K75, Benelli Tre and Yamaha MT-09)
A triple is a good engine compromise, sitting happily between the low-speed torque characteristics of a twin-cylinder (whose larger cylinders give bigger bangs for more punch) and the smooth power of a four (whose smaller reciprocating weight means higher engine speeds and hence more power).

When we think of flexible engine layouts, effortless drive in any gear without compromising top-end power, we think of the three-cylinder engine.

A triple has less vibration than a twin, but more than a four. Triples are also narrower than four-cylinder engines and so easier to fit across the frame.

You typically get an engine with a flat torque curve (good drive when you open the throttle regardless of revs), and in the case of Triumph triples, an interestingly shrill engine note.

Triples are full of character, with enough of a raw edge to make them interesting in a motorbike. Crankpins are offset by 120 degrees (360/3), which is a similar concept to the 90-degree offset (360/4) of the cross-plane crank design, providing the rider with plenty of feel for early throttle mid-corner.

Four

There are currently two types of four-cylinder engines used in motorcycles – in-line four, and V4. In production bikes, vee configuration is currently used by Aprilia, Ducati, Honda and Yamaha (V-Max). MotoGP sees V4 designs from all but Yamaha and Suzuki.

The in-line four is the most popular engine configuration for both motorcycles and cars, offering a good balance between smoothness, longevity and cost.

Currently 600cc is the lowest capacity modern four on sale in Britain, although the Japanese have manufactured a number of smaller capacity four-cylinder sports bikes, 250cc and 400cc variants. Many of these 400cc machines were grey (unofficial) imports to the UK, in the form of Kawasaki ZXR-400, Honda CBR400RR, VFR-400, RVF-400, and GSX-R400.

The four-cylinder engine is incredibly versatile, giving a relatively high performance-to-cost ratio, and has been the power plant of choice since Honda introduced the single-overhead-cam (SOHC) CB750 in 1969. It can be tuned for low-down torque or top-end power, depending on the design and the application. Due to the even firing order it also feels very smooth, especially in 600cc form and below.

Size does matter however, and there is no substitute for cubic centimetres when it comes to engine size, as the laws of physics still apply.

The V4 is like a pair of V-twin engines side by side. The primary decision is whether you have a 360-degree crankpin offset (both move together); a 180-degree offset – which gives a smoother firing sequence but introduces a rocking couple; a 270-degree offset which is found on the Honda VFR800; or a 70-degree offset which is found on the Ducati Desmosedici Stradale V4 engine, which provides a twin pulse firing that mimics the feel of a V-twin and has proven credentials in MotoGP.

Five

As seen in the Honda RC211V 75.5-degree V5 engine. The V5 has three cylinders at the front and two at the rear. Its design is a V4 with an extra piston in the middle of one of the banks. Not currently available in any road bike.

Six

The six-cylinder engine is suited to the larger motorcycle. The Honda Gold Wing has used a flat four and then a flat six engine (as favoured by Subaru and Porsche respectively).

BMW has developed a straight (in-line) six for their larger touring bikes. The Honda CBX-1000 (1978-82) and the Kawasaki Z1300 (1979-89) both used in-line six-cylinder engines across the frame; while Benelli made the first production six from 1972 until 1989, in 750 and 900cc versions. With smaller machines however the additional complexity, weight and cost make four-cylinder engines a better choice.

The perfect primary and secondary balance of a flat six and in-line six engine make them ideal for the smoothness desired in a touring motorcycle, but they are naturally big, heavy and complex power trains so need a big bike to accommodate them.

5. MOTORCYCLE TYPES

The best decision you can make is learning to ride motorcycles. The second best decision is buying the right motorcycle for you.

You must disregard what the rest of the world thinks, and buy what you want. I appreciate that much of motorcycling is about image, but buying the wrong kind of bike and leaving it locked up in your garage is the worst 'look' of all. It not only costs you money, it can irreparably damage your relationship with your hobby so you never really get going.

Do yourself and your biking career a favour, and pick a bike with the specific abilities that you are seeking. Will you be regularly taking a pillion? Are you planning to do some touring, or do you want a 100-percent track day bike? If you do a lot of long-distance riding on motorways and trunk roads, you'll be looking for a fairing, a comfy seat and a riding position which is good for at least a couple of hours in the saddle.

If you ride mostly in town in the summer months, a lightweight naked bike or scooter may be just the ticket. If you want to tour two-up to the south of Spain in extreme comfort, then a single cylinder supermoto will probably not be on your shopping list.

Of course, what you should do is ignore me and buy whichever bike you feel inspired to buy. Variety is the spice of life, and most modern bikes are much more flexible than they first appear.

Ask yourself what kind of rider you are? Do you like to ride on the limit of grip with the engine bouncing off the rev limiter? If so you might find a 1000cc bike a bit of a handful on the road, and a 600cc bike might be more fun.

If you don't like working the engine hard or you use your bike for longer distance work where high engine revs can be tiring, you might look at getting a larger capacity engine with more low-down torque for effortless drive in any gear.

Let's have a look at the broad categories of motorcycle available, their dominant characteristics and what they are typically used for.

Sports Bikes

A broad category indeed: sports bikes are designed to optimise acceleration, braking and handling at the expense of comfort, fuel economy, luggage and pillion carrying capacity. The amount of compromise varies from machine to machine.

Typically engine capacities of 600cc and 1000cc are common in fours and twins, but such is the choice available on the market today that you can get sports bikes with anything from 125cc to 1300cc, with engines from singles, twins, triples, straight-fours and V4s.

Perhaps the most interesting are the new small-capacity sports bike models available from the major manufacturers. Currently 125cc, 250cc and 300cc, 400cc and 500cc bikes are the biggest sellers in the sports-bike world, as newly qualified riders enter the market and want something manageable and stylish to ride.

While being sporty, many sports bikes are also very practical, comfortable, good looking and can be fitted with a top box or hard luggage to improve their usability.

600cc Supersport

Supersport bikes are 600cc (and occasionally 750cc) bikes: showroom models for use on the public road, but also the basis for production-race series, and thus designed and optimised for power, handling, and feedback. The term 'superbike' is often used to describe the 1000cc supersport models, discussed in the next section.

Not surprisingly, supersport bikes are in their element going fast. Tuned for the racetrack, they make most of their power in the upper rev range. You need to spin the engine at more than 8,000 rpm to get the best out of them.

Supersport bikes are light, responsive and powerful, although not so powerful that you'll easily overwhelm the rear tyre. Less commitment is required than with a 1000cc superbike, but sometimes that's a good thing.

Supersport bikes are ideal as your first 'clip-on' type sports bike, usually after a few years on something a bit more user-friendly. If you're used to a twin cylinder engine, while you'll love the lightness of the chassis and the steering, you may find a 600cc a bit gutless low down, or at least hard work to make swift progress. They're great on track when you are 'on it' but can be hard work on the road. If you are in any doubt, I'd recommend you try before you buy.

Superbike

Superbikes are 1000cc production-race bikes (four-cylinder 1000cc or twin-cylinder 1300cc) that get their DNA from the world of road racing and are very fast indeed. They are designed to operate comfortably at speeds in excess of 100mph (at the Isle of Man TT they are pushing 200mph).

They can break the national speed limit in first gear alone, and expect to see well over 160bhp at the back wheel. But they can be frustrating to ride slowly due to their sporty riding position, engine and character.

They are incredible to ride, providing unsurpassed levels of power, feedback and tactility, with rock solid stability at high speed. You will feel everything that is going on with the front and rear tyres. Given their immense ability and high-performance envelope, they really need taking to a track to exploit their full potential.

If you have a few years' experience under your belt, and you're not in the habit of crashing, consider testing a 1000cc bike, but expect to be travelling everywhere extremely quickly. If you do more than a few hundred miles on one, you might find the intense feedback a bit overwhelming, and the seat a bit hard.

They are not designed for touring, but if you're up for the 'iron butt' challenge, they'll do it. They have the engine flexibility to do big distances with ease. Is the superbike one bike to rule them all? Yes, but you'll trade comfort for improved feel and composure at high speeds. Also, the luggage options tend to be limited to soft luggage, so their usability suffers somewhat.

V-twins and fours have different characters; so it's important to try them both to see which you prefer.

Supermoto

The Supermoto is a race-bike in its own right; an off-road bike with road wheels and tyres (usually cut slicks), a chain and sprocket set geared for the road, and a bigger front brake to take advantage of the improved levels of grip on tarmac.

The supermoto is as hardcore in its element as supersports and superbikes are in theirs. Being lighter and therefore more agile than road bikes, they are great fun to chuck about twisty go-kart tracks, but can quickly become tiresome on the road.

These bikes are not recommended for the less-than fully committed rider. They are highly entertaining but also hugely impractical. They are probably the smallest niche of any motorcycle for usability. That can be annoying if you're not in a playful mood.

Larger capacity 'Supermotos' from KTM, Ducati and Aprilia, have little in common with these little terriers, but something of the spirit: long travel suspension and instant power delivery for a committed and entertaining ride.

Touring Bikes

Touring bikes encompass a large engine capacity, smooth and tractable engine, a comfy upright seat and riding position, ample luggage capacity, sometimes even a stereo system, and are as good with two passengers as they are solo.

Heated grips and electronic suspension frequently come as standard. Tourers encompass all of the attributes needed to cover huge distances in supreme comfort, without getting your hands dirty (or cold). Touring bikes can swallow whole continents without burping.

They also make going very fast very easy. Designed for mile-munching in comfort, they have large fairings and screens, large fuel tanks for extended range between fill ups, and deliver easy-to-access power from tick-over to the redline.

You won't get as much feedback from the handlebars, and the significant weight (400kg and up) will make spirited riding in the twisties 'interesting', but to be honest that's not why you buy one.

The engines aren't as exciting as sports bike engines either, but they do suit the bike's character. Tourers aren't designed for scratching foot pegs. You'll feel much happier sitting back in your plush leather armchair, enjoying the luxurious ride and the scenery as the tunes blast out on the stereo.

Sports-Touring Bikes

Combining the attributes of sports bikes and touring bikes, some sport touring bikes are the superbikes of yesteryear, which now look less focused when compared with the very latest evolution of racing machines.

I would also include the 'hyperbikes' in this category (Hayabusa, CBR1100XX Super Blackbird, ZZR1400). With big, strong engines, hyperbikes can also be surprisingly co-operative if you want to be playful. They tend to weigh 250-300kgs so aren't as nimble as true sports bikes, but offer a lot of fun, and cover ground incredibly quickly.

Sports-touring bikes are the best choice for one 'do-it-all' bike. They can commute, they can tour, and they can even do the occasional track day without embarrassing you too much, and at the end of the day you can ride home in relative comfort.

Sports-touring bikes are powerful sporty machines, a little on the heavy side to be really flickable, but with enough comfort that you don't need to visit your chiropractor or attend weekly yoga sessions to straighten yourself out.

'Naked'

A naked bike (sometimes called a roadster) is a motorcycle with little in the way of a fairing for wind protection, an upright seating position and wide flat handlebars.

Now why would you want one of those? That's a good question. I suspect they were invented for people who live near the equator, or who have neck muscles like a rugby prop forward.

Some people like the way they look, others like the upright riding style. It's not difficult to see that they would be cheaper to manufacture, and they certainly add a level of fun to an otherwise serious categorisation and pigeonholing of bikes and their riders.

Suzuki Bandit and Ducati Monster are two examples of highly successful naked bikes, and I would also throw in large capacity supermotos.

While we're on the subject of naked bikes, it's worth mentioning 'street fighters'. Allegedly the street fighter concept came about in the late 1970s and early 1980s, when sports-bike owners couldn't afford to fix up their crashed fairings, so they attached flat handlebars, bolted on some round headlights, and the 'street fighter' was born.

Since then, the 'rough custom' look has given way to a whole genre of production machines from the likes of Triumph, in their hugely successful Speed Triple and Street Triple; Aprilia and their Tuono; and more recently Ducati and their Street Fighter and Yamaha with their MT-09 and MT-10 series.

Street fighters have big engines, sports bike suspension and an upright riding position with lots of leverage at the bars, all of which equals lots of fun. They will also give your neck muscles a workout. If you cover a lot of motorway miles or are over 6ft tall, you may find the windblast tiresome at speed.

Some people like to ride naked bikes as they believe the lack of fairing prevents them from riding too fast. Having tried a few, I'm not convinced they do anything to slow you down, if anything their cheeky nature and lack of wind protection makes you wind the throttle on to get the journey (and the excruciating pain) over as quickly as possible.

If you ride in town and on A and B roads, this kind of bike may be just the ticket, but I recommend you test ride one on a motorway on a windy day before putting down your deposit.

Adventure Bike

Going racing in the Dakar Rally? Following in Ewan McGregor and Charley Boorman's wheeltracks? Then you'll need an adventure bike. Featuring long-travel suspension, they are designed for mostly road use.

Adventure bikes are better off-road than they look, but not as good as a true off-road bike, being too heavy to be continually dropped and picked up. Adventure bikes are a massive growth sector, with all of the manufacturers developing models to try to get a piece of the action.

The majority of adventure bikes will spend more time soaking up speed bumps on the King's Road than vaulting sand dunes in North Africa. For a crossover-type bike, these are hard to beat, although their lofty riding position can take some getting used to, and if you've got short legs you might want to look elsewhere.

Custom

With lots of chrome, a big capacity characterful engine, and low laid-back style, a custom motorcycle is built for cruising.

These bikes do have good performance, just rarely as much as their open pipes would have you believe. They are not the last word in sporty, and have limited ground clearance, but there is no doubt custom bikes have enormous appeal, and are extremely stylish and fun to ride.

They are aimed at a more relaxed rider, and open the door to a different type of motorcycling, one where there is no real pressure to go fast.

Off-Road Bikes

(Enduro, Motocross)
This book is about road bikes, but off-road bikes are great fun too and are worthy of a mention. I lived in central London for many years, and so didn't get much time on dirt bikes, as they aren't really compatible with city living.

In the countryside where green lanes abound, they're really worth a look as an alternative. Find a willing farmer with some land, give him £100 and go and have a day's fun. My enduring memory of riding dirt bikes (and their Supermoto cousins) is that they are just as sharp as road bikes in their own domain.

They might run at lower top speeds, but their power-to-weight ratios, light handling and the punch from those single cylinder engines (and nutty little two-strokes) is legendary. They will wheelie off the throttle in second gear.

They are also extremely physical machines to ride, and the following day, and the day after, and the day after that, you will be feeling the after-effects in your arms, shoulders, legs and back. These bikes give you a serious work out. Physically speaking; riding down the pub on a Sunday on your Hayabusa and doing an enduro event are not even in same ball park.

Riding off-road is all about getting used to the feel of the bike moving around beneath you; riding on the limit and having the back end going faster than the front, or locking up front and back wheels.

When you first get on a dirt bike and you give it a handful of throttle, you will feel like your rear tyre has stepped out a mile. As with all things, your feel will improve with more practice, and falling off is not a huge issue as off-road bikes are designed to fall over.

If you get into off-road bikes, your throttle control will improve significantly. Many road racers start out riding motocross bikes, and still ride off-road as a fun way to polish their riding skills and stay fit.

MotoGP legend Casey Stoner was frequently seen down Kinsham Raceway practicing his skills on his Honda CRF supermoto, and TT legend John McGuinness preferred to train off-road rather than in the gym. How often do we hear about road racers who cannot compete because they've picked up an injury at the motocross track? More often than their team bosses would like.

Riders inhabit a world where the key to success is control at (and frequently over) the limits of traction. There is no better way to practice this than having both wheels continually losing grip. The beauty with dirt bikes and supermoto is you get to practice on the limit, at speeds which are far lower, and therefore with less chance of injury than on a full-sized, high speed 150mph+ track.

The same goes for off-road racing (enduro riding and motocross). When you go into that first corner too hot and lose the front end you can stick your leg out and save it. Try that on an R1. Not you Colin Edwards, you're allowed.

6. CHOOSING YOUR FIRST MOTORBIKE

There has never been a better time to get into motorbikes. The choice of bikes available is better than ever, and bikes are safer than ever to ride, with smart technology like cornering ABS and multi-level traction control. It's still possible to crash them, but it's much harder than it used to be.

The rider equipment, advanced clothing and protective gear available, and the choice and quality of tyres on sale are all excellent. The pedigree of the motorcycle manufacturers has also improved over the last few decades as manufacturing and quality-control processes have matured. Simply put, if you are thinking about getting involved in motorbikes, there has never been a better time to do it.

As with many areas in life, bikers are standing on the shoulders of giants. The motorcycle industry has many decades of successful momentum, leading to the advanced state of affairs that we enjoy today.

As the sport of motorcycling has expanded, so have the businesses that support it. In the UK we have a fantastic dealer network available seven days a week to service our needs, and if we are seeking information on current models, we have a passionate, impartial and eloquent motorcycle press on hand. Modern bikes have the reliability and usability to make them genuinely useful daily transport, with enough choice to suit all budgets and skill levels.

While much of the developing world has not yet reached the place where they can afford to buy a decent car, motorcycles are well within reach of most budgets, hence the global boom in lower capacity motorcycle models. As driverless cars and carpooling become more popular in the coming years, I think we will see motorcycles' appeal increase, as people seek a more exciting way to get about.

Power / Weight = Fun

When it comes to performance, power to weight ratio matters most, and pound for pound, you're going to get a lot more performance for your money when buying a motorcycle over an equivalent priced car.

Even a box-standard 500cc parallel twin will do 0-60mph in five seconds. A sports 600 will do it in four, a superbike in three. When compared with the equivalent performance car, these bikes cost a fraction of the price to buy and run. For the price of a medium-sized family hatchback, you can ride off on a pedigree 180mph superbike with a thoroughbred race tuned engine on board.

If you take the equivalent four wheeled performance alternative; after the hefty outlay, the depreciation in the first year alone would pay for a top end superbike. You are also going to be spending a fortune in fuel and tyres, not to mention the cost of servicing.

Your First Bike

When choosing your first bike, you want to take your time and get the right one. This means starting with something exciting yet manageable, and work your way up to more powerful models as your experience grows.

There are bikes which are suitable for first time riders of all categories; whether you have a restricted licence or an open one which allows you to ride any bike you choose. Let's look at the options.

Open Licence

While can buy yourself any bike you want, you should aim for a bike which suits your requirements as far as design purpose (see previous chapter), and which has a medium sized engine of around 500-800cc capacity.

Picking the right bike will give you room to grow your riding skills to the point that your bike is the weak link in the chain, rather than your ability.

Get yourself something that matches your skill level, a bike which makes you want to get out and ride at every opportunity; something fun, that doesn't take itself too seriously.

If you go on a track day and you manage to ride around sports bikes you feel like a hero, but if they overtake you, it's no big deal. You want it to be about the rider, not the machine.

When you start out, you need confidence by the bucket-load to negotiate the twists and turns that lie ahead. Rather than jumping in at the deep end, get yourself something you can handle, and work your way up to the more exotic stuff after a few years and a few thousand miles of riding experience.

You will get there sooner than you think, especially if you're riding daily, and when you're ready for a bigger bike, it won't feel like such a big deal anymore. Yes, the performance will take your breath away, but the difference is you'll be able to handle it, rather than feeling intimidated.

There is a path of least resistance, a course of progression that will make your experience and personal growth as a rider most fun. Don't try to run before you can walk. If you go out and buy yourself the latest, greatest 1000cc race replica, you'll likely miss out a large part of your essential growth as a rider. You will feel as though you have a tiger by the tail. A tiger that it is trying to kill you at its earliest convenience.

Power is great, but only when you have it under control, and when you're relaxed enough to handle it. Master your control of the machine, and then turn up the power.

When you make mistakes on a smaller bike (and you will make mistakes, it's how you learn) hopefully you won't be travelling very fast, and so the downside of any off is likely to be less serious.

Aim for a light bike with a flexible engine, something that is not so powerful that it will intimidate or overwhelm you, with neutral handling and pliant suspension to soak up the lumps and bumps on the road.

Fit some crash bungs to something like a Suzuki SV650, Ducati Monster 600, Triumph Street Triple or Yamaha MT-07 and get out there and ride. These bikes will teach you everything you need to know about machine control and you won't outgrow them in six months. You don't really need any more than 100bhp in your first bike.

Ideal first bikes have another benefit; they are cheaper to buy, insure and maintain, and there is always good demand for these motorcycles on the used market, so you shouldn't have any issue when the time comes to sell.

Given that you are likely to drop your first bike several times on your way to finding your balance, as well as fitting crash protection, it's not a bad idea to buy second-hand, a bike that already has a few scuffs and scrapes. You won't then feel too upset when you drop it yourself. And you should be able to get a decent discount.

Restricted A2 Licence

Just because you're on a restricted licence, it doesn't mean you can't have fun. Restricted bikes still have plenty of drive even if they run out of steam up top. A number of the bikes previously mentioned are also available in restricted form. You can ride these for two years on your restricted license and then have them derestricted afterwards to save you the trouble of having to buy a new bike.

Many manufacturers are focusing on developing purpose-designed restricted-license bikes (Kawasaki Ninja 300, Honda CBR250R, and Suzuki GSX250R) – desirable smaller capacity bikes for emerging markets. The choice is significant and constantly growing.

The limit for an A2 licence is 46.6bhp (35kW) or less. If you want to ride a bike with more than 46.6bhp (35kW), the bike can only be restricted by a maximum of 50 percent, which means the bike must have less than 93.2bhp (70kW) in its unrestricted form. It must also have a power to weight ratio after restriction of no more than 268.2bhp per tome (0.2kW/kg). This means you have a choice of many older 600cc four sports bikes like early CBR600s, as well as large capacity twins such as Ducati Monsters and supermotos.

7. BUYING MOTORCYCLES

There are two ways to buy a motorcycle; new and used. There are subjective reasons for doing either.

Buying New

If you have the money, I'd recommend you buy new. New motorcycles come with a two-year manufacturer's warranty, are shiny and clean, haven't been mucked about with by anybody, and are unlikely to need any significant work before their first MOT.

You can also test ride before buying, while a private owner is unlikely to let you do so unless you leave a full cash deposit. Take advantage of this by doing your research, draw your shortlist and test ride all of the bikes you're considering.

Large franchised dealerships representing multiple manufacturers usually have a test ride policy, and as long as you meet the minimum age and experience requirements, they will let you test ride any bike, within reason and with a sufficiently large insurance deposit. Ask your dealer what their policy is, get to know them and if you like them, support them with your custom.

If you've just passed your test, you may find your test ride options somewhat limited, but someone out there will want your business, so don't give up if you get a few cold shoulders. Persevere and you will find someone happy to take your money.

When buying new, there's almost always a little room for manoeuvre on the price, so if you don't want to pay full list price, or you're buying in the middle of winter, feel free to haggle.

Use your discretion, speak to a number of dealers and play them off against each other, especially if they are offering older stock, pre-registered or ex-demonstrator models. Make them work for your hard-earned cash. If you keep an eye on the press and find out that sales of a particular bike are sluggish, then use this to your advantage when buying. Supply vs. demand is the biggest factor in determining price.

Finance (PCP/HP)

If manufacturers are offering incentives like zero-percent finance deals, bear in mind the cost of this loan is typically met by the manufacturer to try to increase sales, so don't expect a discount on the list price as well (but fair play if you manage to negotiate it).

PCP stands for Personal Contract Plan. This is a finance deal where instead of borrowing the total sum to buy a motorcycle, the payment plan is staggered to make it more affordable. With a PCP, you don't finance the whole cost, only the 'depreciation' of the motorcycle over the period. This does mean that you don't own the bike until you make the final payment, you are leasing it.

At the end of the term, you make a final lump sum 'balloon payment' to take ownership, or you can hand the keys back and walk away (as long as it is in good condition and mileage is within agreed limits).

It is worth pointing out that a bike on PCP remains the property of the financier until your final payment is made, and if you default on the payments, they will take it back.

This staggered payment system has come from car finance packages, and the final 'balloon payment' is there to make your monthly payments more affordable. At the end of the term, if you want to keep the bike, you can pay off the remainder in cash, or finance it by means of a personal loan.

Negotiating

When buying a motorcycle, many people will find it easier to negotiate over the phone than in person. For starters it is harder for the salesman to read your body language and effectively work you. Putting down the telephone is easier than walking away from a salesman who knows what he is doing.

It is in your interest to support your local bike dealer if you want to make use of his workshop, parts and clothing departments. He won't do a deal with you if it loses him money, so by all means make him work for your hard-earned cash, but these businesses need customers like you to maintain their service levels. If you're buying everything online, don't be surprised if you see your local bike shops closing down.

If he's unwilling to budge on the price of the bike, one potential negotiating point is on accessories or workshop costs. For example, he might not be able to go any lower on the bike's basic price, but he could throw in a half price lock or a helmet, or three basic services to take you up to MOT time.

A number of motorcycles, (large European V-twins, for example) when new, require an expensive first service at 600 -900 miles when the valve clearances are checked, mineral oil is changed etc. Negotiate it into the price when buying new. The last thing you want to do is fork out another £450 three months after paying full whack for a brand-new bike.

If you buy new, you must also be aware that the warranty stands only if you have the machine serviced to the schedule. This usually means you'll be paying quite a bit in servicing fees to keep the warranty intact.

If you're the sort of person who likes to do his own servicing, you can either buy a bike that's a couple of years old, just outside of its warranty period, or you can buy a new bike and pay for the servicing in the first couple of years. It can give you peace of mind, especially if you use it as your daily ride.

Buying Second-hand

For those who can't or don't want to pay for a new motorcycle, there's the used bike market. This could fill an entire book on its own. To the untrained eye, buying second-hand can seem a bit of a minefield.

There are many reasons people sell motorbikes privately: lack of use; raising cash for a newer model; or there may be something materially wrong with the bike that the owner no longer wants to deal with on the grounds of cost or convenience.

If they sell the bike to a dealer and the bike is in a mess, they won't get much in exchange. Selling to a member of the public is far easier.

There is no excuse for buying a bike in poor condition. If you can't afford to buy a decent example, look at a different bike or learn how to haggle. Many motorcycles have had an easy life, having been mollycoddled by their owners to preserve their value. There are always plenty of good-condition, low-mileage examples out there.

Your job as a second-hand bike buyer is to be clear about which bike you're looking for, and to sniff out the machine that matches that. The good news is they're not difficult to spot, and if you manage to prevent yourself from falling in love with the first bike you see, you can get yourself a good bike for a good price.

You can buy second-hand from a dealer, or privately. Given the fact that motorcycle dealers make a living buying and selling used motorcycles, you can usually get a good deal, as they want to turn over a decent amount of stock. Dealers also make more money selling second-hand bikes than new ones. If you haggle hard, you should be able to get a good price as well as leaving them with a decent profit.

You might think this is your one and only chance to buy this bike. But I can tell you now; it is just never the case. Buy in haste, or in a heightened emotional state, and there is a high chance that you will repent at leisure.

A lot of men go into an altered state of mind when buying cars and motorbikes. The section of their brain that deals with logic becomes detached, and the reptilian brain takes over. They start to behave irrationally. I'm sure this is a similar mental state to falling in love.

They will usually have been researching what they want, reading, assessing strengths and weaknesses, so when they turn up to view a bike, there is usually a significant amount of momentum already in place. They will certainly have pictured themselves owning and riding the bike, In essence they've bought into the dream.

A keen-eyed seller will spot an enamoured buyer a mile-off. The 'loved-up' buyer praises the bike, appearing overly keen almost as if he's giving the seller the benefit of the doubt; he has, in a sense, fallen in love with the bike, and in his infatuation, will conveniently overlook the red flags which would otherwise be clearly visible to a normal, conscious human being.

If you fail to ask the right questions, or you ignore any bad vibes you get from the seller, you're asking for trouble. If a private individual sells you a duff bike, you don't have any recourse. Buy a bike from a professional motor trader however, and he has a duty to sell you a roadworthy, serviceable bike, or at least point out if it is not in great condition. A dealer also has his reputation to maintain.

Do you remember the first time you fell in love? That person standing in front of you looked faultless. They could do no wrong. They appeared perfect to you in every way. Until, that is, you started to get to know them. As you did, you started to see them differently, you started to recognise all of their faults. Your initial honeymoon period with your new motorcycle will be over just as quickly, so before the ink has dried on the ownership papers, make sure you know what you're getting yourself in for.

Remember, if you buy a real dog of a motorcycle it's now your problem to deal with, fix or pass on to some other mug. Buy a money pit and you'll wish you hadn't. Ask me how I know.

Research

Before you even pick up the phone, or lift your mouse to look for bikes online, do your research. Every model has an Achilles heel, regular faults and issues, and the internet is full of forums of helpful people willing to give free advice on the bike you're interested in owning, so you will know what to look for when it comes to tracking down a good example.

Always buy as modern and low-mileage a bike as you can afford. The older a bike, the more problems will need sorting out, and buying a cheap bike is almost always a false economy.

Run an HPI check (or similar vehicle history check) to check it hasn't been reported as crashed or stolen, or has outstanding finance; and when you view the bike, check the frame and engine number (if you don't know where this is located, Google it before you visit the bike) against the vehicle documentation.

The vehicle check will not tell you if the buyer has crashed the bike on his own and patched it back together; but you should be able to spot it, and it will certainly feel odd to ride, especially if you try more than one example of the model in question.

The registration document should have the seller's name & address printed on it. If it is different, ask them why. If you're not happy with the answers, walk away.

Keep yourself impartial, and bring somebody with you who is not emotionally invested in the bike, ideally someone knowledgeable who can do the haggling for you. They can play the 'bad cop' to your 'good cop', and bring some balance to the negotiations.

Look for faults as well as benefits, and consider (ideally vocalise) how much money you're going to have to spend putting things the way you want them. It's nice to be optimistic, but the fact remains, you may have to spend quite a bit of money getting the bike up to scratch, and if the current owner doesn't sell the bike to you, at some point he will have to do the work himself.

Don't be rude, and make sure you know what you're talking about, or you'll put his back up. Every bike I've sold there have always been things I could have spent money on, but I knew that I wouldn't recoup the money at sale time, so I didn't bother. The seller is most likely thinking along the same lines.

As the buyer, you are holding the cash, so you are in the position of greater power. The seller may have a bike, but the cash you are holding is more valuable to him; and you as the holder may choose to take your business elsewhere. The seller wants to turn his bike into cash, so use this to your advantage when negotiating.

If you've ever bought and sold bikes, you will understand that you always feel the bike is more valuable when you're buying it, and less so when you're selling it. Desirability bears heavily on perceived value. Use this to your advantage. The seller is at the mercy of the buyers' market because deep down he knows that bike is only worth what someone is prepared to pay for it.

Clever sellers try to use certain tricks to give themselves the upper hand. Take these offerings with a pinch of salt, and see them for what they are, part of the typical sales patter.

Some Favourite Tricks

- ✓ Talking about how it's only just gone on sale, even though actually it's been advertised for weeks or months;
- ✓ Speaking about how many other interested people have already enquired about the bike;

✓ Making up offers from other members of the public or dealers to give the bike a false bottom line. Even mentioning a figure is an attempt to plant an acceptable sum in your head. If he plays this game, do the same yourself to test the water.

✓ Explaining how much he's spent on accessories. If you don't like them, it will cost you time and a significant amount of money to get the bike back to standard, which should actually reduce the value of a tastelessly accessorised bike. For example, if he has decided to powder-coat the swing-arm gold, what on earth are you going to do with that when you eventually come to sell it?

Keep your cool. Stick to your budget, ignore the sales patter and stay focused on what you want to achieve; getting yourself a good quality bike at a price that seems fair to you.

In the cold hard light of day, money talks, and while he may appreciate his bike, waving several thousand pounds of cash in his face is a powerful motivator. If the seller is really playing hardball, and you sense that he's going to drive a hard bargain, unless you really have an immaculate example in front of you, just walk away.

There is a deal to be had, and if you're playing with someone who doesn't want to negotiate, take your money elsewhere. He wants what you have more than you want what he has.

It's worth saying this. There will always be other opportunities to buy similar or better bikes, so unless you feel really happy with the deal, you're likely to get buyer's remorse and feel like you've paid too much (hint: you always do).

You can be sure that there will be things wrong with the bike that the buyer has neglected to mention. You might think that these bikes are as rare as hens' teeth, but almost without exception, the day after buying it, a cheaper and better example will come along.

Mr. Tidy

The main benefit in buying second-hand from a private individual is you get an opportunity to meet the seller to see what he's like, and ask him questions about his bike. This is always a great reflection of how he's cared for his machine.

Is his house a total pigsty? Ask to use his loo, and inspect how clean it is. Is it clean and tidy or does it resemble Scotland's worst toilet? If somebody lives like an absolute slob, how much care do you think they will have taken over their bike? As I said earlier there are plenty of pampered bikes out there, and you want to be buying one of those.

Is all of the paperwork handy? Does he keep receipts or has he just got stamps in the book? Does he know the first thing about his machine when you quiz him? Does he know how to lube the chain and check the oil? Is his bike properly clean, or does it just look clean? Do you get a good feeling talking to him? Do his stories add up, or does it seem like he's trying to hide something?

Is he a well presented clean and tidy guy with a carpeted garage and everything in it in its own designated place? Is he slightly anally retentive? Perfect! This is the kind of guy you want to be buying a motorbike from. First of all, if he is proud of the condition of his bike, he is not the sort to pull the wool over your eyes, and you can bet his bike has been cleaned and polished far more than it has been ridden.

Control the Frame

When you enter any kind of sales environment, you need to think about who is controlling the frame. This is about laying down the foundation for how the situation is going to unfold. There are two ways it can work, you can control the frame, or the other person can.

Watch a good salesman in the flow, they are trying all of their tricks to get you to see them as friendly, to build rapport in as short a time as possible. They shake your hand, ask you what your name is, and get personal with you very rapidly. They start using language which supports their frame, putting words in your mouth, or at least planting thoughts in your mind. They might say, 'When you purchase the bike' rather than 'If you purchase the bike'. Such suggestive language can influence a weak mind. Don't fall for it. Counter with your own frame; 'If I were to buy this bike, what's the best deal you could do?'

When you buy a bike, you are automatically in the stronger position; you have the cash, so you have the power, so you need to be the one setting the tone. You want to bring the salesman into your frame, rather than being pulled into his.

You want to have the attitude, 'My perfect bike is out there at the right price for me, and if it is this particular bike, it will come easily, and the whole experience will be a relaxed easy one.'

If someone tries to get you into an emotional state, they are likely trying to manipulate you into making a decision under pressure. For example, why is a seller interested in a 'Quick Sale', what's the rush? Is there something dodgy going on? Equally if he wants you to put down a deposit before checking out the paperwork, it probably means he wants you to commit to the sale, and feels he has a good price and wants to avoid any slip.

Equally, if someone is piling on the time pressure, along the lines of 'You need to make a decision now, as I've another offer on the 'table', if it feels to you like the other person is trying to pull you into their reality, reassert your position, and stand your ground. If they won't play ball, go elsewhere.

There will be plenty more opportunities and many better bikes available to you as a buyer. If they won't play ball with you, you don't want to deal with them. There aren't many positions where you get to call the shots, but buying a motorcycle is one of them. Set the terms of your engagement and find people who want to deal with you on those terms. Be clear about what you want and who you are before you take any action.

If you approach the seller openly and honestly about what you want, he will naturally feel obliged to behave in the same way. If he tightens up or seems reticent, or has flushed red cheeks, alarm bells should be ringing in your head. You can usually tell if something is amiss. If you smell a rat, be courteous thank him for his time and walk away.

If you're dealing over the phone, ask the seller open questions like: 'So tell me about the bike' and then give him some space to talk, while listening to his response. If something feels wrong or you don't like the way the person is dealing with reasonable questions, go elsewhere.

Only select a viewing which you feel is right for you, and a seller who sounds like a decent person with no ulterior motives. I promise you'll significantly increase your chances of buying a solid bike.

If you buy second-hand from a dealer, they may charge a bit more than a private sale, but you will typically get some sort of warranty for peace of mind.

They should also check out the bike to make sure it is in roadworthy condition before selling it. If it's a real wreck, they probably won't buy it in the first place, or they will advertise it: 'sold as seen'.

Buyer Beware is the motto to keep in mind for a private sale – not always because the seller is dodgy, but often because the seller isn't always aware of the condition of his bike. Get some basic advice on what to check, but as a minimum you should be looking for the following:

- ✓ Mechanical and bodywork damage – scuffed fairing panels, scratches on the frame, swinging arm and forks and rear subframe etc. Is everything lined up, or does it look wonky?
- ✓ Check that the mileage matches the general wear and tear of foot pegs (including the foot peg sliders), throttle grip and key barrel. All bikes will pick up stone chips on their bodywork and forks, just make sure that the mileage and usage that the seller has told you matches the look of the bike. If it doesn't add up, it's either been clocked, raced or crashed and repaired.
- ✓ Check the chain and sprockets for wear, and the chain for general condition and lubrication.
- ✓ Check the tyres for tread and see how far over the bike has been leaned. If the tyres fitted are cut slicks with melted edges, it may not have high mileage but those miles are likely to have been on

track at full throttle.

- ✓ If you get to ride the bike, check the brakes for a pulsing feel through the brake lever which suggests a warped brake disc.
- ✓ Check the suspension and the head bearings for wear; Lift up the front of the bike, and turn the bars side to side about the central position feeling for a notchy point when the wheel is dead ahead.
- ✓ Check the exhaust headers – a new stainless exhaust to replace that rusty steel one will cost £300-400
- ✓ Check the last two MOT's for 'advisory' notes, these will indicate what needs doing. If you ask the seller if any work needs doing, and he tells you no, and you find a list of advisories on the MOT, treat him with caution; he may be concealing something else. In the UK, MOT history can be looked up online, provided you have the registration number of the bike.
- ✓ Check the temperature of the engine when you visit. It should be cold. Start the engine and check it starts first time. Listen for any strange noises, knocking and rattling. When warm, give the engine a good rev to check that it sounds OK and the throttle works fine.
- ✓ Make a note of your observations, so you can compare it with the next bikes you look at.

As far as the suspension goes, any bike with a few miles on the clock will benefit from a suspension overhaul. Add up the money you need to spend to put it right, add 50 percent for stuff you've missed and knock this off what you would consider an acceptable price for the bike.

Used-bike prices can often be found on the internet, or by searching the classifieds to see the going market rate. It really helps if you see more than one example of the bike, so you can tell a good one from a bad one.

Just because it's a 15-year-old bike, doesn't mean it will be knackered. Some old bikes are nearly as good as new, and have lived sheltered lives. Others are neglected, and it shows.

Never buy the first example of any bike you see. You will be excitable, and you will likely miss lots of things. Tell yourself to see at least three bikes before even test riding one. I know it's a pain, but this bike is an investment, and if you buy the first one you see, you won't know a good example from a bad one. When you do find a good example, express an interest to return for a test ride with the cash asking price.

Don't rush into a sale. If this is your bike, it will wait for you. If it isn't, let someone else buy it. There's no rush here. Your perfect bike is out there at the perfect price for you.

The whole process from meeting the seller to test riding the bike to handing over the cash should feel smooth and easy and effortless. If it doesn't, then it's a sign that you're trying to push it. If you buy a bike in a hurry, you will have plenty of time to regret your decision.

Another good idea is to never buy on the day you view. Go home, and sleep on you purchasing decision. If you awake in the morning and still feel excited about buying it, then go for it. As you come back into consciousness, you will be extremely clear-minded, and you should know what to do; whether this one is a 'Buy' or an 'Avoid'.

Some private buyers seem to have an over-inflated idea of the value of their bikes. Just because they bought it, stored it in a garage and never used it, they seem to think that it is worth what they paid for it three years ago. It isn't. It's worth what someone is willing to pay for it. Would you like to pay over the odds for a second-hand bike? Use your head and you'll get the perfect bike for you at the perfect price.

SECTION 2: YOU AND YOUR BIKE

8. RIDER SETUP

*Everyone holds his fortune in his own hands, like a
sculptor the raw material he will fashion into a
figure. But it's the same with that type of artistic
activity as with all others: We are merely born with
the capability to do it. The skill to mold the material
into what we want must be learned and attentively
cultivated.*

-   Johann Wolfgang von Goethe

A successful life on two wheels requires establishing a number of solid foundations out of which riding experience emerges; the first and most important of which is rider training. The biggest risk to your well-being is the 'well-oiled nut behind the handlebars'. You.

You are going to have to put in the hours, risk injury and the possibility of death in order to get the training and the certificate of real-world competence. This path should not be entered lightly, and if you are not prepared to put yourself out there, to fail and learn from your mistakes, then don't start the journey in the first place.

Your development as a rider involves personal development in two distinct categories; your skills, and your attitude. But first, we need to talk about Focus.

Focus

You might wonder why the subject of focus would crop up so early in a book on motorcycles. The answer is simple; focus is what separates the men from the boys. People who ride well are good at focusing. They accept that life is about constantly learning from mistakes, and approach the task of learning to ride with humility and an open mind.

Modern life is packed full of choices; what to buy, what to read, what to think about. Out of this variety of choice comes the potential for a wonderful life, as well as the opposite. What makes the difference between the two is the individual's ability to focus, and the subjects they choose to give their attention to.

Many people are vying for our attention. They have worked out that if they can get their sales propositions in front of our eyes for a period of time, that we're more likely to give them our money. This is why advertising works, and why the press write predominantly bad news.

We are daily subject to a constant stream of information. Free papers feed us 'news', marketing emails promise benefit, and social-media encourage us to share our thoughts with our 'friends'. Who does all of this really benefit? If time is money – and it is – are any of these inputs relevant to us, and do they warrant our precious attention?

Attention is our most precious asset. The thoughts, words and actions that follow on from it are the building blocks of our life, and what make it successful or not. And yet we give our attention up so readily, to things which really don't deserve it.

Media Age

The industrial age has given way to the media age. Our beloved 'black mirrors' take more of our attention than our family and hobbies once did, and yet they are nothing more than a distraction; a technological nervous tick. We are trained to respond to the latest thrill or excitement offered, and grow accustomed to the hypnotic effect of the media drip-feed.

Vanity compels 'users' to produce content for free and give away their most precious personal data willingly, while social media platforms make billions of dollars out of the proceeds. We become so interested in 'liking' other people's lives that we eventually come to neglect our own. We could all do with minding our own businesses a lot more.

The modern office work environment has changed too. Gone is individual space; private room that offers time for profound contemplation. Instead, open-plan offices predominate, busy with chatter and distraction. It's a wonder that workers manage to concentrate long enough to achieve anything meaningful in the modern business environment. Just think how productive society would be if we could only focus and apply ourselves properly.

Buzz Feed

Life in the 21st century has forced us to find a way of dealing with a constant state of media over-stimulation. We exist in a brainwashed, distracted state, flitting from one irrelevant tidbit to the next. In our need to filter this data-stream for the useful 'nuggets', we are losing the ability to focus our minds effectively.

There is no such thing as multi-tasking. You can have one job done properly with your full attention, or two done half-heartedly, and poorly executed.

We have been sold the concept of instant gratification, where 'free next day delivery' is seen as normal. We sense that value can be acquired on credit in the form of 'stuff'. But when the retail therapy fails to do the trick, we don't consider that we might be on the wrong path, instead we double our efforts at acquiring more 'stuff' (ideally on credit).

The advertising executives have brainwashed us into this state of hypnosis; we think a better car will improve our driving, make us better lovers, or make us more interesting. We believe that the acquisition of 'trophies' will bring us the satisfaction that we are seeking. So we move around, seeking a nicer boss, a bigger salary, a better car, a nicer neighbourhood to live in.

We believe that these external changes will lead us towards greater fulfillment, greater self-expression, and ultimately to greater happiness. In so doing, we miss the most important factor of all; if we remain unchanged throughout, then our life is just the same as it was, except we now have more stuff, and the debts to prove we didn't deserve it. I'm not knocking 'stuff'. Stuff is good, as long as it is the means to an end, and not the end itself.

Mastering a skill takes time, and it takes focus. Whether it is motorcycle riding, creating photographic art, playing golf, wine tasting, or playing the drums. These are progressive, tactile experiences, and where your mind leads your body will eventually follow. Sadly few have inclination to pull themselves away from their devices long enough to try.

Motorcycles will give you many gifts, but the biggest of these is the gift of focus. You will learn to focus, or you will fall by the wayside. You may decide after an early tumble, that you want to focus more effectively, or you may decide to throw in the towel.

I hope you choose to continue learning, because going fast and in control is where the real fun of life lies, and those who give up riding in their formative years are passing up more in life than mere motorcycling.

Genius or Personal Desire?

Did you know that genius is just prolonged attention to a subject? In his book 'Outliers: The Story of Success', Malcolm Gladwell poses the theory that it takes around 10,000 hours of practice to become a master at something.

While it's true that some people are naturally gifted in a particular activity, their 'gift' is often cited as the reason behind their apparent genius and the success that inevitably follows. What is frequently overlooked is the encouragement they receive from parents, guardians and peers, and the individual's personal determination to succeed, as well as the many hours of practice they put into their chosen craft.

Personal interest in a subject, and the number of hours spent doing it, are inextricably linked. If you accept this statement as true, then it follows logically that nothing can stand in your way of becoming a master of any subject of your choosing; be it Morris dancing, motorcycle racing, public speaking or playing the piano, except your own lack of interest, and hence your lack of attention to the subject.

A quick study of the autobiographies of successful people reveals they shared a single-mindedness of purpose; an ability to focus wholeheartedly on what they wanted to achieve in the face of many who spoke against them or their vision.

They didn't take 'No' for an answer, and when they failed – as they did a great many times – they got back up and carried on in the knowledge that they would make it one day. It was as though they knew that they would succeed, and so they did. As a result of their determination, and their unwillingness to compromise, they became the masters of sport, music, art, and business revered the world over.

The simple fact is this: If you want to succeed at something, you are going to have to learn to fail at it too. Only by doing things the wrong way, do we learn how to do them the right way. Words don't really teach; it is only through experiencing something in life that we can truly understand it.

If you want to improve your chances of being great at something in life, pick something that you love. The rest of the details will take care of themselves. If you don't enjoy what you're spending your time doing, don't think that perseverance and hard work will bring you to a place of satisfaction. An unhappy journey ends in an unhappy outcome. Relief at the cessation of pain is not the same as joy. Find a way to love what you do, and if you can't go and find something else that you can love. It's not difficult to focus on things that you love, but very hard to focus on things that you care little about.

Learning to Walk

If you're just starting out on two wheels, I want you to know that you're unlikely to get it right the first time. This is just the way of the world, I'm afraid. Learning how to do something new involves making quite a few mistakes.

Your happy path to biking nirvana consists of a very logical progression, a series of incremental steps, which will take you comfortably from where you are now to wherever you want to be.

But just as learning to walk involved a few tumbles at the beginning, you are likely to drop your motorcycle a few times in your early biking career. The key to a successful 'preparation' phase is to be riding at a speed where these falls do not have serious consequences. You also need to be wearing decent protective gear.

When you were a toddler, your parents didn't put you on a tightrope 50 metres in the air. Neither did they leave sharp edged objects or stairs for you to practice walking around. They knew that you would fall over in finding your balance.

Give yourself plenty of leeway when learning to ride and keep the impact of any falls to minor scuffs and scrapes that you can walk away from, having learned a valuable lesson. Please don't buy a brand-new shiny bike as your first motorcycle. Get something you don't mind dropping. If you're going to learn to ride it properly, the chances are you're going to drop it.

If you hold a motorcycle off its stand and let go, it will crash to the ground. Motorcycles are inherently unstable when stationary, gaining stability as they speed up. Motorcycles also weigh a lot; more than you could bench press. If you've never sat on a motorcycle, you might be surprised at how substantial they are. Managing this heavy, unstable weight at low speed can prove challenging.

Muscle Memory

When you start out, the whole activity will feel alien, especially if you are used to driving a car. You may be used to riding a bicycle. With a motorbike, instead of pedalling, you are now charged with operating four controls; one for each hand and foot, and trying to stay as relaxed as possible as the bike moves about beneath you.

As you put in the hours, you will become more comfortable with the movement and in translating the feedback, and your ability to control your bike will improve.

As you train your muscles and your mind to respond in particular ways, you will develop the 'muscle memory' that athletes talk about. It takes time and practice, but once the neural pathways are connected, riding motorcycles will feel as easy and comfortable to you as walking does now. Your motorcycle will feel like an extension of your body.

Life on two wheels has enormous benefits to you as a rider, but there is no doubt it's a riskier proposition to the unfocused individual than say, driving a car. The potential pitfalls have more serious consequences, which can bring you to a short sharp end before you've reached your full potential, and we don't want that to happen.

Intuition

Your single biggest asset in any activity is your intuition. In the previous section we discussed the worldly assault on your senses, the barrage of information trying to worm its way into your consciousness. Other people want you to do what best suits them. What they are offering may certainly have some benefit for you, but their predominant interest is a selfish one; they want to benefit themselves.

Learning to ride means learning to concentrate for extended periods on the task at hand; being able to develop your mind to focus without distraction. Training mind and body to deal with the mental and physical elements of riding is essential, just as an athlete or football player must practice the movement of his sport, so the motorcycle rider must polish his riding skills out on the road.

What I want to encourage, above all else, is an individual who is able to take his training and experience, and develop an attitude that allows him to perform to the best of his ability. As riders, we want to be operating not from a place of fear or trepidation, but from a place of intuition, and knowledge of our own power.

Intuition is developed in an individual by a simple process of de-hypnotising. The media onslaught fills our minds with emotionally charged rubbish, which sways our thoughts, words and actions. We are brainwashed, conditioned to respond to these stimuli, not normally acting in our right minds, but according to the messages others have put in our heads.

The solution lies in cleaning the slate, to create the space for the mind to reset and to act from our place of assured confidence. If you want to foster your own intuition, you will need to learn to quiet the buzz of your over stimulated mind. Once you have 'turned down the volume', you will be able to hear the small quiet voice within; that is your intuition.

Why Intuition?

Your best work in life comes from a state of inspiration, of intuitive knowing. The musician who hears a number-one hit playing in his mind and writes it down; the best-selling author who takes notes on the stream of ideas entering his mind; the football player who anticipates his opponents' every move; all of these individuals are acting from a place of intuition, from a place of 'instinct' if you will.

You want to be in such an intuitive state of mind when you ride. Operating from a place of intuitive knowing, you are at your most gifted, and the additional sensory perception afforded by your expanded state of awareness gives you an advantage over 'mere mortals'.

When you operate from a place of intuition, you know what is appropriate, and you know what is not. You can sense when the police are aware of you, and when they are not, whether there is a tractor round the next bend, whether that van is about to pull out, and you can take the appropriate action. Intuitive people don't think as much as feel their way along the road.

Increased Sensitivity to Life

If you tend to blunder around, knocking lumps off yourself and others, the chances are you are not sensitive to your intuition; either that or you have a high emotional pain threshold.

One way to increase your sensitivity is to meditate daily to tune yourself up, to let the higher, purer frequencies return. Those that you had when you were younger, which the media and the many distractions of your life have crowded out.

As you practice clearing your mind of any thoughts first thing in the morning, you will find it benefits your entire life one day at a time. Find a quiet room early before the children awake, or before you need to walk the dog and spend 20 minutes in a comfortable position with your eyes closed, focusing on your breathing. As thoughts come into your mind, as they naturally will, just release them and focus back on your breathing.

You will feel the success of quieting your mind-chatter when you feel your energy level rise, a sense of lightness of spirit. As though you have awoken refreshed from a nap, except you were conscious throughout. This is the perfect state of mind for riding motorcycles. It is the perfect state of mind for other things too, it's just that when you are wielding a powerful tool with a sharp edge, which has the ability to cause you and others great harm, you want to be firing on all cylinders.

I will not go into great detail about meditation and inspired living; there are many excellent books available on the subject, only recommend meditation as a daily practice. In my experience, this one activity has done more to improve my life than any other. Being clear-minded is something that money cannot buy.

Once you have cleared away the negative chat in your head, and your mind is refreshed and alert, you can give your full attention to the task at hand. Everything that you think, say and do evolves out of your state of mind; your attitude to risk, your ability and willingness to learn, your perception of the world, what other road users are about to do. Your 'biker-sense' if you will.

If you've had a row, or find yourself annoyed by something, take the time to centre yourself, to re-calibrate your emotions before you climb aboard your bike, and your ride will be more meaningful, more fun, and far less likely to kill or injure you.

As you see the correlation between your frame of mind and the results that you get – not just on two wheels but in life in general – you will think twice before doing anything important from an emotionally charged state of mind: Not talking to your partner or children, not meeting with clients, not making important decisions, not using a sharp knife or operating power tools, and not riding motorcycles.

Would you get out a chainsaw or even a gun if you were in a really bad mood? When the family arguments start, it's good to know that the gun cabinet is locked. If you are upset, dealing with a potent weapon like a motorcycle is best left for a time when you have come back to your senses, when you are able to make better decisions. Treat your motorcycle in exactly the same way as you would a lethal weapon. Be in your best frame of mind when using it; which means trying to avoid any mind-altering influences: alcohol, heightened states of negativity, and manic moods are best avoided.

9. FEAR

Many would-be bikers never even get to swing a leg over a motorcycle. They are too afraid of what might happen if they did. Either they don't trust themselves or they don't trust other people. While this is a missed opportunity, I'm guessing that if you're reading this book, you probably don't fall into that category.

'I'd love to get a bike, but I'd probably kill myself', isn't just a clear sign of a pathetic loser with no control over their life; it suggests that people who ride have no choice about how they behave either, which is clearly nonsense. People who ride motorcycles feel most acutely the choices available to them, and they exercise those choices every time they ride.

For those of us who choose to get into motorbikes, the excitement and adventure of learning to ride outweigh any fears we may have had in the beginning. Of course, we know that people get killed and seriously injured riding motorcycles, just as with any exciting and fun activity in life, but we are confident that we will use our skill and judgement to beat the odds. If we weren't, we wouldn't have started out riding in the first place.

The good news is there are techniques to stay safe out on the road, and they are neither difficult to understand nor hard to apply. The key to success lies in training mind and body to respond in appropriate ways to the situations we face on a daily basis. Some of this is learned behaviour, as we will discuss later in the book, and some of it is common sense. The previous chapter introduced the concept of riding with intuition. The greater our level of intuitive behaviour, the greater our level of common sense. Now we need to talk about fear, and why it is important to you as a rider.

What is Fear?

We use language to try to communicate with other people, not just what we want, but how we are feeling. Our emotions are labelled many things; happy, sad, proud, embarrassed, depressed, content, shocked …

At the top of the emotional scale are the good-feeling, self-empowered emotions, often called happiness, joy, elation, and bliss. In the middle are more average emotions called contentment, and satisfaction. Heading down the scale we have boredom, with frustration, irritation, anger and resentment further down, and eventually at the lower end of the scale, fear and depression.

This spectrum of emotions has the high-flying, good feelings at the top, and the low, bad feelings at the bottom. Another way to look at it is this: a feeling of total empowerment lies at one end of the scale, feelings of complete powerlessness lie at the other.

When you feel powerful and in control of your life, it's fun to go fast. You want to go out into the world and take whatever it has to offer you. But when you feel completely out of control, it feels scary to go fast. You hole up inside your house, draw the curtains as if you have the worst hangover of your life and just want to be left alone to die.

And so it is with motorcycles. When you feel great you feel as though you can do anything, you are clear headed, in the zone and firing on all cylinders. When you feel totally out of your depth, you advance with trepidation.

When you start riding, you will experience fear. Fear is your indication that you are not up to speed with the situation that you find yourself in. I remember how my brain was frazzled the first time I rode a motorcycle, as I tried to manage the combined activities of steering, changing gear, accelerating and braking, all out on the public highway.

Each hand and each foot had something to do; I was fully engaged in the process and way out of my depth with this strange new activity. 50mph (the top speed of the bike I was riding) felt more like 120mph. Even though I had five years of driving experience under my belt, I was scared of this little 125cc bike, and I was grateful to have an experienced guide to follow me and keep an eye on what I and other road users were doing.

As time passed, I grew more comfortable, and my ability to read the road ahead improved. Even so, I stumbled unwitting into a number of situations where I exceeded my ability and experience, and found myself doing the 'grip of death', where my arms froze up solid on the handlebars. I was incapable of doing anything; not accelerating, not braking, and not even steering. It was like being a passenger rather than a rider, watching myself do absolutely nothing to stop the situation which was unfolding.

Frozen fear is a natural response to finding yourself in a situation that overwhelms your senses and your capacity to cope; deer often experience this when caught in the headlights of an oncoming car.

At panic stations, all logic goes out of the window, and we instinctively do the worst thing possible, we freeze up and do nothing. All our training is for naught, we are incapable of responding in any positive way. Mere bystanders, as events unfold before our eyes.

The leading edge of fear is your understanding that you are moving towards something that is not going to end well.

If you feel that sense of edginess, as you will invariably in your early days, wind your aspirations back a notch, approach the task in hand a bit more gently, and you will find your progress easier. Trying to push through an uncomfortable feeling is what gets people into trouble. You probably forgot to meditate this morning. Not to worry, just take it easy today, and remember to get yourself in a better frame of mind before your next ride/race.

You cannot necessarily train yourself not to have a 'death grip' reaction, except by putting yourself into progressively more advanced situations, until you grow comfortable with them and they no longer surprise you.

Freezing up, or panicking, is caused by a lack of experience, and being overwhelmed. More experienced riders don't freeze up because they normally ride within their comfort zones, having pushed their limits in a safe environment such as a closed track (more of that in a later chapter), or progressively on the road.

Imagine if, as a junior employee on your first day out of school in the corporate world, you were suddenly asked to be the CEO of the company that you had just joined. You would most likely be plunged headlong into fear; the leap from office junior to the ultimate 'buck stops with me' big boss, is too big a jump to take in one step. Making decisions on business strategy, answering the questions of the shareholders, and directing the executive board in a high-power, high-money environment are not easy when you have no business experience, don't speak the lingo and don't understand how things work around here. You would be standing there with a dry mouth, trying to explain things you didn't understand, and feeling like you wanted the earth to open up and swallow you whole.

It is far more satisfying, as well as being less straining on your nerves, to gradually work your way up through different positions of the company, learning different skills and gaining experience, and an understanding of the culture that will make that top appointment one day feel like the next logical step.

It goes without saying, but you really want the same smooth progression in your biking career, so you don't seize up when the situation calls you to perform at your best.

By all means have excitement in your riding, but there is a difference between the feelings of fun, and the feeling of trepidation. Aim for the former, avoiding any big jumps. Focus instead on a gradual development of your skills and experience as you broaden your biking horizons day by day.

That's not to say you can't make your move in a year if you have the desire to move that fast, just know that the office junior and the CEO have disparate roles as far as others' expectations of them, their decision-making ability, their public speaking skills, credibility, and understanding of the business at hand. You get to choose to progress as quickly or as slowly as you choose, just remember to keep it feeling good, and you'll stay out of trouble.

The truth is we already use our emotions to guide our daily lives; choosing to move forward with things that we like the sound of and avoiding things that we don't. We may consider the majority of our decision-making comes about as a result of facts and logical reasoning, but there is an underlying knowledge or experience of what is good for each of us, as individuals, and this broader understanding expresses itself through our emotions.

If you can learn to get back in touch with and use your sensitivity, you can guide yourself about many things in life, not least; your choice of bike, when to buy and when to avoid, when to go out for a ride, who to go out for a ride with, how fast to corner, when to stop and have something to eat or drink.

Use your training by all means, and use your eyes, your ears and your road sense, but learn to listen to your inner guidance to lead your actions.

If you are unable to hear any kind of emotional cues, you need to slow your mind down; get into the habit of meditating every morning when you awake, until you are clear minded and present. Clear-minded happy, fun people make good decisions. Confused people make poor decisions. Be clear minded, have fun and ride as fast as it feels good.

10. BASIC BIKE SETUP

Have you ever spent the time to setup your bike properly? Do you know that you can tailor your machine to your own requirements? I'm not just talking about twiddling suspension adjusters, but the more basic control layouts and touch points. Are you worried that any fiddling will make things worse rather than better? In this chapter we discuss the rudiments of bike setup, what you can change to get things the way you want them.

Ideally your bike should feel as comfortable to you as your favourite pair of slippers. When you feel comfortable riding your bike, you can focus completely on the task at hand, rather than the fact that your wrists ache.

Controls

The first port of call should be bike's controls ... adjusting brake and clutch lever span, and clutch biting point.

Next have a look at lever and bar positions. Many people buy sports bikes and then complain that they make their wrists hurt, not realising that often the levers are putting their arms and hands into unnatural positions. The nerves that we use to sense the controls run through the wrist. Placing these under stress can lead to numbness and pain. Lever position is adjustable up and down, to give your arms and wrists the optimum angle for your normal riding position.

With your bike on its stand, climb aboard and adopt your normal riding position. Try adjusting the angle of the clip-ons, and the vertical alignment of the levers until you have found a setting which you like and which makes operating the controls easier at the angle your arms normally take. Tighten all of the bolts back up to the recommended torque setting.

If you have a lot of trouble reaching the bars, or you find the race crouch position of sports bikes too uncomfortable, you can fit a set of custom-made clips-ons which raise the handlebars to a more comfortable position.

If you have particularly broad shoulders, you might want to consider buying longer clips-ons to give your arms a more comfortable riding position rather than forcing your wrists to take up an unnatural bend. Twist grips of different thicknesses are available, if you like a thicker grip, then just swap them over.

The seat is another feedback surface, which lets the rider know what is going on at the back tyre. As a result, the seats on supersport bikes tend to be harder for more direct contact, while touring bike saddles are geared towards comfort. If you want a more comfortable seat on your sports bike, there are plenty of people who can take your original seat and place padding to make it just the way you like it.

Foot Pegs

Position of control inputs is equally important to your comfort and grasp of the machine. You will be supporting your bodyweight, pushing off the foot pegs, and they need to be at an angle which allows plenty of blood to flow to your legs and feet. There's no point being in a race crouch with your knees by your armpits if your blood supply to your legs has been cut off, and you can't feel your toes.

Most road bikes have plenty of additional ground clearance below the foot pegs. Manufacturers typically fit sacrificial 'sliders' to the underside of foot pegs to let you know that you are approaching maximum lean angle. Foot pegs can usually be lowered without sacrificing too much ground clearance.

Some bikes have alternative mounting holes in the footrest brackets. If your bike doesn't come with adjustable foot peg brackets, consider having some brackets made up to get the pegs where you want them (whether higher or lower, forwards or backwards).

The rear brake pedal is height adjustable to allow a comfortable reach for your foot. Make sure once you have adjusted it, that the brake light switch is working properly.

Some motorcycles have adjustable headstocks to change the steering head angle to sharpen up steering response. Raising the forks up in the triple clamps can have a similar effect, in that it decreases the steering head angle while also lowering the front of the bike.

Rear shocks of some bikes have adjustable links or shim stacks, which can be inserted to raise or lower the rear ride height, which also has the effect of changing the handling geometry. Take that owner's manual and read it thoroughly so you understand your own bike's level of adjustability.

Suspension

Suspension has two principal functions. It is designed to provide a level of comfort for the rider when traversing less than smooth terrain, and it is designed to keep the tyres in contact with the road surface during acceleration, braking, and cornering manoeuvres.

Suspension has two essential components; a spring and a damper. The spring allows vertical movement of the suspension (and the wheels which are attached to it), and the damper damps the oscillation, absorbing the energy. Without the damper, the spring and most likely you too, would be pogo-ing down the road after the first bump. If you want to see this in action, take a look at cars with worn out shock absorbers.

Springs

The majority of suspension springs are linear, that is they deflect linearly or proportionally under load. The stiffness of a spring is normally stated in kg/mm or lbs/in. A 1kg/mm spring will deflect 1mm for every 1kg loaded on top of it. A 100kg rider will deflect a 1kg/mm spring by 100mm or four inches. Share that same load between two fork springs and the total deflection will be halved.

Once underway, the bumps in the road, braking and accelerating forces all exert more force on the spring, compressing it further. Put simply, the faster you go, the more force the suspension has to deal with. This is the reason that race bikes have stiffer suspension springs than road bikes; they are used under more demanding operating conditions.

If you buy an aftermarket shock (the common term for a rear spring/damper unit), you will typically be asked for your weight, whether you ride solo or with a pillion, whether you carry luggage, and how fast you ride. The suspension expert's aim is to provide you with a spring that is appropriate for your weight and riding style. If you weigh 17 stone (108kg) and ride like Michael Dunlop then you're going to need a stiffer spring than if you weigh seven stone (44kg) and ride like a policeman.

Put on the same bike, the 17-stone rider may bottom out the suspension, while the lighter rider may not deflect it at all. Luckily, most bikes in their stock form can be made to work well for a wide range of rider weights.

Dampers

The other part of suspension is damping. Damping is achieved by pushing viscous oil through small apertures. The thicker (more viscous) the oil or the smaller the aperture you're pushing it through, the greater the damping effect.

The cartridge inside a telescopic fork deals with damping, and works on the upstroke (when the fork or shock spring is compressed), and the down stroke (when it rebounds).

Some shocks and forks, especially on production-race bikes designed for road racing, have multi-adjustable damping on forks and rear shock, for fine tuning at the racetrack for different riders and different surfaces.

Indeed more and more high spec machines nowadays incorporate high- and low-speed compression damping; the high-speed damping takes up the big sudden bumps, while the low speed compression damping deals with fork dive and extension during braking and acceleration.

Sag

To set your bike's suspension up correctly, the first thing to adjust is the static sag. This gets the suspension in the right operating range for your weight. It ensures that that in normal operating conditions the suspension doesn't bottom out under braking or bumpy conditions, or top out when accelerating hard out of a corner, something that can induce a tankslapper.

Most motorcycle suspension is designed for a wide range of rider sizes and styles and incorporates suspension preload adjustment to allow the correct set up of sag.

There are two sag measurements to take into account, *rider sag* and *static sag*, and they are measured from the suspension when it is fully topped out.

Rider Sag is the amount the bike sits down on its suspension with the rider (in full riding gear) in the saddle.

Static Sag is the amount the bike sits down on the suspension under its own weight, rider removed.

To set up sag you will need the assistance of two strong friends; one to hold / lift bike to fully extend the rear shock / forks, and the other to take measurements. With the rider off the bike, measure the suspension fully extended (L1), and then measure the suspension length with you on board in your normal riding gear (L2). The difference between these figures (L1 – L2) is rider sag.

Rider sag should be between one third and a quarter of total suspension travel. For a street bike a good starting point is 35-40mm rider sag at the front and 30-35mm at the rear.

Many people wrongly assume that they can make a spring stiffer by adding preload to it. It doesn't help that the forks are often marked 'stiffer' and 'softer'.

When you add preload to a linear spring, you are not increasing the stiffness of the spring, all you are doing is compressing the spring, or 'pre-loading' it a certain amount. If an 80kg rider climbs aboard a 1kg/mm spring with no preload, he will compress the spring 80mm.

But if we add 10mm of preload to the spring, when he climbs aboard now, the spring will only compress by 70mm.

For the first 10kg of the rider's weight, the spring was already pushing back with 10kg of force. It only started deflecting once more than 10kg was added.

This preload does have the effect of making the suspension feel stiffer, but in reality it just takes more force to get the suspension to initially deflect.

Adding preload cannot help you get over a too soft a spring for your weight and riding style, neither will backing off the preload help if the spring is too hard. You will need to set up your sag, and work out whether your springs are appropriate for your weight and riding style.

It's worth bearing in mind when setting up the sag that adjusting preload does affect suspension geometry. The majority of bikes will not have the means to adjust shock length (aftermarket shocks often have lengthening bars fitted), but almost all can drop the front end by raising the forks in the triple clamp to sharpen up the steering by increasing the steering head angle.

Damping Settings

Besides sag settings, damping needs to be set up for the road conditions. My biggest recommendation here is to buy yourself a setup book and carefully and gradually adjust settings, one at a time until you have something that feels better to you. The subject is complicated, and benefits from a whole book's explanation.

It might seem daunting to tweak your bike, but unless you get out there and adjust your bike, and more importantly understand how the adjustments that you have made translate to rider feel, you will never know the ability of your machine.

You could turn your bike from a bucking bronco into a sweet handling ride, but if you don't try these things, you will never know how good it can be.

There are two useful books that I have listed in the *Recommended Reading* chapter at the back of this book, which explain in significant detail how to setup your sag, your bike's geometry and your suspension's damping to your liking. Take the book with you, find a road that you enjoy riding and ride it multiple times, adjusting your suspension each time so you can compare settings in consistent conditions. You could do a similar thing on a track day, measuring either levels of confidence, or lap times to determine the success of your adjustments.

11. ESSENTIAL MACHINE CONTROL

There are six basic controls on a motorcycle. Throttle, clutch, front brake lever and rear brake pedal, gear lever and handlebars: all are essential to machine control. There is a job for each of our hands and feet to do, and a right way to do that job.

Working with the bike rather than against it is the key to becoming a smooth rider. There's no doubt that you need to be sitting in the saddle or you can't operate the controls effectively, but the best thing you can do as a rider is to give the bike control inputs as smoothly as you can, and then try to get out of the way.

When riding, think of yourself as the pilot of your bike, much as the rider of a horse is there to steer but not strongarm the beast. If you don't wrestle with your bike, it will respond much better to your control inputs. In essence that means a relaxed, light touch on the controls, and progressive use of the throttle, brakes and steering.

Imagine you have found a new-born chick on the ground. Maybe a few days old, its bone structure has not yet formed, and it must be handled very delicately. This is how lightly you should operate the controls of a motorcycle.

The light touch is good for two main reasons; Firstly, the motorcycle has dynamics that work best without the rider on board – the handlebars want to shake for example – and secondly, the more relaxed you are, the more you are able to feel what is going on, getting feedback from the bike and road below through those same controls.

Counter-Steering

I wasn't taught about counter-steering when I learned to ride, which strikes me as odd, because counter-steering is effectively how you steer a motorcycle. Until you can deliberately steer your motorcycle where you want it, you don't have full control.

Counter-steering is quite simply steering the handlebars in the opposite direction (counter) to the way you want to turn. It sounds complicated but it isn't. Unlike a tricycle, which steers like a car with the front wheel turning in the direction of travel, counter-steering is essential to cornering on bicycles and motorbikes.

Don't get too hung up on the 'counter' bit, just think about using your arms to actively steer the bike. If you can't deliberately steer your bike to put it exactly where you want it, then you need to get out there and practice actively steering until it becomes a reflex response.

If you have ever ridden a bicycle, you will have used counter-steering, although you're probably not aware of it, as the forces involved are so small that they are barely noticeable.

But on a motorcycle, wheels and tyres are heavier, and greater lean angles are required to make a turn, so the effects of counter-steering are far more pronounced and much more obvious to the rider.

The reason counter-steering is necessary is because of something called gyroscopic precession. That spinning mass of front wheel and tyre is rotating beneath the handlebars, when the bars are turned to the right, the bike leans to the left, and the tyre's contact with the road does the rest.

The best example of counter-steering in action is to watch slow motion video of top-level motorcycle racing. As the bikes exit a corner at full lean, you can see them steering their front wheels in the opposite direction to the way they want their bike to lean to stand their bikes up. Observe the front wheels' direction as they are skipping along the top of the tarmac. Even when the front wheel is airborne, it still has enough gyroscopic influence to stand the bike upright.

You don't need to understand counter-steering, you just need to know that it works, and practice it until it becomes second nature. The best way to think about steering a motorcycle is as follows:

If you want to lean the bike to the left you need to push the left handlebar, and if you want to turn the bike to the right, you push the right.

If you shift your weight to the inside of the turn, this can also reinforce the behaviour of pushing the inside bar.

When you ride, consciously steer your motorbike with positive inputs through the bars to lean the bike where you want it. Do this every time you ride and before long it will becomes a natural reflex response.

Power-Steering

For truly effective steering, use both of your arms. To turn right, push on the right bar at the same time as pulling on the left, and you will get twice the turning effect. It's the equivalent of power steering for bikes.

If you ever see racers 'flip-flopping' from fully leaned over one way to full leaned over the other, this is exactly what they are doing; wrestling their bikes at speed by applying a considerable force to the bars to counteract the stabilising effect of the rotating wheels.

Top Tip: For maximum efficiency when steering your bike, make sure that you are pushing at right angles to the front forks; for sports bikes with low set clip-ons, you will need to make sure your arms are below the horizontal, with a 90-degree bend in your elbow. It will make the turning effort far easier.

If you ride with your arms straight, pushing at an angle of 45 degrees above the forks, you will need over 40 percent more effort to achieve the same steering input (you see, trigonometry can be useful).

So to effectively turn a sports bike you need to get your body and your arms lower and flatter to the tank.

The leverage effect of wider-set handlebars also helps to reduce the amount of steering input required. This is the reason that bikes with wide, high set handlebars seem so easy to turn, whereas a race replica feels heavier. It is also the reason why John McGuinness favours wide handlebars on his TT bikes; it makes his life easier over the gruelling 37.73 mile TT course.

Stability at Speed

Unlike a car, which becomes increasingly unstable at high speed, motorcycles become more stable: as the momentum of the rotating wheels and tyres increases, a greater force is required to turn the bike off its line.

If you are struggling to turn at speed, use your foot pegs as a base from which to push more effectively with your arms. Motorcycle racers regularly wear through the soles of their boots because of the force and leverage required to get bikes turned at racing speeds.

The bike will also turn easier when rolling off the throttle, decelerating or braking. You should be aiming for smooth arm inputs to get the bike cranked over. When you have mastered actively steering and it becomes second nature, you can put the bike exactly where you want it, and your riding will become a more precise and more fun activity.

Throttle

The throttle provides accelerating and decelerating force via the rear tyre. That's obvious enough. But as mentioned in the previous section, the throttle is also used to arrest the fall of the bike as it is being steered to its maximum lean angle in a turn, to steady the balance of the bike, and to stand the bike up when driving off the corner. Motorbikes feel most composed during cornering when on a light constant throttle.

As you approach a corner, roll off the throttle and apply the brakes progressively, building more power as you progressively load up the front tyre. You should be aiming to do most of your braking before you start leaning the bike.

Once you are happy with your entry speed, actively steer the bike into the turn at the rate you want. You can trail brake into the corner if you want, gradually releasing the brakes as you approach your maximum lean angle.

When you have reached your maximum lean angle, crack open the throttle ever-so slightly, to stabilise the bike and arrest the fall, and when you see a clear line out of the corner, roll on the throttle to stand the bike up and, once more upright, use the bars to steer out of the corner.

Often the transition from closed to open throttle can take a while to master, especially when you have all of the other elements of cornering to consider, and some snatchy fuel-injected bikes make this a more daunting prospect than others. But the sooner you crack open the throttle, the sooner you can pick your exit point and start driving off the corner.

Throttle response is dependent on engine type, the torque curve of the engine and the engine's speed. Motorcycle engines are highly tuned, and therefore produce more power as engine speed increases.

In this regard gear selection is essential; you want to be in the correct gear to give yourself sufficient drive when you roll on the throttle, but you also want to know that when you crack open the throttle at full lean that you are not going to unleash too much power onto the rear tyre, overload it and cause a slide.

Front Brake

The front brake is a phenomenally powerful tool. It is so powerful that it can break traction at the front wheel, causing a front-end off, lock the front wheel, or stand the bike on its nose.

The front brake should be used as progressively as possible; gradually squeezed and gradually released rather than grabbed, to prevent shock loading of the suspension and front tyre, which risks breaking traction. Imagine you are squeezing the arm of someone to give them reassurance, or squeezing the juice out of a lemon.

Because the weight of the motorcycle is thrown forward during braking, the front tyre has the most grip, and does the majority of the work in slowing the bike.

Learning to trail brake into corners is worth practising once you have a bit of riding experience under your belt, as it gives you an extra insurance policy when cornering.

In the beginning, trail braking is best practiced on the track. But if you get all of your braking done before you enter a corner, you have little opportunity to fine-tune your corner entry speed. When you have mastered control of the front brake, and feedback from the front end to the point that you can trail-brake deep into the corner, not only can you enter the corner at a higher speed, but your trail braking will steer the bike more keenly as the front suspension is more compressed. Trail braking is discussed in more detail in chapter 13.

Rear Brake

The rear brake is far less effective than the front, as evidenced by the smaller size of the disc. It is useful to slow the momentum of the spinning rear tyre and wheel, especially at high speed, but there is little weight over the rear tyre when braking.

In heavy braking situations the weight is thrown forwards, and there is little weight over the rear tyre so it is easy to break traction and cause a rear wheel skid. When carrying a pillion or luggage, the increased loading on the rear tyre means the rear brake can be used more effectively without locking the wheel.

If your motorcycle has a tendency to wheelie under power, a gentle dab of rear brake pedal is an effective, smooth way to bring the front down, the same applies to the often-clunky gearshift between first and second through neutral.

When manoeuvring at low speed, the rear brake can be used in conjunction with applying the throttle and slipping the clutch for fine machine control.

Racers advocate using the rear brake to stabilise the rear when braking into corners, or when they want to 'back it in' to get a better angle coming into and out of the corner.

Top Tip: As there is so little traction available at the rear tyre, if you are riding a bike without ABS, the rear brake can be used to test available grip at the road surface. It may be wet, or you may be riding on a surface that you are unfamiliar with. If you're tip-toeing around, and you want to know for sure how much grip there is, try locking up the rear momentarily. Trying this in various situations will quickly give you a gauge for how much grip is available. Once you have locked up the rear tyre, you should release it immediately, or you risk losing the stabilising effect of your rear tyre's rotating mass.

The Six P-s - Developing your Motorcycle Roadcraft

To perform any activity well, we must first adopt the rule of six P-s: Proper Planning and Preparation Prevents Poor Performance. Out on the roads, this translates to an awareness of hazards which may catch you off guard and cause a panic situation, and making sure your machine and your riding skills are in tip-top condition. If you are able to anticipate everything that you might reasonably come across, and you have the ability to safely manage it, you will come to no harm.

If you can get your hands on a copy, I recommend reading Motorcycle Roadcraft: The Police Rider's Handbook (2013), which the UK motorcycle police use as a system to negotiate the roads safely. It's not the most dynamic work, and you may not agree with everything inside, but there's no denying it makes a lot of sense, and as a system used by professional riders, it clearly works.

Motorcycle Roadcraft centres around a five point system: Gathering **information**; being aware of the road conditions and having good hazard awareness (this comes with increased riding/driving experience), making sure you are in the correct **position**, at the correct **speed**, and in the appropriate **gear** to negotiate the hazard, before **accelerating** away to safety. I won't go into huge detail here, but in a nutshell the five points are as follows:

1.   Information

The information phase is never complete as long as you are aboard your bike. If you're riding down a public road, you are either taking in information, or giving out information to other road users (positioning, body language, lights, indicators, horn and appropriate hand signals).

You are gathering information to assess the road conditions ahead, giving more careful attention to the potential hazards you identify. Some conditions require more concentration than others, and the faster you ride, or the busier the conditions, the more you will need to focus. Your eyes should be constantly scanning, anticipating potential hazards, but you should also be using your nose (diesel) your ears (other road users) and your sixth sense (your gut).

The more you drive or ride, the better you will get at spotting potential hazards and successfully negotiating them. The key to efficient information gathering is about knowing where to put your attention. You only have a certain amount of attention to give to the hazards out there, but the more experienced the rider, the more adept they are at risk assessment, dismissing hazards that are not relevant, and focusing on those that are. This is something that comes with practice.

As with everything in life, the better the communication, the better the execution of the task at hand.

2.   Position

Correct road positioning is essential to riding safely and efficiently. Unlike a car driver who has little opportunity to move around in his lane, a biker's smaller footprint, at least when upright, makes it easier for him to move around the road space to improve the data gathering information step, and to spot hazards early and deal with them appropriately.

The ideal position when riding is the one that gives the rider the most benefit. This will vary depending on where you find yourself. When riding in a straight line, you will want to position yourself to get the best view ahead, usually between the middle of the lane, and the centre-line of the road.

When approaching a junction, you may choose to move over further to the centre to give yourself more space in case a vehicle should pull out. If you see a patch of gravel on the road, you may choose to position yourself over an area with more grip. When passing a line of parked cars or a delivery van, you may choose to give them a wide berth in case a door should suddenly open, or an obscured vehicle pull out without indicating. When overtaking, you may choose to move onto the other side of the road to improve your visibility of the road ahead before committing to the manoeuvre and applying the throttle.

Because of the increased road space required for cornering, you will naturally move to the right-hand side of the lane when taking left hand corners and to the left of your lane when negotiating right-hand corners. This positioning also gives you a better view around the corner, so you can see oncoming vehicles earlier, and assess the corner better before deciding when to make your steering input, and the best line to take.

When planning an overtaking manoeuvre, you can use improved road positioning to see past large vehicles obstructing your view of the road ahead. As you are smaller and harder to spot, put yourself in a position where other road users can see you more easily. If you ride directly behind a large vehicle which is hiding you from plain sight, and that vehicle pulls onto a side road, give other road users a chance to spot you, because they won't expect you to be there.

3.   *Speed*

Always ride at a speed that is appropriate to the road conditions. This sounds obvious, I know. Take into account the available grip, your ability, other road users, and any hazards in your frame. Just because you can negotiate that hazard ahead, doesn't mean the person in front of you can, so don't be surprised if they suddenly brake.

If the rest of the road users are travelling at the speed limit, and you are going significantly faster, they may not be expecting your excessive speed, or they may not have the skill or perception to spot someone travelling that fast. Sometimes the excuse 'Sorry, I didn't see you' may actually be true.

You may be travelling too fast for your own ability or the road conditions, particularly in corners. Adopt a 'slow in - fast out' approach to cornering on the road and keep brown-trouser moments to a minimum. As a rule, ride to the road space you can see ahead, and make sure that you can comfortably stop in the clear space.

If you are travelling too fast to negotiate a hazard, you will need to brake / decelerate to reduce speed, which hampers your ability to negotiate the hazard ahead. But if you are travelling at the right speed, you can focus on the issue at hand. You don't want to be changing down gears during a corner, you want the bike settled on its suspension and you want to be focused on turning and driving off the corner.

4.   Gear

There is an appropriate gear for you to be in at any point during your ride. As motorcycles have sequential gearboxes, you have to be on top of your gear changes. You can't change from sixth to first in one swift movement like in a car's manual gearbox; you need to work your way down through the gears like a sequential auto or modern dual-clutch gearbox.

Motorcyclists should take advantage of motorcycles' inherent benefits to stay safe, and one of these is their swift acceleration. To make this benefit count, you will need to be in the correct gear so that when you do want to accelerate briskly you can open the throttle and go. The Speed and Gear steps really come together as one.

An easy way to make sure you are always in the correct gear is to get into the habit of using engine braking to adjust your speed, in combination with the brakes.

5.   Acceleration

Once you have identified the hazard and assessed it, put yourself in the correct position, at an appropriate speed and in the right gear, you can negotiate the hazard before accelerating away.

12. GEAR

While car drivers move around in climatically controlled boxes isolated from the world outside, bikers are exposed to the wind and rain, the hot and the cold.

Motorcycle riders rely on their protective clothing to keep them comfortable. To do this their gear needs to deal with the changing atmospheric conditions and temperatures they will meet. It should also incorporate body armour and abrasion resistant materials to protect the rider in the event of a fall.

In the UK the only legal requirement is that you wear an approved helmet for head protection (except if you're a Sikh wearing a turban). In the rest of the world laws regarding protective equipment differ, or are completely absent.

In my mind, protective equipment is essential. The best protective gear works so well that you don't even notice it is there. While it's nice to feel the wind through your hair, nothing fills you with confidence like wearing a full set of leathers, boots, gloves and a full-face helmet. We don't give it as much attention as we should, but our mental comfort when riding sets the tone for everything else which follows. When you're warm, dry and comfortable, you can keep your mind focused on the road ahead, and not on how cold your hands and feet are.

Leathers or Textiles

When it comes to protective clothing you have two choices; leather or textile materials such as Cordura®. Both can be purchased as one-piece or two-piece suits, and good examples of each are comparable in cost.

The one-piece leather suit is a fitted cut, normally highly ventilated with stretch panels in the right places for optimum manoeuvrability and comfort, and is typically used for track riding and racing.

The one piece textile suit is designed as a waterproof over-suit which can be worn over your normal day clothes, and you can typically step out of it without taking off your boots; ideal if you are commuting to a work meeting, although you will still have helmet hair and a crumpled suit to contend with.

Two-piece leather and textile suits are similar, and usually zipped together to keep drafts out. The trousers differ in cut and some textile suits incorporate braces to keep them up. Textile suits tend to have a more relaxed fit, designed for sports-touring or touring motorcycles. Go and ask your clothing dealer for advice and try on some different suits.

If you want to look the part, you will want to wear clothing which is appropriate for your motorcycle, so you probably wouldn't choose one-piece race leathers if you were going touring on your Harley to the south of France, although don't let me stop you if that's the way you roll.

If you're going touring, you may appreciate the plethora of pockets, the looser fit, better insulation properties and waterproof lining that a textile suit offers, over the out-and-out race performance of a leather suit.

If you are only planning to buy one outfit, I would recommend a textile suit. If you ride all year round - there are some nice biking days in the winter months too - you will eventually end up buying one anyway. If you are planning to do track days, you will need to buy or borrow some leathers; either a one-piece or two-piece suit with a joining zip, before they allow you out onto track. These can be picked up fairly cheaply on eBay.

Textile gear is waterproof, windproof and more comfortable to wear for longer periods. Due to the inclement nature of the UK weather, a textile suit will get you off to a good start as it is much more flexible, not to mention warmer than a pair of leathers.

If you only ride in the summer, then a set of leathers combined with a waterproof over-suit in case it rains, can work perfectly well too. A well-worn set of leathers fits like a favourite pair of jeans, and your leather jacket can be styled with a pair of Cordura jeans for a more fashionable look around town.

Leathers

- ✓ Excellent abrasion resistance
- ✓ Distinctive 'biker' look
- ✓ Breathable
- ✓ Armour in key areas (knees, elbows, shoulders), and the armour is comfortable
- ✓ Waterproof - up to about half an hour
- ✓ Track use necessity
- ✓ One-piece leathers for the 'Road Racer' look
- ✓ Some have removable linings for winter and summer use and some

have a back hump (not ideal if you want to drive a car)
- ✓ Minimum of pockets
- ✓ Tight fitting
- ✓ Not machine washable
- ✓ Leathers are available with waterproof linings but these are prohibitively expensive.
- ✓ Take a long time to dry

Textiles

- ✓ Incorporate Gore-Tex® or other waterproof membrane to keep you dry for more hours
- ✓ A more relaxed fit
- ✓ Can incorporate full CE approved armour (knee, hip, back, shoulders, elbows) though doesn't fit as well as leather armour
- ✓ Lots of pockets (including some waterproof ones)
- ✓ Trousers and jacket of same make zip together
- ✓ Removable thermal liners
- ✓ Machine washable - quickly and easily restored to 'as-new' condition.

Waterproof Gear

It used to be the case that no waterproof clothing was completely waterproof. Given long enough outside in the torrential rain, the wetness would eventually start to soak through. I'm pleased to report that this is no longer the case. I have personally tested my gear riding through one of the wettest and windiest UK winters on record, and it never once leaked, keeping me completely dry.

The solution is modern wonder fabrics such as Gore-Tex® Pro Shell. These are available in motorcycle gear and they really do work. In the older designs of Gore-Tex jackets, the waterproof membrane sat underneath the external layer of protective textile material. Once the outer material was wet through, it could not quickly dry out, and the membrane by osmosis eventually passed the water through to your skin. If you ride all day in the rain with one of these older suits, you will eventually get wet, and the weight of the wet jacket will tire you out.

But Gore-Tex Pro Shell is different because the waterproof membrane is incorporated into the external shell material, so water runs off the surface of the suit rather than soaking into it. This keeps the wet weight down making it more comfortable to wear, reduces drying time to overnight, and reduces wet-induced windchill to a minimum.

I wish I could say the same about gloves. Your gloves will eventually get wet, and when they do they will cool your core body temperature down. Your hands have a huge number of nerves, and a correspondingly good blood supply. This coupled with their high surface area means they act as a pretty decent heat-exchanger. We dunk our hands into cool water on a hot day to cool ourselves down, and put our gloves on in chilly winter weather to keep ourselves warm.

Cold, wet gloves are a heat sink that you could do without if you want to stay warm. If you are planning a long trip and the weather looks variable, take a spare pair of gloves or two, or get yourself some handlebar muffs to keep the wind and rain off your hands, just test them at speed to make sure they don't obstruct your controls. I am really looking forward to seeing Gore-Tex Pro Shell gloves on the market.

Textile gear is perfect all-year-round gear, and when buying, you generally get what you pay for. Some equipment is made to a budget and will fall apart in a matter of weeks (make sure you get a warranty on any clothes). Other manufacturers expend an enormous R&D budget on their product lines, and back them up with a five-plus-year warranty.

The best thing to do is to go and see for yourself the quality of what is available. You cannot shop for motorcycle gear online, unless you know the brand and the fit, or have a free no-quibble returns policy. Get out to the shops, try on some suits and see which fit you the best, which feel comfortable, good quality and worth the money.

You want to trust this kit if you have an accident. You also need to consider what you'll be wearing underneath (a shirt for work or perhaps a fleece in the winter), and whether the legs and arms are long enough when you're wearing the suit in your riding position, and not just standing up in the shop.

For sports bikes you will be in a more pronounced crouch, so you don't want too much jacket material at the front, or it will bunch up. Equally you might want a bit more jacket material at the back to avoid displaying any structural cracks.

Helmet

When it comes to protecting your 'little grey cells', you have a lot of choice open to you. Before you rush online looking for bargains, hang on a second.

People's heads, like the bodies they are attached to, come in different shapes and sizes. Fortunately, there are a number of helmet manufacturers out there who cater for this variability in the shape of the human skull. The best thing to do is get yourself down to your motorcycle accessory dealer and try some different makes out until you find one that fits you.

Don't take recommendations of helmet fit from anyone else, as the ones which work for them won't necessarily work for you, and few people can tell you the shape of their head.

The best helmets are light and therefore easy on the neck (important if you are wearing it all day long), quiet (within reason and with earplugs in), well ventilated in hot weather, with a comfortable lining (preferably removable for easy washing), with a decent double-D fastening system.

They should also come with a visor insert (called a pin-lock) to prevent the visor misting up in cooler weather. If your helmet doesn't come with a pin-lock insert, then you can buy sticky inserts yourself that perform the same function.

When it comes to quality helmets, I always look to see what the road racers are wearing. They rely on their helmets, so they need to be comfortable, and do their job properly when it comes to the crunch. Some well-respected brands worth checking out are Arai, Shoei, Suomi, AGV, Shark, HJC, Caberg, Schuberth, X-Lite, and Nolan.

My head is more oval shaped, and I find a lot of helmets can press into the front of my forehead, so I like the fit of Arai and Shoei helmets, try some out and see which ones work best for you. If your head is shaped more like a ball, you may find other helmets fit you better.

As far as colours go, the choice on offer is mind blowing. If you want a classic look, you can go for a solid colour or a classic gloss or matt black or white, but you will probably at some point be lured by the plethora of funky painted designs. Some manufacturers paint their helmets in the colours of their sponsored racers, other designs are more 'alternative'. Find something that represents who you are, or blend in with a classic.

How far you go here is really up to you, if you have deep enough pockets, there are even a number of designers who will custom paint your lid to any design you like.

While the asking price for a decent helmet may look expensive at over £500, you really can't put a big enough price on your head, not just for crash protection should you be unlucky enough to fall, but that a cheap poor quality helmet will distract you from your riding.

If you ride around town, if you like the feeling of the wind on your face, or if you like to be seen, then an open face helmet is a stylish way to ride, though you may need some goggles to keep the bugs out of your eyes.

If you do a bit of town and a bit of motorway, and you like the extra protection of a chin bar, consider getting a flip-up lid; they are slightly heavier due to the chin bar mechanism, but this can be preferable to taking off your helmet every five minutes.

Neck Warmer

Neck warmers are essential in the spring, autumn and winter, and also in the morning and evening in the summer when it can get pretty cold, especially at altitude.

Boots

Good quality boots, if well looked after, will last you a long time. Once broken in they will feel as comfortable as a favourite pair of slippers. Leather is good, although many of the sportier boots use plastic, metal or even carbon-fibre reinforced plastic to protect vulnerable parts of the foot and ankle from crushing forces.

As your legs are the most exposed part of your body when you ride, especially when you're in town, it pays to have a good quality waterproof boot with a grippy sole (no flip-flops please!).

I say waterproof, because unless you're just using the boots for racing, and you live in the UK, you're going to end up riding in the rain at some point, and having wet feet is not much fun.

Plastic armoured boots do tend to creak like a pirate ship's rigging, so if you enter late or exit early, you might want to buy something all-leather, or keep a little can of WD-40 handy to quiet things down.

If you do end up riding in the rain, make sure that your trousers are also waterproof and that the rain runs outside the boots. Waterproof boots are waterproof, whether the water is on the inside or the outside, and once they fill up with water on the inside, they take an age to dry out.

Gloves

Gloves can be divided into three broad categories; winter, summer, and all season gloves. If you ride only in the summer, you might get away with only one pair of all-season leather gloves. If you ride in the winter, you'll definitely need some winter gloves to keep your hands warm, so you can control the bike properly and not lose all sensation in your hands.

In extreme summer conditions or if you live near the equator, you can wear summer gloves that are highly ventilated, either with lots of tiny perforations in the leather, or textile backing and a leather grip, to keep the hand cool in the breeze.

Finding a good glove is paramount, as you will sense all of your steering and braking feedback through your hands, so they should be a good fit and give you lots of feel. As the size of gloves varies significantly from brand to brand, be sure to try some on from different manufacturers to find the right size for you.

Some glove manufacturers, Held for example, manufacture gloves with two functions, they can be used as a ventilated glove, but also incorporate a Gore-tex liner within the main body of the glove in case it rains or gets cold. It's effectively two gloves in one. It's a brilliant idea in theory and it works really well in practice. The system is called Air 'n' Dry, and is definitely worth a look.

Handlebar Muffs

If you want to know what effective winter gear looks like, take a look at those who ride all year round. Motorcycle couriers are big fans of handlebar muffs. These are material sleeves that fit over the handlebar, protecting your hands from the direct effects of the wind and rain.

Muffs are usually attached by means of the handlebar end-weight, so shouldn't interfere with the brake and clutch levers. These are much more effective than gloves in cold wet weather, but you will definitely lose points for style if you fit them to your Panigale, and I'm not sure how well they work at high speed.

Heated Accessories

Heated jacket, heated grips, heated gloves are all useful weapons in the arsenal of the winter biker, and can extend your riding pleasure if you ride all year round and you feel the cold.

Some people are extremely hardy, don't feel the cold and certainly wouldn't bother the doctor with a 'mere flesh wound'. Others are more sensitive to their surroundings, and will feel pain and the effects of cold temperatures more readily.

On a cold winter's evening, after about an hour in the saddle, you will start to feel the cold. If you get wet, the effect will come on quicker. In these situations, having a little bit of extra warmth can raise your spirits, and hence the quality of your riding. If you are warm and comfortable, you will probably also be more relaxed, and can focus on your riding instead of how cold your hands are.

Most heated equipment plugs into a fused loom which is connected across the bike's battery. As long as the engine is running, the battery will be charging. If you stop for a long period of time, or if you have bike with a small engine (less than 250cc), make sure your heated gear is not putting too much strain on the battery and charging system.

GPS

Ideal for the navigationally challenged, but becoming the standard nowadays, satnav is a godsend. How did we ever find our way before?

I use the TomTom app on my phone, which is mostly right; Google and Apple have satnavs built into their mapping apps, but these do need an internet connection to work unless you have downloaded an off-line map (the TomTom app doesn't, so is more effective when abroad or in the highlands of Scotland).

The phone goes in my pocket and I have to decipher the verbal messages to make the right turning rather than looking at the pictures. At least I can keep my eyes on the road ahead.

You can of course buy dedicated satnavs for motorcycles; the TomTom Rider and the Garmin Zumo are designed for use with gloved hands and are fully waterproof. These plug into the battery or a 12V accessory socket (if your bike has one), and sit on your top yoke.

If you like maps, get yourself a MapsMan waterproof map, and put it inside a magnetic map case on the fuel tank.

Hearing Protection

Above about 50mph, motorcycles get pretty noisy, even if they have a fairing. To protect your ears, keep your brain comfortable and to stop yourself from getting fatigue, you are going to need some ear protection.

There are a number of disposable earplugs which are suitable for motorcyclists, Earsoft FX are excellent, and reduce the noise to very comfortable levels, though they are large and can be uncomfortable if you have small ear canals. Moldex is another good brand. You can buy earplugs in small quantities, but they are much cheaper if you buy a large box of 200 pairs from a PPE (personal protection equipment) specialist online. If you ride regularly you will need a constant supply of fresh plugs to stop yourself from going deaf. Reusing old earplugs is not hygienic.

Battery Trickle Charger

Unless you ride every day, you will probably benefit from a trickle charger. As bikes get progressively lighter, especially sports bikes, the quest for weight savings has hit batteries hard.

The batteries on most motorbikes are too small, and those on modern sports bikes are frankly pathetic and will go flat if left alone in the cold for a period of a couple of weeks without starting the engine. Imagine a battery the size of a carton of orange juice having to crank a 1,000cc engine with a high compression ratio.

These batteries are not cheap either; so if you don't ride at least every other week, buy yourself a trickle charger before you have to buy yourself a new battery as well as a trickle charger.

There are a number of chargers on the market. If you have access to a power source, you can use a mains-powered trickle charger. If your bike is situated outdoors in your garden or in the shed, you can buy solar panel trickle chargers which also work quite well, though in winter it's best to take the battery indoors and plug it into a mains charger as the solar energy that makes it down to your battery may be enough to keep the battery alive, but not enough to keep it in a state where you can actually start your bike and go for a ride.

Once a battery is dead, it cannot be revived. Get yourself a trickle charger sooner rather than later. Halfords, Acumen, Optimate, and Oxford are some well-known UK brands. You might also take the opportunity to buy yourself one of the handiest bits of kit you can buy, a portable power pack: An all-in-one tyre compressor, battery charger, battery jump pack, light and 300w 240v inverter. This can pump up your tyres, charge batteries or start a car or bike with a flat battery. Available with different cranking capacity for different sized engines.

13. TYRES (& THE ROAD SURFACE)

The last 20 years have seen a massive leap in tyre technology. As advancements in engine design have increased horsepower, tyre manufacturers have had their work cut out producing tyres that can put that amount of power down on the road.

Much high-performance tyre technology has come to us courtesy of the racetrack, where manufacturers have been asked to produce tyres able to handle the 200bhp+ of modern bikes. Grand Prix riders of the 1970s and 1980s would have given their left arm to race on the kind of rubber you can buy in your local tyre dealer today.

Tyres are engineered for a particular purpose; be they all-season road tyres, racing slicks, motocross tyres, or road-legal track-day tyres. There's a tyre for every occasion, and a direct correlation between the tyres' grip and how long they will last; the softer the tyre the more grip but the quicker the wear. But there is more to the story than grip versus longevity. The biggest and most important factor in tyres is design operating temperature.

Design Operating Temperature

This is the most important design feature of a tyre. It sounds obvious, but tyres are designed to work at a particular temperature. When a tyre corners, it holds the bike by the friction force generated between the tyre and the road surface. Likewise when you accelerate or brake, the tyre 'bites' into the road surface to get the purchase needed to speed up or slow down the bike.

The more work the tyre is asked to do, the hotter it will get. If you've ever rubbed your hands together to warm them up, you have experienced the conversion of kinetic energy (motion of your arms) into heat (your skin) via friction at the skin's surface. Design temperature is where the tyre gives maximum grip.

Riding around town at speeds of up to 50mph with gentle accelerating, braking and cornering means less friction, less power dissipated through road tyres. The tyre won't generate as much heat, so a lower design temperature tyre is preferable.

Throw in the variability of ambient conditions such as air temperature, diverse road temperatures and the potential for a wet surface which can cool the tyre significantly and it's easy to see that a road tyre might have to deal with a multitude of different operating conditions.

At the other end of the scale, race slicks are best used after baking in tyre warmers to get them up to their extremely hot operating temperatures before going out on track. A high-speed session on track with significant lean angles, high cornering speeds, full-throttle acceleration and heavy braking will get the tyres extremely hot. Clearly in this situation a high design temperature is desirable. Using a road based tyre would surpass its optimum temperature. It would overheat, and grip would be compromised.

The "Holy Grail"

The 'holy grail' of tyres, is a tyre that warms up quickly, has incredible grip in both wet and dry conditions, lasts a long time and can be used occasionally on the track. Most manufacturers can make sticky rubber with ease; the real problem is making them last more than 1000 miles. Consider that MotoGP rubber allows lean angles of 64 degrees, and harnesses over 250bhp at the rear tyre and the stopping force of carbon discs, but wears out in less than 80 miles.

With the introduction of dual- and even triple-compound tyres, we are getting closer to this 'Holy Grail' formula. In a multi-compound tyre, the middle section of the tyre, where the bike spends most of its time, is made of a harder wearing compound, the next band(s) out get increasingly softer for better cornering grip when leaned over.

A modern fast road tyre should be able to handle all year-round riding, including a few track days and occasional riding in the wet. It will probably be somewhat compromised in the wet when compared to a road-biased sport-touring tyre, but will be ridden more in the dry so this is an acceptable compromise. When you consider that a spare set of wheels with dedicated track day or winter tyres is going to set you back at least £500 second hand, it's nice to have a set of tyres which can handle almost anything you throw at them.

Tyre Pressure

Tyres have a semi rigid carcass construction, and they are designed to flex a certain amount, but they rely on the pressure of the air inside them to work effectively. The tyre's carcass is what gives the rider feel from the road below. To allow the suspension to work effectively you need your tyres to press into the road, and not flex too much. That happens at or around manufacturer stated tyre pressures, the pressures the tyres were designed to operate at.

You need to keep your tyres inflated to the correct pressure; too little and it will affect the bike's suspension and grip (think about how you would move around less effectively if your shoes had mushy soles).

People might recommend that you drop tyre pressure for a track day. As you work the tyre very hard, the tyre – and the air inside – warms up significantly. When air is heated, it expands increasing the pressure inside the tyre. If you check your tyres directly as you come into the pits on a track day, your tyre pressures should be around the recommended levels. As they cool the pressures will drop.

In the absence of expert information, it's better to run your tyres at the recommended pressures. An over inflated tyre is better than an under inflated tyre. Tyre fitters at track days have experience of recommended tyre pressures. When you check your tyres, make sure you use a properly calibrated gauge; many petrol station compressors are not accurate, those that offer free air are not legally required to calibrate their gauges.

Grip and Contact Patch Size

How often do you hear TV commentators and pundits marvelling at the tiny contact footprint of a motorcycle tyre? We are supposed to be amazed that something so small can grip so well. Well, I've got news for you, a larger contact patch size does not necessarily mean more grip.

To prove this we need to go back to physics class. The formula for grip, or Friction is $F=\mu W$, where F is the friction force the tyre can generate (i.e. its Grip), μ (Greek letter mu) is the tyre's coefficient of friction and W is the weight. You will note no mention of surface area.

Therefore there are only two ways to increase grip:

1. Increase the coefficient of friction of the tyre compound, μ
2. Increase the weight of the bike and rider, W

If you want to know why racecars use aerodynamics, here is your answer. You adopt the stickiest tyre you can (highest μ value) with sufficient endurance, and you make the car artificially heavier – adding weight without increasing mass – using aerodynamics. The same technology that gets a 500-tonne Airbus A380 airborne can also make F1 cars weigh significantly more in motion than when stationary, increasing their cornering grip.

If a bigger contact patch doesn't increase grip, does this mean that a narrow tyre has the same grip as a wider tyre? As hard as it may be to believe, this is true, but it's a simplistic view of what is happening in practice. It can only be viewed as correct at the instant the force is applied through the tyre. In dynamic conditions, the ability of a tyre to maintain that coefficient of friction is determined by other factors.

If grip is not dependent on contact patch size, why are high performance cars and motorcycles fitted with wider tyres? Well, $F = \mu W$ applies to friction at the road surface, but there are other factors which come into play. We must also take into account the rubber's 'Shear Properties'.

Imagine walking up a steep bank which was coated with sandpaper. You would find it grippy and easy to climb. But if the sand, instead of being glued to a strong fibrous paper, was loose, arranged in the form of a sand dune, you wouldn't find your climb as easy.

Even though your foot has excellent grip with the sand, the problem is how the sand interacts with the other grains of sand in the dune. A sand dune has very low shear strength, and allows significant movement. It supports little force. You wouldn't build a house on a sand dune.

If a powerful racing motorcycle was fitted with something resembling a bicycle tyre, it might grip if the power was applied very gently, but if you unleashed full power, the tyre would not be able to withstand the huge forces at play. It would distort, most likely be destroyed, and in all the distortion would leave little rubber in contact with the road.

The more robust construction of a wider 200-section motorcycle tyre is better able to put that power down in the first place without shearing. It's the difference between running the 100m sprint in a pair of athletic spikes, or in a pair of loose fitting shoes with marshmallows for soles. Power is nothing if you can't put it down on the road, but it's not the size of the rubber patch per se, it's the compound and the tyre construction behind the contact patch which matters.

At this point we should also bring in tyre design temperature. Wider tyres also have benefits as regards operating temperature. Tyre coefficient of friction (μ) varies with temperature, it improves as the tyre warms up to its design temperature, but drops off if the temperature rises too far above that point and the tyre overheats (the tyres are 'cooked').

Tyre designers also aim to dissipate the heat produced to keep the tyre within its optimum design operating temperature range. A larger mass of tyre will absorb and dissipate this heat produced more effectively than a smaller one, just as a heavy-bottomed saucepan is used to absorb and distribute heat more effectively to avoid burning food.

The tyre profile is also key to the way the motorcycle steers, and in providing rubber at the sort of extreme lean angles that can be achieved. A wider more substantial tyre also provides better stability over surface imperfections – stones, debris etc. – and gives more stability due to the larger rotating mass of the wheels.

Wider tyres also help when it comes to the rate of wear. Stickier tyre compounds wear quicker than harder, and while a bigger contact patch doesn't necessarily provide more grip, it does spread that tyre wear out over a bigger surface area. The tyre lasts and maintains its profile for longer.

How Tyres Grip During Cornering

To understand how tyres grip when cornering, we can use the example of a basic friction experiment. Imagine you have a rubber brick on a level concrete table, and that brick has a large weight on top. A horizontal cable attached to the brick is pulled by a stack of weights hanging from the table edge. As more weights are added, eventually the sideways force exceeds the rubber block's grip. It breaks traction and slides across the table. Adding more weight to the top of the brick increases its grip.

The rubber brick represents the tyre, the weight on top is the weight of the bike and rider, and the grip it produces is calculated by the formula $F=\mu W$.

The cable which is trying to pull the brick over the edge of the table represents the cornering force which acts parallel to the surface. When the sideways cornering force exceeds the grip available at the surface, the tyre breaks traction.

A cornering bike is subject to inertial forces. These act sideways. No part of this cornering force is acting downward ... cornering doesn't improve grip, except on a banked track, like the UK's Oulton Park. In this case, some of your cornering force does increase your effective weight (also see: Wall of Death).

If you add more weight to the bike in an attempt to increase its grip, that same weight must also be accounted for in braking, accelerating and cornering forces. This cancels out any benefit.

In our rubber brick example, if we add another weight to the top of the brick, we must also add the same weight to the weight stack hanging off the edge of the table, as the centrifugal force this represents is proportional to the mass of the object cornering. Double the mass and you double the cornering force.

If you take the preceding to be true, it follows that a lighter motorcycle racer like Dani Pedrosa has no additional benefit over heavier riders. While he may accelerate and brake more easily as he is a lighter package ($F=ma$), he also has less grip to play with ($F=\mu W$) when accelerating and braking. During cornering, as we have discussed, there is no benefit. It is worth saying that a lighter rider may reduce wear and tear on the bike, tyres and brakes, depending on his riding style.

Crank it Over

There is a simple formula that we can use to work out the maximum theoretical lean angle achievable with a specific tyre fitted. If you want to read the science behind it, have a look in the Recommended Reading chapter at the back of the book. Calculators set to degrees:

$\mu = \tan(\emptyset)$

Where μ = the tyre coefficient of friction and $\emptyset$ = lean angle

A coefficient of friction of 1 allows a lean angle of 45degrees (modern sports tyre). If you want to reach 64 degrees like a MotoGP bike, you will need a super-sticky coefficient of friction of 2.05.

This simple equation is the reason manufacturers can state the maximum lean angles their tyres can achieve. They know the coefficient of friction, and they have scientific calculators.

How do You Want to Use your Available Grip?

Imagine you have a wooden post in the centre of your garden lawn with a rubber band pegged to it. This rubber band can be stretched one metre in any direction, but beyond that it will snap. It represents our theoretical tyre's available grip.

Pulling the band forwards from the peg one metre simulates 1g of braking force. Pulling the band one metre to the rear represents 1g of acceleration. One metre to the sides represents 1g of cornering force.

As the rider, you can choose to stretch your rubber band within this imaginary circle in any direction you want. You can use 1g of braking force, or 1g of cornering force, or you can choose to use 0.7g of braking and 0.7g of cornering force. 0.7+0.7 = 1.4. It is easy to see the benefits of trail braking into corners, and getting on the power earlier during cornering.

Some modern traction control systems do the maths for you. For example the BMW S1000RR's TC works in a number of different ways, one of which measures lean angle (and therefore how much grip is being used to corner), and restricts the power available once a predetermined lean angle is exceeded.

The threshold depends on the riding mode selected. Rain mode allows 38 degrees of lean (μ = 0.78), Sport mode allows 45 degrees (μ = 1), Race mode allows 48 degrees (μ = 1.1), and Slick mode allows 53 degrees (μ = 1.3). These are the threshold values and probably conservative for the conditions, as they are incorporated into a production road bike.

Tyre Types

Those little black hoops on your bike are the only thing keeping you and your bike 'shiny side up' as we say, so as well as keeping tyre pressure in check, it's worth picking the right tyre for your type of bike and riding. We'll discuss the tyres as they broadly fall into the following categories; in no particular order:

Sport-Touring Tyres

High-silica compounds promote excellent wet-weather performance, quick warm-up: popular with commuters and year-round riders. Modern sport-touring rubber is excellent for fast road riding on a number of different bikes.

Sport-touring tyres suit a broad range of motorcycles, riders and riding styles. They also offer a good compromise between grip and longevity. They tend to have a rounder profile, which gives the feel of a gradual roll into a corner, rather than the 'falling off a cliff' feeling you might get with more aggressive profiles.

Manufacturers put significant time, effort and money into developing sport-touring tyres that grip well in all seasons and last. This longevity is typically reflected in their retail price, so expect to pay top dollar for these frankly brilliant tyres, which just continue to improve year after year.

Sport-touring tyres also adopt dual-compound technology, with a harder compound in the centre of the tyre for more durability when upright, and a softer compound on the shoulders for improved cornering confidence. This dual-compound design evens out wear and prevents the tyre from squaring off too early, maintaining beneficial steering and handling characteristics for longer.

These tyres have considerable grip, and should provide enough performance for the majority of road riders, but if you ride very fast (i.e. knee down) on the road, or like the fast-steering feel of race oriented tyres on your sports bike, these are unlikely to be on your shopping list.

If you ride a good number of miles a year, sport-touring tyres will save you a lot of money. While softer stickier tyres might have more outright grip, if you never use it, you're just paying for tyres that will wear out more quickly. You should look for a pair of tyres with a level of grip that you can use all of, i.e. you should be approaching the limit of grip of the tyres in normal conditions.

Sport-touring riders are more likely to ride all year round, so they demand a tyre which operates well in the colder, wetter months of the year, which lasts a long time and wears evenly. A generous tread pattern has two main benefits: First it provides a good exit route for water to disperse, and second because the blocks of rubber between the tread pattern are allowed to move about more under acceleration and braking, they encourage heat to build up in the tyre.

Getting tyres up to a good operating temperature is key to good performance in the colder months. Have a look at Michelin's Pilot Road 4 tyre, and its sipe (thin slits) design, which car winter tyres adopt with equal success.

Fast Road Tyre

Acceptable cold-weather performance, warm up quickly, but are optimised for dry weather riding. Popular with sports-bike riders who do the occasional track day.

These have a good balance of grip and tyre life. They are typically aimed at production-class machines and sporty road bikes, the riders of which will not usually ride all year round, and may find themselves doing a number of track days a year. The design is a compromise between outright grip and tyre life. While life is limited, they usually last long enough that you only need one pair of tyres a year, and that will suit the majority of riders.

Different manufacturers use different profiles and carcass constructions which give you more or less extreme steering characteristics, a rounder-profile sports tyre will gradually lean the bike over into the turn, whereas a sharper, more triangular profile steers more quickly, feeling more like the bike is falling over into the turn. The sharper profile gives excellent grip at full lean angle but is less stable when braking in a straight line.

Your favoured profile depends on personal preference, and how the tyres work with your particular motorcycle geometry. Ask your tyre dealer about feedback from his customers, have a look at his tyre stock, and try to gauge other owners' or motorcycle journalists' opinions.

Modern sporty road rubber is also available with dual-compound technology. Like sport-touring tyres, these are designed for long life while providing maximum grip where it is most needed.

As tyre technology improves, the lines are becoming blurred between these popular classes. When a dual-compound sport-touring tyre can provide enough grip all year round for most bikes in most conditions, we will see technology from these sport-touring tyres working their way into the sportier ranges; with increased use of silica, dual-compound technology, less aggressive profiles for confidence inspiring tip-in, and with a softer, higher friction coefficient compound on the tyre shoulders.

Road Legal Track Day Tyres

Track day tyres are essentially slicks with a minimal tread cut into them to make them road legal. These tyres are very sticky and relatively soft, providing incredible levels of grip when worked hard on track, but tend to have a short life. Not so good in the cold or the wet, and not recommended for normal road use as they are unlikely to reach their operating temperature.

Very sticky rubber like this will highlight any suspension issues you may have. Where a road tyre moves around a lot, a very sticky tyre will transmit greater forces through the suspension. Don't be surprised if you need to tweak your suspension to tighten things up before getting the best out of these frankly incredible tyres.

Race Slicks

Strictly reserved for racers and hardcore track-day riders. These untreaded tyres are designed to operate at the high loads and temperatures experienced from continued high speed cornering. They are used with tyre warmers to keep them at their optimum operating range.

The difference between a cold race tyre and a hot one is significant, so it is important to keep them hot so they don't catch you out on the first lap. Tyre warmers reduce 'cycling' of the tyres and can prolong their useful life as well as your useful track time, as you don't spend two laps tentatively warming them up.

Wet Slicks

Wet slicks are heavily treaded tyres for racing in the wet, and provide huge grip under these conditions, but use them in the dry and they will quickly disintegrate as speeds and temperatures build, and there is no surface water to cool them. A very expensive option, and only really useful for racing in the wet.

Touring Tyres

Touring tyres have a harder compound and are designed for heavier motorcycles, in both carcass construction, and in grip compound. Heavier bikes wear tyres out faster than lighter ones, but their heavier weight means they can get grip from a less sticky tyre.

Long tyre life is more important than outright cornering edge grip. Touring bikes have limited ground clearance when leaned over, and spend little time at the edge of the tyre.

Tyre designers select a profile which matches these handling characteristics. Big touring machines tend to put in the miles too, so riders demand decent longevity from their tyres, and the ability to handle big power outputs.

Trail Tyres

We are talking about tyres for the 'Soft Roader'. Think BMW R1200GS rather than an enduro bike. They are aimed at large capacity, 600cc+ bikes with off-road pretensions that will mostly be used on the road.

The tyres are more heavily treaded for ride-anywhere grip, and warm up quickly. Useful for occasional green-laning or dirt trails. Anywhere dusty unsurfaced roads abound – like South Africa – these tyres are very popular.

Large Supermoto Tyres

The genesis of the large supermoto type bike (KTM Supermoto, Aprilia Dorsoduro, Ducati Hypermotard) has spawned a new breed of tyres. These use a sticky compound tyre with a larger block tread pattern, not as much as the trail bike example, but they do have a grippy compound that works really well and looks the part.

Some things Worth Knowing about Your Tyres

1.   *Your Bike was designed around a Specific Tyre*

When manufacturers develop motorcycles, they do so in conjunction with a tyre manufacturer, and will recommending an OEM tyre replacement which has been tested with the bike during its development. If you choose to adopt a different tyre, you may find your sweetly set-up bike no longer inspires confidence. Approach new tyres with caution, take advice from tyre manufacturers, other riders, and tyre dealers. Be prepared to set up your bike around your new tyre choice.

2.   *They are Brilliant*

It's worth emphasising this point. The tyres available today are extremely good, and give a level of grip that racers 20 years ago just didn't have. Shop around by all means, and pick a reputable tyre dealer, but the chances are the tyres are not going to be the weak link in the formula. More likely you have neglected to service your suspension, and you're blaming it on your tyres.

3.   *Compounds*

In the search to give the consumer 'one tyre to rule them all', manufacturers have been developing tyres with two and even three rubber compounds in the same construction. They use a harder compound in the centre section of the tyre for longevity, and increasingly stickier compounds on the shoulders where greater grip is required, and where the bike spends less time.

Dual or triple compounds improve grip and tyre life and keep the profile of the tyre sweeter for longer. But if you're not going to use of the additional grip available, you might consider using a harder compound tyre and change tyres less often.

4.   *Profile*

If your journey, or your riding technique, doesn't involve much in the way of cornering – mainly motorways and A-roads – then you are going to square off your tyres, which affects handling. A new tyre has a 'pointy' profile, for want of a better word. How pointy depends on the manufacturer, and the tyre's intended use. A pointy tyre gives quicker turn-in and, once leaned over, a larger contact patch. They can feel a bit too nervous for some, the bike feeling as if falling over as you lean.

Road oriented tyres on the other hand tend to have a more shallow, rounded profile with a more gradual steering feel and less dramatic response when leaning. As the centre section of the tyre wears, the profile can flatten and the motorcycle will not want to turn until leaned over significantly, which can be disconcerting.

If you have a supersport bike and you fit sport-touring tyres, you will get more mileage and better cold and wet weather performance, but your choice of tyres may dull the super sharp handling characteristics and make it feel more like a gentle relaxed sport tourer than a thoroughbred race bike.

5.   Feel

Riding motorbikes is all about feel, and feel is a personal thing. Choosing a tyre which works for you, which gives you the right amount and type of feedback is not as simple as choosing the tyre which won the tyre test in the latest bike magazine.

It depends on your bike, your suspension setup, when your suspension was last serviced, your riding style, and your personal preference. You need to get out there and try a few brands, and see which ones you like the feel of. The bad news is that tyres are expensive, the good news is that if you ride even a moderate amount you will be changing your tyres fairly frequently (every six to eight thousand miles on average), so you will get the chance to try a few brands out.

6.   Your Bike

The profile and construction of your tyre plays a huge part in the steering geometry and the suspension of your machine, and can change how it steers, accelerates and brakes. Changing from one tyre to the next could require suspension tweaking, and could make your bike steer differently. It is likely to require some getting used to. Tyre manufacturers have fitment guides and tyre recommendations for different machines: check out their websites for more information.

7.   Tyre Recommendations

To keep abreast of what's going down in the world of two wheelers, check out the UK Motorcycle press (digital and print magazines as well as online).

We are extremely lucky in the UK with a long tradition of extremely high-quality motorcycle journalism. These guys practice what they preach; they ride a lot of miles in all seasons, they club-race, race at the Isle of Man TT, commute thousands of miles a year, and regularly take trips abroad to attend the latest bike and tyre launches (it's a hard life, I know!).

They live and breathe bikes, so their judgement on tyre choice is definitely worth a listen. Motorcycle magazines typically run a fleet of test bikes, assessing different tyres and other accessories.

Also check with your motorcycling friends, for the choice is wide. All the major auto tyre manufacturers are accounted for; Dunlop, Pirelli,

Continental, Michelin, Bridgestone, Avon as well as some other cycle only brands Metzeler, Maxxis, Mitas.

14. MOTORCYCLE MECHANICS: SELF SERVICE

A bike on the road is worth two in the shed

-   Ogri

Motorcyclists today expect reliability and performance and usually get it, but it was not always so. Once upon a time, a biker was often by default also a motorcycle mechanic. One reason a biking fraternity arose was because riders were frequently in need of the assistance of fellow biker to get them up and running again.

Just as with cars, motorcycle reliability has come on a long way in the last 50 years. Improvements in design and manufacturing quality have made modern motorcycles dependable. The majority of quality Japanese and European bikes will cover at least 50,000 road miles before requiring any major work, but they do need to be regularly maintained by people who know what they're doing to remain in good working order. These are, after all, high performance machines.

When it comes to servicing your own machine, you can do as little or as much as you like. You might wonder why anyone would consider servicing their own motorbike. Wouldn't we all be better off paying someone else to do our dirty work for us? What if we did something wrong?

It's true that some people out there would never consider raising a spanner to their pride and joy, in case they caused irreparable damage, but they would be missing out.

Being a biker and doing a bit of basic spannering go hand in hand. It's a great opportunity to learn more about your bike and keep on top of its condition so that you know that everything is working at its optimum. It's also far cheaper, so when money is tight you can be sure that your bike will not suffer as a consequence. Motorcycle dealerships have high overheads to cover; premises, workshop technicians, showroom staff, but time taken away from the TV or your phone costs you nothing, and can actually be much more fun.

You're in Charge

There are elements of servicing that you, as an owner should be keeping an eye on. This isn't really servicing per-se, it's basic care: keeping tyre pressures adjusted, cables, brakes, and chain and sprockets inspected, cleaned and adjusted.

You can also keep an eye out for corrosion and nip it in the bud. Of course your local workshop can do all of this for you, but I doubt you'll be booking your bike into your local dealership to have the brake pistons cleaned every three months. If you understand the condition of your machine when you take it to the workshop, you'll be well-informed about the difference between work that actually needs doing, and when your mechanic is just pushing for a bit of extra cash.

If you've checked them the week before, you won't fall for "would you like us to change your front brake pads sir, they are dangerously thin". If you keep a spare set of front and rear pads in your toolbox, you can swap them out in half an hour, and keep running costs to an absolute minimum.

You can't blame workshops for wanting to help you out, they have no idea how often you service your bike. If it's once a year, they will advise you that your pads are low when they're about half worn. They are running a business and want to help you to keep your bike in good condition. But when you're knowledgeable about the state of your bike, you're in charge of what needs to happens, and when.

The other thing servicing bikes will give you is mechanical sympathy. Before they delve into the workings, most don't really think about what makes their bike stop and go. But when they start taking them to pieces, they discover that motorcycles are marvels of mechanical engineering; collections of metal, plastic and rubber, that work in understandable, albeit amazing ways. They also realise that motorcycles are designed to be serviced by human beings.

With just a little understanding of what's going on, and a few tools in your toolbox, you will get the satisfaction of learning more about your machine, save yourself a significant amount of time and money (thousands of pounds over the years), and keep a much better eye on the condition of your bikes now and in the future.

Self-servicing will give you an unexpected level of connection with your machine, respect for the engineering that goes into it, and a satisfaction for your own skill and ability to keep it in tip-top condition. You will know how the bike has been maintained, as you have taken responsibility for its upkeep.

It can feel daunting at first. The skimmed knuckles, the moments of dread when you've lost that important bolt in the leaves of your garden patio, or dropped a washer into the bowels of the machine and you know that until you find it, you can't put the bike back together. It's also getting dark, and you need your bike in order to get to work tomorrow. No pressure!

When you've worked on your bike a few times, you will know your way around it; how to get the fairings off, how to get the air box removed (with its associated Medusa of euro emissions gubbins), and how to get the service parts swapped.

When you get the hang of things you'll learn that there is a method to carrying out these fairly simple tasks, and as long as you follow the instructions (I know it's difficult gents, but trust me on this one), changing your spark plugs and air filter can be a quick 45 minute job, and checking the valve clearances on a V4 can take an afternoon.

If modern, equality diversity and inclusivity life has left your manhood feeling a bit limp, there are few things more likely to put lead back in your pencil than learning to take your motorcycle to pieces, and then putting it back together again. After that you can club your woman over the head and drag her into your man cave.

Where to Start?

Before you start dismantling your trusty mechanical steed, buy yourself an instruction manual and a rudimentary tool kit to you can do the job properly. I'll run through a list of basics as we move through the tasks.

Begin with simple and easy jobs and get your confidence and your skills up. Engine oil and filter changes, fork oil changes, spark plug changes and brake maintenance are all good places to start before working your way up to the trickier stuff like changing a clutch and checking valve clearances.

It's also worth saying that there are no bonus points for having a gung-ho attitude when you start out. If you really don't know what you're doing, or you decide that you want to use brute force or improvise instead of equipping yourself with the right tools, you may discover that you can cause a lot of very expensive damage, very quickly.

Start off steadily, follow the instructions in your service manual, and you won't have to turn up to your local motorcycle mechanic with your tail between your legs.

Benefits of Home Servicing

The following are some benefits open to the do it yourself mechanic.

✓ You can keep on top of what servicing needs to be done to your bike, and when. You need not take anyone else's word for it and you're in the know.

✓ You can save yourself a decent amount of cash by carrying out the basic tasks yourself. An older bike will cost more to service in three years than the bike is worth, which makes DIY far more appealing.

✓ Attention to little tasks keeps your bike in tip-top condition

✓ You have the fun of learning more about how motorcycles work.

✓ If your motorcycle is your only mode of transport, it may be more convenient to do your own servicing than making an appointment at your dealership, and getting lifts to and from there.

✓ The first time you service your bike is hard work, but when you've done it once, it's far easier to do again the next time

✓ Put the money you save on self-servicing to one side and spend it on upgrades to your bike like a new rear shock or front fork re-valve.

I won't go into too much detail on the tasks outlined below, as there are plenty of guides (like Haynes Manuals and the manufacturers' workshop manuals which the workshop technicians use) which describe with step by step instructions what to do in any task, from adjusting the headlight to rebuilding an engine from the bottom up, but you should get a flavour of what's involved should you be curious about trying the jobs yourself.

How-to Guides

Manufacturers' workshop manuals are available relatively cheaply in electronic format on the world-wide-web. While they aren't as good as having the workshop manual in paper form, you can print out the pages that you need for the particular task in hand, and when (not if) they get covered in oil grease or brake dust, you can just throw them in the bin. Much of the service book you will never use anyway, so you're being resource friendly by printing pages to order.

If Haynes has produced a workshop manual for your bike, this is a good starting place. I believe Clymer do similar manuals in the USA.

I've a lot of time for Haynes 'how-to' publications. They are clearly laid out, methodical and will give you tips and workarounds for the tasks at hand, as well as warning you of any special tools you need before starting the job.

I know you are eager to get started, but make sure you read the whole procedure beforehand, including the references to the other chapters and their procedures. For example, changing the spark plugs is easy, but it may involve lifting the fuel tank, swivelling the radiator or oil cooler, subjects that are covered in separate chapters with their own difficulty levels and tool requirements.

If one of these preparations turns out to be a 'five-spanner job', you might want to know this before you take your bike to pieces on a Saturday, don't have the tools to finish the job and need your bike to get to work.

Set Aside a Workspace

If you plan to do a lot of work to your bike, set aside a workspace and try to keep it tidy to avoid losing tools, nuts and bolts. This will help you to get the jobs done neatly and with everything to hand even if you're not a methodical tidy person.

If you have a garage, this is the perfect workshop, a flat floor is ideal for using stands to lift bikes, but a driveway, or even a reasonably flat section of public road can work too, just don't work near a gulley drain where you can lose tools, nuts and bolts or even bike keys.

The Right Tool for the Job

You can improvise with some tools, but you will definitely need at least one torque wrench to tighten bolts correctly. Of course it's clockwise to tighten, and anti-clockwise to loosen fasteners, but how tightly should you do them up?

Designed for lightness, motorcycles use a lot of aluminium. Over-tightening bolts a can easily strip aluminium threads, leading to potentially irreversible damage, or an expensive repair bill. Threads can be re-threaded, but it really doesn't bear thinking about.

Buy a couple of torque wrenches, and torque your bolts up to the values listed in the maintenance manual so you know you've done it right, and that your wheels aren't going to fall off when you're travelling along at three figure speeds.

For UK residents, your local Halfords is a good starting place for tools and workshop manuals, they frequently stock semi-professional tools which will last, and which are high quality. They are also open at weekends so you can visit them on a Sunday afternoon for that obscure tool you need to finish your weekend job.

Warning!

When screwing down bolts, take note: if it feels like too much effort, then something is wrong. These fasteners should go in easily perhaps not by hand, but relatively easily with a tool. Even inside the engine, you should only be applying significant effort when torqueing down the bolt once it is seated.

If the bolt isn't seated and it is proving to be hard work, you're either cross-threading the bolt or the screw, or the bolt you're screwing is too long for the hole you're trying to push it into, and you're stripping the threads or trying to push it through the other side of the block. Ask me how I know!

Get into the habit of doing up the bolt as tight as you can by hand, before even reaching for the spanners.

When removing nuts and bolts, bag them up and label them to remember which ones went where, bearing in mind that some bolts are longer than others: they may all look the same, but be slightly different lengths.

Maintenance Procedures

There are a number of jobs that you can do with a minimal effort and minimal tools.

Lubricate and Adjust the Chain

Lubing and adjusting your chain is something that you should do regularly, and it's more about keeping your bike in good working order than it is about servicing. If you really can't be bothered, fit an automatic chain-oiling system to do the job for you (see chapter 16 for Customising Your Bike).

Chain oilers are particularly beneficial if you do a lot of mileage or ride in the winter months … the last thing you want to do after a wet ride home is clean and lube your chain in the dark. If you really can't be bothered with any of it, buy a bike with a shaft final drive.

Get yourself some gear oil, which tends to be cheaper and better than expensive chain lubricants, and apply it after cleaning your chain in paraffin (kerosene) and wiping it clean with an old rag.

It is always best to lubricate your chain directly after a ride when the chain is hot. The lubricant will stick to the hot chain and will be absorbed into the nooks and crannies. Lubricate the chain when it is cold, and you will get a lot of lube flying off onto the rear wheel and tyre edge.

Put your bike on its centre stand (if it has one), and spin the rear tyre while applying the oil to the chain. If your bike only has a side-stand, you will need a rear paddock stand and some swing-arm bobbins to raise the rear wheel off the floor so you can spin it. Or solicit the help of a friend.

In the second case, put the bike on its side-stand and standing on the left of the bike with the handlebars turned to the right, hold the right handlebar in your left hand, and the rear right pillion foot peg bracket in your right and pull the bike forward to lift the rear wheel off the ground, rotating the bike around the side-stand. Now your assistant can spin the rear wheel while oiling the chain.

As long as the side-stand is securely down, the bike can be pivoted around it. You can actually use this technique to spin a bike around on the spot if you're brave enough. Ducatis and other bikes with return-sprung side-stands need extra care, for obvious reasons.

Adjustment of the drive-chain slack involves releasing the tension at the rear axle (for a traditional swingarm) or releasing the rear axle pinch bolt (for single-sided swing-arms) and turning the adjusters until the chain has the desired amount of slack; normally 20-30mm in total, then re-tightening the bolts.

Clean the Brakes / Change Brake Pads

You will need: brake piston pusher tool; torque wrench; brake cleaner spray; copper anti-seize grease; cable ties; old toothbrush; protective rubber gloves; eye protection

Keep your brakes in tip top conditions by regularly inspecting and cleaning the brake pistons and brake pads.

For reasons that only God knows, even though it is the 21st Century, motorcycle manufacturers still don't use rubber dust boots on motorcycle brake caliper pistons – it seems to work well enough on every car ever built, even high-performance ones. Perhaps they don't yet see motorcycles as standard transport, perhaps they want to give their mechanics something to do when servicing them. Perhaps the temperatures are too high? Answers on a postcard please.

The upshot of this omission is that the caliper pistons exposed to road grime and the elements are going to get fouled, caked with crud and salt and brake dust. This is less of an issue if you only ride in the summer, but if you ride all year round, you will need to clean brake pistons regularly to keep even wear on the discs and a good lever feel. Dirty pistons equal dragging brakes or a wooden lever feeling, as one or more of the pistons sticks or is harder to move, and the rest of the pistons have more braking work to do. If neglected the brakes will become ineffective.

This is a fairly easy, albeit fiddly process. Here's how to do it:

1. Working on each caliper at a time, first loosen the pins holding the brake pads in place while the calipers are still in place on the forks (usually an Allen-key fitting). Then loosen the bolts which hold the caliper to the forks/swing-arm and slide the caliper off the disc, supporting it with a cable tie to take tension off the brake hoses and unions. Remove the brake pad pins, the brake pads and rear metal spring plate, noting which way round the pads go (they may be asymmetrical).

2. Place a small piece of wood or a piston pusher tool in between the pads, and pump the brake lever to push the pistons out until you can see clean metal, taking care not to push them too far. If some are coming out unevenly, push them back in and try again until they are all showing some clean piston.

3. Clean the pistons with an old toothbrush and some warm soapy water. The toothbrush helps you get into the tight spots. Once you have scrubbed off the muck, rinse with clean water. Wear eye

protection to stop getting any crud in your eyes.

4. Push the pistons back into the caliper body with a piston pusher tool. You can improvise here with plastic or rubber faced tools, but anything metal is likely to damage the caliper pistons and it's a pretty tough job, so I recommend you buy a tool. You'll be doing this a lot to keep your brakes in good nick so it's a tool worthy of investment.

5. As you are pushing brake fluid back up the lines, there is the potential for overspill at the master cylinder reservoir. Keep an eye on the fluid level in reservoir, and if it gets too high, siphon out some of the fluid to maintain the correct fluid level.

6. Now clean the brake pads, scraping the crud out of any cooling/wear indicator grooves with a suitably sized flathead screwdriver. Clean the pads thoroughly with brake cleaner and rough up the surface on a stone or some grit paper. Clean the spring plate too. Spray the brake disc with brake cleaner and use a Scotchbrite pad to remove any glaze from the disc before wiping with a clean cloth.

7. Put the spring plate back into the caliper, followed by the brake pads (or new pads if you need them), insert the brake pad locating pins through the holes in the brake pads and the holes in the spring plate (apply a smear of grease on locating pins, this keeps them free moving)

8. Locate the caliper back on the brake disc, tighten the caliper mounting bolts to the specified torque using a torque wrench, and pump the brake lever to move the pads onto the disc. Your brakes should now feel like new.

9. Repeat on the other side, and on the rear caliper.

10. Remember to take it easy with braking for the first hundred miles until the pads are fully bedded.

Change the Engine Oil & Filter

You will need: fresh oil and filter; oil sump plug removal tool (this will usually be a normal socket fit, but check the manual as you might need an Allen or square socket); torque wrench; oil filter wrench; oil drain pan; rags to mop up the inevitable spills; plastic funnel; protective gloves.

Changing your oil and filter is an easy, if slightly messy job, but it is the number-one thing that will keep your engine in good condition. Oil is used for lubrication, but also for cleaning, and heat dissipation, and in a motorcycle engine it gets a hard life, and needs changing regularly.

1. Get your engine up to operating temperature before switching off. Remove ignition key and put it in your pocket.

2. Locate and open the oil filler cap (this helps the oil to drain out

quicker).

3. Remove fairing panels and guards as necessary to gain access to the oil sump plug and oil filter.

4. Locate your oil pan under the motorcycle and undo the sump plug to drain the engine oil, making sure the hole is at the lowest point to drain effectively. It goes without saying that a lot of hot oil will be coming out very fast, so get your hands out of the way, and get ready to mop up the spills. Don't do this job for the first time on your mother's pristine driveway. She won't thank you for it.

5. Once the majority of the oil has drained, undo the oil filter with a filter wrench and drain the contents of that into the pan.

6. Wipe the mating surfaces of the oil sump-plug drain hole and oil-filter mounting clean with a rag.

7. Take the new oil filter and smear some fresh engine oil on the rubber gasket at the mating surface. Install the new oil filter. Torque the new filter up to the recommended setting. If you can't reach to do so, tighten it by hand as tight as it will go, making sure your hands and the filter are clean, and then an additional three quarters of a turn. Due to access issues, I have hand tightened oil filters for years and never had a problem with any leaks, but if you can access it properly, use a torque wrench.

8. Refit the engine oil sump plug with new sealing washer. Tighten the plug to the specified torque. If you don't have a new sealing washer, it's not the end of the world. I have re-used old washers without any problems, just make sure you torque it back correctly.

9. Measure out and pour in the recommended amount of oil into your engine checking that you don't overfill. The amount will differ depending on whether you are replacing the oil filter or just the oil.

10. Check the oil level is between the high and low levels, replace the oil filler cap and start your engine.

11. The oil pressure (red) light will stay on for a couple of seconds longer than normal as the oil filter is filled with oil, but should go out. Let the engine idle for a couple of minutes and switch off.

12. After 10 minutes, measure the oil level and top up as necessary, making sure you take measurements on level ground. I try to aim for halfway between top and bottom levels, but if your engine burns oil, it's probably safer to set it to the top level to give yourself a margin. Use your judgement. If you have over filled your engine, don't panic. You're going to have to try to drain some oil out of the sump, which is going to be messy. It's better to start off with too little oil, and add a little bit at a time while continually checking the level.

13. Pour used oil into a plastic bottle (The container your previous oil

came in is perfect, but at a push PET bottles work too. Just make sure the oil is cool or the bottle will melt), and mark its contents clearly. Dispose at your local tip.

14. Clean up the oil pan and funnel with rags and check the bike for oil leaks. The exhaust may smoke if oil has fallen onto the header pipes.

Change the Air Filter

Special tools required: a friend; long screwdriver; new air filter; patience.

The air filter is normally located above the engine, under the fuel tank. Changing the air filter can be a very easy one-man job or a rather difficult two-man job depending on your make of bike, and whether it has been designed for ease of servicing.

Some brands make their motorcycles easy, designing fuel tanks with a simple pivot at the back, and a support rod at the headstock to prop them up. Other makes can be harder to service, and the act of removing the fuel tank will likely involve supporting the tank to prevent damaging it: beware of inadvertently pulling off hoses from the underside of the tank.

The air filter usually sits inside the plastic air box. Remove all the screws holding the air box lid down (not forgetting there may be one in the centre for which you will need a long reach screwdriver). Inspect the old filter and, if dirty, replace it with new.

You can buy aftermarket air filters, like K&N, which are excellent free breathing filters requiring minimal maintenance for life, but sometimes the original filters from the manufacturer work best (after all the engine has been designed and tested as a piece with its ancillaries). Reassemble the same way you took it apart, making sure all the hoses go back where they came from.

Service the Forks

Special tools required: motorcycle stand capable of lifting the front of the bike; torque wrench; fork-oil-level tool (or a metal ruler)

The forks do a huge amount of work, and benefit from fresh oil as frequently as the engine; every 6-8,000 miles. If you want to learn to ride well, whether on track or road, consistency in front-end feel is paramount. Keep your fork oil fresh and you remove one of the variables, giving you a solid basis on which to build your experience.

The procedure of changing fork oil is not difficult, but you do need a stand to lift the front end of the bike off the ground and allow the front wheel and forks to be removed.

1. Raise the front end off the ground using a lift.
2. Remove the brake calipers and support them with cable ties.

3. Undo the front-axle pinch bolts, remove the wheel spindle and drop the front wheel.
4. Remove the mud guard and any associated brake hoses bolted to the forks.
5. Loosen the fork top caps.
6. Loosen the triple-clamp bolts (lower and upper) and the handlebar clamp bolts.
7. Supporting the fork in one hand, remove the circlip at the top of the fork and drop the fork out of the triple clamp. Reinstall the circlip in the top of the stantion.
8. Remove the top cap, taking care as there may be preload on the spring.
9. Remove the spacers, washers and spring, noting which way round they go.
10. Invert the fork, draining the oil from the fork and pumping the fork to assist drainage. While fluid is draining clean the washers, spring and spacers.
11. Refer to your manual for the type and level of oil required to refill, and add fresh oil to the fork, pumping the fork to distribute the oil. Once air has been removed, use an oil level tool to set the level correctly. While it can be difficult to get the level exactly right, the most important thing is that the level is the same in both forks.
12. Reinstall the spring, washers and preload spacer and screw down the top cap to the specified torque
13. Reinstall the forks and tighten the triple clamps, install the front mudguard, front wheel and brake calipers.

Change the Spark Plugs

Special tools required: torque wrench, spark plug socket, extension bar, lots of tools to find the right combination)

Changing your spark plugs is a pretty easy task on most bikes. The biggest problem is getting to them – taking the tank out of the way and removing the airbox to get access. How easy this is depends on your bike and the engine configuration. Flat twins are the easiest as the plugs are exposed. V-engined bikes offer easy access to the front spark plugs, but those under the seat/tank may be harder to get to. To access the spark plugs on inline fours requires removing the airbox.

A decent automotive toolkit will come with a couple of spark plug sockets. These are longer than standard sockets with a little rubber insert which lightly grips the spark plug connector so you can thread it into the cylinder head without it falling out.

Always use a torque wrench to tighten the spark plugs to the specified torque. If you don't have a torque wrench do not carry out this task until you have one.

Clear any debris from the area. You don't want any foreign objects falling down the spark plug holes into your cylinders.

HT leads attach to the top of the plugs, and must be removed. The spark plugs sit deep within the recess of the cylinder head. Using the socket extension bars from your toolkit to find a combination which allows you access, remove the plugs by turning anti-clockwise, they should come loose very easily.

Once removed, check the gap is as stated in your maintenance manual. You can use flat feeler gauges, but if your plugs have iridium electrodes, or multiple electrodes around a centre electrode, use an inexpensive wire type gauge tool to measure / adjust the electrode gap. Also check the plug condition against a chart to see how your engine is performing. A worn spark plug can diagnose myriad issues with an engine.

If you have a compression tester, then this is a good time to test your cylinder compression. If a cylinder is not pumping properly, the valve timing may be out, a valve not seating, or you may have worn piston rings. You workshop manual will explain the methodology.

Change the Chain & Sprockets

(Special tools: assistant; torque wrench; chain splitter and riveter tool; breaker bar; socket)

Before you change your chain and sprockets, consider whether you might benefit from a gearing change. Going up a tooth or two on the rear sprocket can give your bike a bit more shove in the lower revs, but make the effective revs higher at cruising speeds, as the final gearing is changed.

Always change chain and sprockets as a set as they wear together. If you change one and not the other, wear on the new item is accelerated, so you'll just have to change them all again.

If you're thinking of changing your front sprocket for a smaller one, bear in mind that changing the size of the front sprocket will affect the squat/anti squat characteristics of your bike, and may put undue stress on the chain due to the more acute angle at the sprocket.

Before you split the chain, take off the front sprocket cover. Get your assistant to sit on the bike and press the rear brake with the bike in neutral and the rear tyre on the ground, and using a breaker bar to loosen the nut holding the front sprocket to the crankshaft. If you wait until after you've split the chain, this nut is going to be hard if not impossible to remove.

It is best to loosen the rear sprocket mounting bolts when the chain is still on, as they will be tight and will not want to budge once you have taken the rear wheel off.

Once your sprockets are loosened, split the chain with the chain tool, making sure you're using the right part of the set. You're effectively looking to push one of the rivets through the back of the tool.

Remove front and rear sprockets, and replace with new sprockets and a new chain. You can buy lighter aluminium sprockets, but I prefer steel ones as they last longer. Some OEM front sprockets (Honda for example) use a rubber cush drive incorporated, which aftermarket sprockets won't have.

At this stage, adjust your swing-arm chain adjustment to its original position; there should be marks on the swing-arm or notches. As the chain extends over its life you want to have plenty of adjustment available. You may need to remove a link or two from your new chain to get it to fit properly, just do as you did when you removed the original chain, making sure the two ends can be mated up with the soft link provided. You only have one soft link, so measure twice and split once.

Install the new chain using the soft link supplied to join the ends of the chain, making sure you include the O-rings provided. Push the front plate onto the soft link using the tool, and then rivet the soft link heads to hold them in place.

The chain-riveting tool has a backing plate that should be solid, and a front plate that should also be solid with two holes to allow the links to push out whilst you're pressing the front plate onto the rivets. Push the plate onto the front of the soft link until it aligns with the chain links adjacent. Then using the riveter and the solid back plate, mushroom the soft links at the front to hold the front plate in place. If you're not sure what it should look like, check the old chain for reference.

If you feel at all uncomfortable doing this activity, leave it to your dealer, or bring a friend who knows what he's doing and has the necessary tools. It's not difficult, but it can be a bit fiddly first time you do it, and you don't want to mess up a chain and have to wait for some new soft links to arrive. There are many videos on YouTube explaining how it's done.

Once the chain is on, torque all the sprocket nuts up to the required torque settings and replace the front sprocket cover.

Throttle body / Carburetor Balancing

(Special tools required: vacuum gauges)
Vacuum gauges work as well with carbs as they do with throttle bodies. Full instructions are supplied with your workshop manual, and your specific vacuum tool. You may need to lift the tank and remove the airbox to get access to the throttle bodies/carbs vacuum hoses. Balancing carbs / throttle bodies will give you smoother running and idling, and you may get more mpg to boot!

Valve Clearances

In my experience, these rarely need adjusting but they should be checked to give you peace of mind. I had a Honda CBR600F which did 47,000 miles, and the valve clearances never once needed adjustment. I also had a Honda VFR800, which are legendary for never needing adjustment, but at only 42,000 miles, 10 of the 16 VFR valves were out of spec and needed adjusting.

If you can check the valves yourself, it is worth learning how to do it; there is nothing more annoying than spending hundreds on a valve clearance check and getting nothing in return.

Valve clearance checks are an unwelcome expense, and most people would say that you would know if your engine valve clearances needed checking. If your bike if pulling like a train and everything is running smoothly, chances are they're fine. If you regularly check your engine compression at service time you should know whether your engine is pumping properly. If it is, then your valves are probably fine.

If after checking them, you need to have your valve clearances adjusted. You can either do it yourself or you can get the garage to do it for you. Most modern engines use shims to adjust their clearances. The shim is a little metal disc of a precise thickness, which is swapped out with another disc until the clearance is correct. Shim-under-bucket type engines require the camshaft to be removed to access the shims to measure them before deciding which replacement shims you need.

If you do it yourself, you will need to make a note of the valve clearances, compare them against what they should be for inlet and exhaust valves. You will then need to take the camshafts out, and have a look at the shims that you have in there. You can then calculate what size shims you need to adjust your valve clearance to within spec.

Most engines tighten up over time, requiring shims to be swapped out for smaller ones. If you do this yourself, mark up the shims and buckets for each cylinder, and make sure they go back where they started, likewise camshafts (should be marked IN and EX for inlet and exhaust)

You can buy yourself a motorcycle shim kit for £100 or ask your dealer nicely if you can swap shims with him. He may be happy to swap with some of the shims you have, but don't be surprised if he isn't. As most engines tighten over time (as the valves bed into their seats), dealers end up with a lot of the same type of shims which are no use to them, so don't be surprised if he would rather you buy your own.

Brake Fluid Change

This is an easy two-man job, but you can do it on your own. The most important thing you need is patience, as it can take a while to bleed the system. Just when you think you've got all of the bubbles out, more will appear.

Brake fluid is nasty stuff, so protect your hands and eyes, and cover vulnerable areas of bike where drips are likely to occur. If you upgrade your old brake hoses to stainless steel or replace anything inside your calipers, you will need to do this hydraulic bleed as part of the job.

If your brakes are really spongy and you have air trapped in the system, or if it has been over two years since the last change, it's time for a brake fluid change. Brake fluid is hygroscopic, which means it has an affinity for water. Over time, water in the atmosphere will make its way into your brake fluid. If you then ask a lot of your brakes, the heat produced can boil the brake fluid, and you will find your brake lever doesn't work.

You will need: clear plastic tubing; container to collect the spent brake fluid; tiny ring spanner; fresh brake fluid; rags to protect your paintwork; syringe/water bottle and plastic tube; PTFE tape to seal leaking bleed nipples).

1. Cover the vulnerable areas of your bike with rags and towels. Brake fluid is corrosive and will damage paintwork.
2. If you can get your hands on a brake fluid changer, effectively a hand operated vacuum pump, this will make your life so much easier.
3. If you don't have a brake bleeder kit you can perform this task with the help of friend, one to pump the handle/lever, the other open/close the brake bleed nipple with the little ring spanner.
4. Before you get started suck out the old brake fluid in the reservoir with a syringe, and fill it with fresh brake fluid, taking care not to overflow the reservoir.
5. Keep the reservoir topped up as you go through the process to avoid entraining air into the lines.
6. The bleed sequence is as follows:
   - Open bleed nipple,
   - Pump lever until clear fluid runs
   - Close bleed nipple
   - Repeat on other caliper
7. Eventually you will have no more bubbles coming out of your clear plastic tubing, a solid feel at the lever/pedal, and fresh fluid emerging from the plastic/rubber tube.
8. Use your workshop manual for the correct bleeding sequence. If you have a Honda with linked front-rear braking system, the process can be a bit more complicated. Other machines are a bit easier to deal with.

Change Tyres

This is one for the expert (and strong) DIY man. If you're concerned that you might cock it up, or you have a nice pair of carbon wheels, don't take the risk, get your friendly tyre dealer to do it for you.

Changing your own tyres won't save you a lot of money, but it will give you more flexibility about swapping tyres and maximising their useful life. If you're into stunting, chances are you will already change your own tyres, and you'll be good friends with your local tyre dealer, raiding his pile of used hoops for anything with a bit of tread left on them.

With a bit of practice you'll soon get the hang of the technique. Check out the many useful videos on YouTube showing the process in action. You can fork out hundreds of pounds for specialist equipment, but people change tyres with very little in the way of tools (even a van can be used as an effective bead breaker)

Here's what you'll need for the job:

- ✓ Front and rear bike stands (either front and rear paddock stands or a frame stand)
- ✓ A bead breaker (a long lever, or a press if you can get one)
- ✓ Window cleaner or soap spray
- ✓ At least three tyre levers
- ✓ A valve core tool
- ✓ Two lengths of 2×4 to protect the discs when you're changing tyres
- ✓ Rim protectors (these will protect a little bit, but you will eventually take chunks out of your rims if you change your own tyres, unless you're fitting very soft or flexible tyres)
- ✓ Balancing weights
- ✓ Wheel balancer
- ✓ Very strong arms
- ✓ Strong boots, and knee crawlers

While it is true that a little technique accounts for a lot of strength, when you change your own tyres for the first time, you are going to be sweating. A lot. So make sure you have at least three Weetabix for breakfast. It's a good workout, and you will need patience, patience, and more patience, to make it work without destroying your rims.

Here's what you do:

1. Support your bike on stands to remove the wheels. Ideally use front and rear stands, an Abba stand or a bike lift. I wouldn't recommend improvising here as the bike can easily topple over if you get it wrong.
2. Remove the wheels from the bike, making sure to account for any spacers / speedo cables that may fall out. You will need these when you put the wheel back on.

3. If you're doing this job in the winter, put your new tyres, and your old wheels with tyres on inside your warm house overnight to get them up to an easy to work temperature and make them more pliable. Borrow some tyre warmers if you can.

4. Working on one tyre at a time, let the air out of the tyre, and then use the valve core remover to remove the valve core completely. Set this core aside in a safe place.

5. Lay the two lengths of 2×4 on the floor, and place the wheel on top, the rim of the wheel resting on the wood, the discs off the ground. This protects the brake discs as you manhandle the tyre onto the rim.

6. Using a bead breaker, break the bead of the tyre on both sides. It sounds easy, but this is the hardest part.

7. Take your tyre levers and using rim protectors, spray up the bead with window cleaning spray or a water / detergent mix and use your tyre irons to lever the tyre over the lip of the wheel. Hold one and work your way round. Useful if you have three hands or an assistant standing by. Check out YouTube for practical demonstrations. Work around the wheel progressively, and don't try to take too much at a time.

8. Once the first bead is entirely off, flip the tyre over and do the same on the reverse. The second side should be much easier than the first. Remove the tyre from the rim. Getting the tyre off is the easy bit.

9. Once the tyre is off, clean up your wheel, check it for damage and check the condition of the valve. Replace if damaged.

10. Get your new tyre, and making sure it is facing in the right direction (there is an arrow indicating the direction of travel on the tyre), lubricate it with some window cleaner and push the tyre onto the rim. It should go on fairly easily with enough force. Line up the dot on the tyre sidewall with the valve stem. The dot signifies the lightest part of the tyre, so it should be lined up with the heaviest part of the wheel (usually where the Schrader valve sits).

11. Spray the bead up liberally. Now push the bead down at your knees and kneel on the bead so that it sits in the centre of the wheel (in cross section). This will give the bead at the opposite side of the tyre enough room to pop over the rim. If the bead nearest you is too close to the edge, you will not get the tyre on no matter how hard you try.

12. Work around in one direction, using your knees to keep the bead pressed down where you are, and the rim protectors to keep your rims from getting scratched. Work around slowly, not getting ahead of yourself. Soon enough, you'll pop the bead on. The tyre bead is

braided steel wire. The rim is aluminium. If you try to force it, you will damage your wheel.

13. Check again that the mark on the sidewall lines up with the valve stem and reinstall the valve core.
14. To seat the beads, spray some lube on the bead on either side of the tyre and pump the tyre up. You can use a big bicycle pump (the tall ones with foot plates), a home compressor or the petrol station tyre machine if you have a car and can transport your wheels there.
15. You will hear a loud pop as each bead seats on the lip. If you don't hear two very loud pops, stop pumping air in, release the air, and re-lubricate the beads and try again. If you have not seated the beads with 35psi, deflate the tyre, re-lubricate the beads and try again. Keep your hands well away from the unseated bead and the rim.
16. Put the wheel on your static wheel balancer, spin it and let it come to a natural stop. Using chalk or a white marker, mark the lowest point of the tyre. This is the heavy spot. Weights will need to be added to the opposite side of the wheel (opposite your mark) to balance the wheel. You need to determine how many weights are required. Using some duct tape, stick a few balancer weights opposite the heavy spot, adding / subtracting as necessary to balance the wheel. The wheel is balanced when it can be turned, stopped and released at any point on its circumference, and it remains stationary.
17. When you are happy that you have sufficient weights, attach them with permanent adhesive. Race teams use static wheel balancers, and they work very well.
18. Reinstall the wheel making sure all the spacers go back in where they came from.
19. If you're doing both tyres, repeat the procedure with the other wheel. If not, you're done and ready for a hot shower and a cold beer!

Change the Coolant

Changing coolant is a simple job, done every couple of years to keep the inside of the engine clean and corrosion-free. It might look the nice bright colour of fresh coolant in the radiator, but when you get it out, it will resemble dirty mop water.

Buy premixed engine coolant or mix your own antifreeze with demineralised water suitable for your engine. Here are the steps:

1. Let the engine cool down
2. Remove the fairing panel (if you have one) so you can get access to

the radiator cap and the rubber coolant hose which is attached to the engine at the coolant pump, usually by a hose clip.

3. Remove the radiator cap, if it hisses when you first untwist, leave it a few minutes to cool some more.

4. Place a container under the engine to catch the used coolant

5. Unscrew the hose clip or drain bolt and drain used coolant into the container.

6. Release the hoses from the overflow reservoir (the expansion tank next to the radiator) and drain coolant from that too.

7. Using a hose, flush out the radiator by jetting into the radiator filler hole. Flush out the expansion reservoir too from the top bung and capture the liquid. Reinstall all hoses.

8. Slowly refill the radiator from the filler cap. The trapped air will bubble out as the coolant is introduced. Rock the bike backwards and forwards to get the air out of the system. Take your time and let as much air out as possible. Fill the expansion reservoir up to the fill line.

9. When the radiator is full, leaving the radiator cap off, start the engine, making sure the you blip the throttle a few times to help to clear any air locks from the cooling system. Once the engine has run for a few minutes but the coolant system is not pressurised, stop the engine and refill the radiator from the filler cap.

10. Once your system is fill of coolant, depending on your bike design, you may need to bleed off any excess air from the high point of the system – check your service manual. Replace the radiator cap, and locate the bleed screw. On many bikes this will involve lifting the tank. The bleed screw is often located on the thermostat housing on the back of the engine, or the top of the rear cylinder. If as you unscrew the bleed screw there is a hissing sound, and then fluid emerges, it's a good sign you've effectively bled the system. If you open it and nothing happens, repeat earlier steps remembering to blip the throttle to dislodge trapped air, until the air is released and coolant comes forth from the bleed screw.

11. Retighten the bleed screw, lower the tank and replace the fairing, disposing of the used coolant at your local tip. Coolant is toxic but sweet smelling and should be kept away from pets and inquisitive children.

12. Before you take your bike on a large and important journey, start the bike and let it get up to temperature until the coolant fan kicks in. It should come on just over 105C and cool to just below 100. Take it for a test ride to check everything is working OK. If your fan doesn't come on, or the bike is overheating, you may have an air lock which needs releasing.

13. Repeat the earlier steps as necessary until the air is bled from the system. The whole process should take one to two hours on your first attempt.

Cable Maintenance

The mechanical connection between twist-grip and throttle bodies or fly-by-wire throttles is operated by cables and you will need to check them regularly for condition, to make sure they're not fraying or about to snap, and to make sure that they are clean and adequately lubricated. Throttle cables come in pairs, one to open the throttle and one to close it.

Release the end of the cable, as per your maintenance manual, and using a cable oiler, force the cable lubricant into the top of the cable until it comes out of the other end. Using the right lubricant is essential to prevent the build-up of dirt and grime, which can lead to accelerated cable wear. Use lubricants which are suitable for your cables. PTFE lubricants are good, or better still a PTFE lined cable, if you can get your hands on one, which will reduce the amount of lubrication required.

If your cables are starting to fray, they are on the way out. Either replace them yourself or take your bike down to the local workshop and get them to help you. If your clutch cable snaps you're stranded. If your throttle opening cable snaps, you can use the close cable as an open cable 'bodge' repair, as the throttle has a return spring which will close it, until you can get a replacement.

Cables are not the only parts of your bike that would benefit from lubrication; levers, footpegs, ignition, basically anything that moves benefits from some oil to keep it free and loose. Your workshop manual will have a list of clean-lubricate-and-adjust tasks.

Clutch Change

Changing the clutch sounds like a nightmare job, but it's not that hard really. If you do a lot of town riding or race starts off the traffic lights, the chances are you will have to change your clutch plates. I've seen them last well over 70,000 miles even on big heavy bikes, but of course it depends on your riding style, how much town riding you do, and whether you have a slipper clutch fitted.

You can change the clutch with the engine in the frame in most cases, but you will need to drain the oil if you have a wet clutch (if your bike sounds like a bag of spanners at idle then you probably have a dry clutch). The clutch is made up of an alternating stack of clutch friction plates and drive plates held in a clutch basket with clutch springs to actuate the assembly. As clutch designs differ from bike to bike, it is best to find a workshop manual to carry out a clutch replacement. Wet clutch plates will need soaking in oil before you use them. It's not a difficult task, but you may need a replacement clutch cover gasket to prevent engine oil leaks on reassembly.

Warranties

If you have a new bike with a manufacturer's warranty, there are likely to be conditions which typically translates to an approved workshop carrying out your servicing. You can still do minor checks, lubrication, keep the chain and brakes in good condition etc. and not invalidate your warranty. Speak to your dealer if you're not sure of the rules.

I hope this has given you a sense that performing these tasks yourself is not only achievable, but it can be satisfying and even fun. If you're the sort of person who learns from doing things, give yourself several hours, take the pressure off, watch a few YouTube tutorials, and have a go at doing it yourself. If it all goes horribly wrong call out a mobile mechanic to help you put it all back together.

15. TOOLS

To carry out your self-servicing tasks, you will need a handful of tools as listed below. While these may appear expensive to buy, good tools properly looked after will last a lifetime, and you can hand them on to your grandchildren so they can perform the minimal service tasks required on their electric cars.

If you cannot afford to buy tools new then consider buying some second-hand ones, or better yet find someone with a significant tool collection that you can make use of until you can afford to buy your own decent ones. Just remember to clean them before you give them back!

Get yourself the following basic tools and you'll be able to do most maintenance jobs:

Automotive Socket Set

The Automotive toolkit contains large sockets, including two deep sockets for spark plugs (usually 16 & 21mm). They are typically 1/2" drive, with a two-way ratchet, extension piece, T-bar and universal joint. Buy the best quality you can afford and clean it after use and it will outlast you.

Mini-Socket Set (1/4" drive)

This is an absolutely essential bit of kit for the home bike servicer. The mini-socket set is useful for a multitude of different duties from removing fairings panels, battery terminals, brake pistons, brake caliper pins, adjusting brake levers, removing air-box housings etc.

It has a number of fittings which can be attached to a screwdriver or small ratchet including mini-sockets, flathead and crosshead screwdrivers, hex, star and torx drivers. I have used both Proxxon and CK tools and both are high quality sets which have lasted over 10 years and still look like new.

Spend upwards of £50 and get something really good.

Torque Wrench

A torque wrench is an essential tool for the home mechanic. Use your torque wrench to tighten all of your nuts and bolts to the specified torque settings in your manual. If they are left too loose they may come undone, too tight and you risk stripping out threads. In the UK, Halfords do a range of excellent Halfords Advanced torque wrenches which cover the range of torque values you're likely to encounter. Have a look in your service manual before shopping to make sure your wrench covers the torque range you require.

Breaker Bar

24" or 600mm long with a 1/2" drive at the end. This is essential to undo tight bolts such as rear axle nuts, wheel-nuts, sprocket nuts, suspension brackets etc.

Long Philips Screwdriver

A long crosshead screwdriver is invaluable for those difficult to reach parts of a motorcycle, when trying to undo screws around the fuel-injection and intake system. You could use a socket set with umpteen extensions, but a long-shaft screwdriver is less wobbly.

Piston Pusher

Until the motorcycle manufacturers do the honourable thing and put gaiters on their brake pistons to prevent them from getting covered in road grime, you are going to have to clean the pistons regularly yourself.

For this purpose, you will need a piston pusher. There really is no substitute for this tool, you can certainly try to improvise, but may end up damaging the pistons.

Large Flat Bladed Screwdriver

More useful than you could possibly ever imagine, probably the most useful tool in the box. A magnetic end is a nice touch for picking up screws and making them stick. Used for screwing, but also for levering, twisting and as an impromptu punch and cold chisel.

Magnetic telescopic tool (with inbuilt LED light)

At some point you are going to drop a screw or bolt into a tight space and need to retrieve it. This handy tool will save your bacon. It's dark inside the recesses of your motorcycle, even on a bright sunny day, and even if you have hands like Chopin, there are still some places you won't be able to reach, but this little tool will. Mine has paid for itself many times over.

Oil Filter Removal Tool

Required to drain fluids from your bike and perform an oil change, the filter removal tool can take the form of a socket which fits on the end of the filter, or a chain or rubber strap wrench, which is more universal.

Spanners (open and ring)

For the removal of general nuts and bolts, and where a socket set cannot reach. If you can afford a set, ratchet spanners are excellent at undoing nuts in the very tight spaces found on motorcycles.

Pliers

(Needle nose, circlip, normal etc.), useful for removing hose clips, and general gripping duties. Buy a good set like CK or Snap-on.

Feeler Gauges

A necessity for checking valve clearances, feeler gauges come in a range of thicknesses. Make sure your feeler gauges have the correct range of blades for the engine clearances that you are measuring. If used infrequently, keep them well oiled.

LED head Torch

This is another must for the home servicer. Being so far up in the Northern hemisphere, the UK is blessed with long summer evenings, but our winters leave little light for the home servicing mechanic.

After the clocks change around Guy Fawkes Night, we lose light around 3:30pm. If you are still working as light begins to fade, a head torch can make the difference between getting the job done or not. If you want to do some work on your bike after work in the winter, you'll be doing it in the dark. Unless you have a well-lit garage, a head torch is compulsory wear.

If you do have a garage, consider getting some floor mounted LED lights. These can provide you with plenty of lighting so you can see what you're doing, summer or winter, night or day.

Nitrile Rubber Gloves

The business end of a motorcycle is not a nice place: engine oil, grease, brake dust, brake fluid, coolant, metal paste, and road grime are all present, and you should look for ways to protect your hands when working on a bike. You can buy vinyl gloves, but nitrile rubber gloves are a better fit and far more resilient, so you won't go through as many pairs.

If you really dislike wearing gloves, you can buy some high quality construction PPE at DIY stores, which won't make your hands sweat, or use barrier cream to protect your hands and rub Swarfega generously into all of the nooks and crannies of your hands after you have finished working to clean your hands and then moisturise your skin. Dermatitis is not a good look.

Threadlock

Sometimes you want to make extra-sure that a bolt or nut will not come loose. The service manual will typically indicate where Loctite or similar adhesive is required. Components which are under a lot of load and vibration can work loose and fall out, make sure that you use a nutlock or threadlock to hold them tightly in place.

Copper Slip

There are also components that you would like to be easy to remove when required. These are typically not load-bearing parts but are in areas where they exposed to the elements such as exhaust brackets and suspension linkage nuts and bolts. Using copper slip will prevent fastener threads from rusting together and make them easier to remove the when the time comes around. Not recommended for parts that you do not want to come lose – like anything holding critical parts on your bike, e.g. caliper mounting bolts.

Automotive Multimeter

For the diagnosis of electrical issues, battery voltage and current, current continuity, charging system, and fuel injection system issues.

The Right Tools for the Job

Make sure you have access to the right tools before you start any home servicing job. If you're unsure, try to have access to somebody who has lots of tools, or at the very least access to a car in case things go wrong and you need to go to your local Halfords on Sunday, when everywhere else is closed.

If you use your bike to get to work, the pressure is well and truly on. Give yourself a back-up, or an extra day to sort things out if they don't go according to plan (in the beginning, things rarely go according to plan, but we only learn from making mistakes)

Sometimes you can improvise on tools, but there really is no substitute for having the right equipment. Tools are designed for a particular reason. That reason, as you will come to appreciate, is that there is no other way of doing that specific job than with that specific tool. When you've been servicing your bike for a few years, you will gradually collect all the tools you need to take on everything but the most specialised task.

16. CUSTOMISING YOUR BIKE

When motorcycle manufacturers design motorcycles, they are designed as a complete package, but also to a bottom-line cost. Industry margins are tight, and every penny counts.

When it comes to building motorcycles on a budget, the first things to suffer cost-cutting are materials, suspension components, and the quality of finish. The more specialised a motorcycle's design, the fewer customers it will attract, so typically sales volume and cost are inversely proportional; as production numbers rise the recommended retail price falls.

As you get accustomed to your new bike with a few thousand miles under your belt, you will start to explore the performance envelope. It might be perfect for you, but the chances are there will be things you want to tweak to make it better.

You may want it to handle better, or fit your body better. You may want improved comfort over distance or to be faster around a racetrack. Human beings are hard-wired to find better ways of living; it's part of the evolution of the species.

Fortunately, a multi-million pound aftermarket accessories industry exists to give us bikers anything and everything we could possibly think of bolting onto our motorbikes; from pink anodized aluminium engine casing bolts, to full exhaust systems made out of the most esoteric materials known to man. If you want it, somebody out there will make it for you, the only limit is your ability to dream and the depth of your pockets.

Establish a Benchmark

Before we explore making things better, it is worth checking that things are as good as they can be in standard trim; that your machine is in good working order with a properly adjusted and lubricated chain, the steering-head bearings in good condition, suspension pivot points are greased, and your tyres at the correct pressures and condition, and your forks have fresh oil.

There's no point looking to improve your bike if you haven't got the basics in order. There might be nothing wrong with it that a little TLC wouldn't cure. By all means make changes, but understand the context in which you are making them. All good? OK, let's have a look at some of the more popular modifications and accessories available, what they do, and whether they are just cosmetic or actually improve your machine's performance.

Tyres

The OEM tyres your new bike came on were part of its original development and set-up. While they may not be what you might choose for yourself, they have been tested extensively with it.

My first bike came with awful tyres, giving no feel whatsoever and therefore little confidence. They felt hard and plastic rather than supple and elastic. It wasn't a great start to my biking career. I think the main problem was the bike-plus-rider package was too light to get any useful heat into the tyres.

Long story short, once I skipped them and put on some modern sporty rubber, it was a revelation. Finally, some grip! Now I understood why people enjoyed riding motorcycles. One track day at Brands Hatch Indy later and the sides of the tyre were melting! If you haven't tried a new tyre, it should be your first port of call.

Your choice of tyre will affect the characteristics of your machine. See chapter 13: for more detail. Tyres are one thing, but how do we make sure that they keep contact with the road to begin with? That'll be the job of your suspension.

Suspension

Production motorcycles are usually set up for average riders and average conditions. They are also built to a budget. Because a rider's weight makes up such a large proportion of the overall motorcycle package, suspension needs to be adjustable to suit different sizes and shapes of rider (with and without pillion and luggage).

Getting your suspension sorted for your body weight and riding style is the best thing you could do to improve your bike's performance. A sweet handling bike is a joy to ride.

Even as new, most OEM shocks aren't great, but if your bike is a few years old, you might want to consider having the suspension overhauled, at the very least by putting fresh oil in the forks, and oil/gas in the rear shock, and changing the springs for new ones suited to your body weight and riding style.

If you're feeling flush, you might also consider getting a cartridge kit for the forks and a new rear shock, just make sure you are actually upgrading to something better than stock.

Modern bikes come with many different types and qualities of suspension. Some items are low-budget and frankly feel it, while others will be fairly decent quality kit that will last well if properly serviced. Before making any rash decisions, work with what you've got to try to get something usable out of your standard equipment and available adjustability. See chapter 10 for more information.

It might appear to be expensive spending £800 on suspension. While it may not be visible to the casual bystander, from behind the handlebars you can really feel the benefit of suspension work. Find someone who knows about suspension for some decent advice about setting up your bike the way you want, or improving the suspension system if it's a bit floppy after 30,000 miles of use.

If you have decided that you want to upgrade your suspension, try to get a few opinions from other owners about what has worked for them. Unless you know and trust the suspension expert you're speaking to, remember that they want to sell you a new shock or fork cartridge, so they may be quick to rubbish what you've currently got on your bike. Ask around on some internet forums, or speak to your biker mates who have the same bike as you. Ask them for a test ride on their bike if they have had suspension work done. Try to pick someone around your size and weight so that the bike is set up about right.

New aftermarket suspension will be tailored for you and will depend on your weight, and on how you use your bike. You don't want to spend thousands on a super-adjustable shock with high and low speed compression damping if you mostly only use your bike for commuting or gentle rides to your local bike cafe. Super-trick suspension with major adjustability is useful for track riding and racing teams, as settings can vary significantly from track to track.

When I was looking to improve the stock suspension on one of my bikes, I asked a local suspension dealer about buying a new shock. I was told that the stock OEM rear shock was rubbish and that I should buy a new shock from them. I decided to get a second opinion, so I approached someone I had used in the past with good results. He told me that the existing shock could use a recharge of gas, but that it was actually better quality than the shock the other garage was trying to sell me, and certainly more than adequate for my needs.

While they will give you advice, remember dealers are also running a business, and they may be less interested in principles than in selling to you, regardless of whether you need it or not. Any workshop worth its salt will set up your bike how you like to ride it, and will agree to improve the setup if things change over time. If you have any problems, for example if it's too hard or too soft or your riding improves and you want them to tweak it some more, they should be happy to set it up again free of charge.

I once made the mistake of believing the hype surrounding car suspension. I decided to have a set of coil-overs fitted to my car. Many sources, including ones I trusted, stated that coil-overs were an effective and logical upgrade from standard suspension. The standard springs and shocks weren't a disaster, just showing their age after 120,000 miles of UK road use. £600 and a drive up to Leicestershire later, and I had a very uncomfortable and regretful journey back to London.

The car rode like a go-cart, and felt as though it had its suspension welded solid. The ride was so appalling that I used to wince driving over the battered potholed roads of North London.

Suffice to say I will never fit coil-overs to any car, ever again; they are not compliant enough for road use. I removed the iron girder suspension myself, mainly because I couldn't bear to throw good money after bad, and bought some Eibach standard replacements. I couldn't believe that anyone would consider that coil-overs gave any improvement over standard settings. Don't believe the hype, test these things out for yourself. Of course coil-overs vary from brand to brand and spring rate to spring rate, but the ones I tried were terrible.

Forks

When it comes to telescopic forks you have many options: keeping the original forks you can have new springs fitted to suit your weight, you can re-valve them for compression and / or rebound damping (sometimes only one of these needs re-valving), you can fit a new cartridge kit (brand new internals). All rebuilds will come with a fresh fill of decent quality fork oil.

Your fork oil takes a hammering over the miles, and by the time it comes out it typically resembles dirty washing-up water. Replacing it with fresh oil every 6-8,000 miles will make a huge difference to performance and durability of your forks, even if you decide to do nothing else.

Rear Shock

The OEM rear shock absorber can often be serviced by suspension technicians, but replacement parts are not always available. Shock servicing involves fresh oil / gas, and it may be worth getting a better spring fitted at the same time. For a bit more money, you can upgrade to an aftermarket shock from: Ohlins, WP, Maxton, K-Tech, Nitron, Bitubo etc.

With aftermarket shocks, you get what you pay for. If you don't need the functionality, don't pay for it. If you only use your bike for touring, get a shock with basic adjustability, and if you regularly take a pillion, consider a remote preload adjuster.

Aftermarket shocks are rebuildable and will last for years. If you sell your bike, reinstall the original shock and sell the aftermarket one to recoup some of the cost. If you buy the rear shock online or mail order, make sure you know how to set it up, or get a knowledgeable biker friend to set it up for you.

If you don't have it set up properly, your modification is pretty much worthless. Track days are a good place to do this, as the service is offered for a nominal fee, and you can test the suspension changes on the same track. Sadly most people who ride will never get their bikes set up properly, and will never know how good their bikes could handle.

Check out the Recommended Reading section at the back of the book for in depth guides into setting up your suspension.

Exhaust

Aftermarket exhausts generally come in two flavours: an end-can (muffler) or a full system (from header pipes from the exhaust manifold all the way back to and including the muffler). This is probably the most popular modification, as it can be easily seen and heard, and many bikers are strutting peacocks at heart.

I admit, some engines do sound good with free-flowing exhausts (Honda V-fours; Yamaha's R1, especially the cross-plane crank engine which sounds like a MotoGP bike; large V-twins). I find modern four-cylinder screamers less appealing, but that's just because they get REALLY LOUD at high revs, and that is usually how their owners like to ride them.

There are many bikes, especially modern classics which I think sound fabulous in stock trim, (e.g. 2005-2006 GSX-R1000, R1 2004-2006) before the Euro-3 emissions regulations stifled engines with large cumbersome catalytic converters.

End-cans come in 'road-legal' and 'race' varieties. The latter are typically marked as such; or 'not for road use', because they are antisocially noisy and have the potential to be particularly intrusive. They are loud, regardless of what bike they are fitted to; the smaller engines with fewer cylinders end up sounding even more annoying. If you ride on the road with a race exhaust you are breaking the law. While it is unlikely in this day and age that you would be stopped by, let alone see, a policeman, if you are pulled over you may get a warning or some points on your licence.

The biggest issue you will have is on track days which have noise limits as part of their planning conditions, (check max dB online before you set off), and getting your bike through its MOT (or your environmental emissions test). If you have a race can, reinstall the original exhaust at MOT time. Take your original number plate too.

If you are buying an end-can, check the original exhaust as it may require cutting to fit the aftermarket part, which might dissuade you against the modification, as it can look a bit messy when reverting to the original, particularly on naked or semi-faired machines. It may also require, and should come with, a link pipe to attach it to the exhaust headers.

Many large capacity sports bikes have exhaust control valves. These provide back pressure at low revs and improve low down torque, as well as providing noise attenuation at the resonant 3-5k, to meet stringent drive-by noise regulations for new machines. If you buy a replacement end-can it is unlikely to come with an exhaust control valve (some non-OEM cans do have these but they are rare), so be prepared for more boom at low revs!

One thing is certain, if you run a noisy end-can, you will attract attention to yourself. This may have been your intention all along. A four-cylinder motorcycle which revs to 14,000 rpm will make a considerable amount of noise with an open race pipe, and they will all hear you coming and going; your family, the neighbours, the villagers, the police …

Forget about sneaking out early in the morning or sneaking in late at night, and forget about having an extra-marital affair; everyone including the village goose will be up to speed with your comings and goings.

Unless my bike has a particularly pathetic sounding exhaust, I prefer to keep the original, for a number of reasons:

1. I like to ride bikes as their creators intended without the concern that I'm making a terrible racket and drawing attention to myself. If anything, I want to sound like I'm going slowly, not fast. I would rather be operating in 'stealth mode' not 'look-at-me' mode. I can't wait until production electric motorcycles come out. These are the stealth bikes of the future.

2. The second is purely for reasons of comfort. I once owned a V-twin with a cheap race pipe with very little internal baffling, and the exhaust was so loud that I used to get a headache riding the damned thing (even with the best earplugs I could find stuffed deep into my ear canals!). Those sound pressure waves coming out of the exhaust were too much, and I just found it annoying.

3. The third reason is social. I lived in central London on a busy roundabout for many years, and found myself cursing loud motorcycles that woke me up in the early hours of the morning. That rider could be heard from a couple of miles away, and I don't doubt that he felt safer broadcasting his arrival to the world, but when he ran past my house (and quite a few others') at 5am with what was effectively an open race pipe, I felt sad that a fellow biker was giving the rest of us a bad name.

Like it or not, we are all ambassadors of our sport, and we should act in a way that matches how we want to be perceived. I accept that modern exhausts are bulky and seriously heavy. Changing them for a carbon-fibre or titanium end-can sheds kilos, and can significantly improve the looks and handling of your bike. I choose road legal exhausts to keep my neighbours and myself happy, and keep myself under the radar.

As well as shedding weight, hopefully, the exhaust will help your engine to breathe more freely, which can release more power. If you put on a freer-flowing exhaust, you may need to re-jet your carburettors or tweak the fuel injection system by fitting and setting up a Power Commander, which adds additional cost but ensures that the fuelling is right and that your well-meaning modifications are going to yield positive results.

Other Engine Modifications

Motorcycle engines come in a pretty high state of tune as standard. A freer flowing air filter and exhaust can help an engine to breathe more effectively, and setting up the fuelling correctly with a Power Commander will optimise those changes.

If you start to look further inside the engine to improve performance, think first whether you might benefit from buying a more powerful machine, or look at ways to reduce your current ride's weight to give a better power to weight ratio.

If you're serious about engine tuning, look at the race teams who take a standard bike and make it go as fast as possible, and assess what they do to get their bikes working well, and more importantly how much they spend. Look at newer machines, or look for a motorcycle with an engine which has character that suits your riding style.

Would you rather spend £20k of your own money developing the right bike, or would you rather Kawasaki Heavy Industries did it for you? Unless you are racing in a production class, your money would probably be better spent on some advanced training, suspension work or on honing your skills at a trackday; the majority of which in the UK have marshals on hand to provide feedback on riding style and cornering lines.

Brakes

Most motorcycle brakes are well up to the task of stopping the bike they are fitted to, and providing they are properly maintained and serviced, will continue to perform well. If you find your brakes wanting (and if you have a particularly heavy bike or do a lot of track days you might), your first port of call should be a brake fluid change, followed by a different brake pad material to improve stopping power and feel.

Brake pads come in two basic types; organic and sintered. Organic pads are not as hard as sintered pads, have more feel and a more progressive action.

Sintered pads are much harder, bite more into the discs, but are less progressive and will wear out your brake rotors more quickly. Somewhere in the middle is a hybrid semi-sintered pad material which aims to give the best of both worlds, progressive action, good bite, and reasonable rotor wear.

You can buy after-market brake rotors for your bike too, but the standard OEM rotors themselves are typically high-quality items, so I would only replace disc rotors if they have exceeded their maximum run-out.

If you have a particularly mushy feel at the level or pedal, first bleed your brakes to make sure that you don't have air trapped in the system. If you are still in need of more control, you can upgrade rubber hoses to braided stainless-steel brake hoses. Some machines come with braided hoses as standard, but most Japanese motorbikes use rubber, which lose stiffness over time.

If you're upgrading your hoses, ask yourself whether you need additional braking force at the rear. I prefer to run with a less sensitive brake, as it reduces the chances of rear lock-up. I frequently leave the rear brake hose as the standard rubber OEM item when upgrading the front lines.

Standard DOT4 brake fluid as used in cars and motorcycles is glycol based. It is hygroscopic, absorbing water from the atmosphere and from within the braking system over time. This ensures that the critical brake systems are protected against water in the brake lines, which can corrode components or freeze in winter and block the system.

Consequently, it is recommended that you replace brake fluid every two years. – DOT standards for brake fluid state a dry and a wet (3=percent water) boiling point.

As you can see from the table below, wet brake fluid has a significantly lower boiling point than fresh dry brake fluid. If you work your brakes hard and you have sintered pads, the temperatures generated can boil fluid and give you that mushy feeling at the lever and zero braking effect. If your fluid has never been changed, or you have no record of it being changed, then it's worth getting some fresh fluid in there.

Fluid	Boiling Pt (dry)	Boiling Pt (wet)
DOT 3	205C (401F)	140C (284F)
DOT4	230C (446F)	155C (311F)
DOT5	260C (500F)	180C (356F)
DOT5.1	260C (500F)	180C (356F)

With the advent of sintered brake pad materials and the increased heat produced, DOT4 (department of transport) brake fluids were developed and DOT4 replaced DOT3 as the minimum standard.

DOT5 fluid is a silicone based brake fluid which is not hygroscopic but it is twice as compressible as glycol based fluids, which can result in a spongy, inconsistent feel at the lever. Harley Davidson motorcycles specify DOT5 silicone brake fluids.

If you want a high-boiling-point traditional brake fluid, then look for DOT5.1 brake fluid. DOT5.1 is a traditional (non-silicone) glycol based fluid, which exceeds the DOT5 standard. The DOT marking is a minimum standard, some brake fluids will have a much higher boiling point than the minimum. For example, Castrol Racing SRF has a dry boiling point of 320C and a wet of 270C.

Screen

There are lots of options available for aftermarket screens. These are typically made to order from a number of manufacturers. You can buy screens of various shapes sizes and colours, from touring flip-up screens for maximum wind deflection, to double-bubble screens to the bespoke screens used by road racers.

If you're buying double-bubble, my advice would be to buy a genuine manufacturer's screen, or a dark aftermarket one, I've had issues with screens refracting the sun's rays like a magnifying glass and melting the clocks in the cockpit.

There's no doubt a double-bubble or race screen will give you much more wind protection, especially on an exposed sports bike. If you're buying an aftermarket screen, make sure that it has a black painted area at the bottom of the screen to mimic the original. This dark painted area shields unsightly cables and clock mounting brackets from view.

Chain Oiler

If your motorbike has a chain and sprockets and you do a fair amount of mileage, you might consider the benefits of an automatic chain-oiler. Fitting one not only saves you the hassle of lifting your bike and cleaning and lubricating the chain, it will make adjustment of the chain a much rarer occurrence, and the chain and sprockets will last longer.

The biggest benefit I have found is a smooth and vibration free drive at all times. If you think your bike feels a bit rough running, get yourself a brand-new chain and sprockets and a chain-oiler and your bike will feel brand new.

It might be a bit mucky down at the business end, and some systems, if improperly set up, can leave a damp oily patch on the driveway or garage floor, but set them up properly, and top them up once a week, and they will keep your chain in good nick.

Some systems have a valve which is opened by the vacuum of the engine. When the engine is running, the oiler runs, and when you switch off the engine it stops releasing oil.

Electronic systems are also available which don't require cutting into a throttle body or carburetor vacuum hose. Instead they work via accelerometers in the control box which detect when the bike is moving, opening an electronic valve to dispense oil. It's not as neat an installation as the vacuum system, as you have to find somewhere to mount the control box, but it should be more accurate at dispensing oil and will avoid those unsightly puddles.

Chain oilers aren't cheap, but if you do a lot of mileage or if you're lazy when it comes to chain maintenance, they will pay for themselves in no time. You can also buy manual oilers which you will need to either give a squeeze, or remember to open and close yourself when riding.

Horn

Why is it that the largest vehicles have the loudest horns? HGV's, with their formidable road presence and well-protected driver usually have terrifying air horns, whereas motorcycles and other small and vulnerable road users have little tooters more appropriate for a child's tricycle.

Motorcycle horns are difficult to hear at speed on fast roads and motorways, where trucks and cars could use more warning of your presence. They may not be able to see you, but at the very least they should be able to hear your horn if you use it.

The standard horn on your motorcycle will likely use direct current from the battery, and this is the reason it is so weedy. If you install an aftermarket horn, you will need to install a relay to keep the current flow through the horn switch to a minimum, and allow maximum current from the battery direct to the horn.

The hardest thing you will find when installing an aftermarket horn (or two), is somewhere suitable to mount it. If you have a faired bike or a sports bike, you will have some space behind the radiator or under the front forks triple clamp. If you want an idea where to mount it, have a look where the original horn is installed.

If you have a naked bike, there is plenty of open space to install aftermarket horns, but aesthetics will come into play more, so look for something chrome which will blend in with your bike's style. You will want to install your horns in as open an environment as possible to make the most of the increased horn sound; if you tuck them away in the tail fairing, they might be easier to fit, but you will lose much of the benefit of increased volume.

When you buy aftermarket horns, you will probably get just a horn, no wires or relay. They are typically sold as replacements for cars, which already have the necessary relay, wiring and connectors.

To install them on your bike, you will need some cabling, thin stuff for the relay actuation (3A), and a thicker cable to and from the horn (17A). You will also need a four-pin automotive relay, assorted blade connectors, heat-shrink, cable ties, nuts and bolts for mounting and nut-lock. Look online for an auto electrics supplier to source this equipment, and cut and crimp the wires to suit.

If you want to save yourself a load of bother, buy yourself a relay wiring loom harness off eBay, these are often available for wiring up motorcycle fog lights. This is ideal if you want to install two horns as it will already have two pairs of wires running from the relay which you can plug into the horns. Be prepared to do some fiddling about with connectors, and tidying up long wires, but having a ready-wired wiring loom makes the job of installing a horn an awful lot easier.

If you're wiring it yourself, a standard automotive relay has four terminals marked 85, 86, 30, 87. Connect your original horn switch to terminals 85 and 86. On terminal 30 of the relay, install a fused lead to the battery positive terminal. Terminal 87 is for the cable which goes to your horn(s).

You will also need a connection from the other side of your horn(s) back to earth or the battery negative terminal. If you connect two horns, connect them in parallel, leads from 87 to both positive terminals, and one lead from the other terminals to earth. If the horns have no positive or negative terminals, it probably doesn't matter which way round they are connected.

Test your wiring. When you push your horn switch with the ignition activated, the relay should 'click'. This 'click' indicates the main circuit is opening and will allow the horns to be fed directly from the battery.

If you're going to fit a horn, do a proper installation. Use insulated connectors, and cover them in heat-shrink tubing and use a heat gun (a hairdryer will do) to seal them up. Also buy adequately thick cabling to keep your voltage drops to a minimum. When you have measured your cables and you're happy with the lengths, wrap the cables up into a proper wiring loom using cloth tape (available from auto electricians). This not only makes it easier to thread the cables through the bike, but it keeps their size to a minimum. Once in place and wired in, cable-tie the loom in position for a nice neat installation. Beep Beep!

SECTION 3: RIDING

17. CORNERING

Motorcycles corner by moving the centre of weight to the inside of the turn. The faster you want to take a corner on a motorcycle, the greater the lean angle required to make it round the curve.

Unlike a car which will steer more or less the same radius curve regardless of speed, a lean angle of 45 degrees on a motorbike will steer a small radius at low speed and a large radius at high speed.

When it all comes together, few things are more exhilarating than a well-executed corner. Cornering is the skill which separates the men from the boys, and is usually the technical area most lacking in new riders, and therefore most likely to cause problems.

It's not difficult to master cornering as long as you understand some fundamental points and have some tricks up your sleeve which you can apply each time you corner.

Motorcycles are single-track vehicles, unstable when stationary, but increasingly stable as speeds climb. If you've learned to ride a bicycle, you've discovered that stability increases with speed. The same is true for a motorcycle, the rotational inertia of the wheels and tyres keeps the bike upright, and the faster you go, the faster the wheels rotate and the more stable the machine.

If you're travelling at speed, it is possible to ride with no hands, steering the bike's course by shifting your body weight to one side or the other. As you slow down, things start to get a bit wobbly and you find yourself reaching for the bars as the gyro-stabilising effect of the wheels falls away.

Just as a rolling coin falls over as it slows down, so a bicycle wheel is more affected by gravity as it loses its rotational inertia. With this in mind, a bike will turn most easily when the engine is decelerating with the front brake applied.

Grip Is Not Infinite

As we learned in chapter 13, cornering is made possible by the friction between the tyre and the surface of the road. This friction force is what prevents the bike from continuing to go straight when it enters a corner. We know this because of what happens when you remove this force – observe a racer going straight on into the gravel when losing the front trail-braking into a corner.

The amount of grip available from a tyre depends on a number of factors in any moment: the temperature of the tyre, the tyre compound, how old the tyre is, how many times it has been heat cycled (heated up and cooled down), the temperature of the road surface, the condition and make-up of the road surface, whether the surface is wet or dry, and the weight of the bike and rider, passenger, luggage etc.

On any given ride, you will need to take all of these factors into consideration when assessing how fast you can take a corner. A well set-up bike will give you plenty of feedback from the bars and the seat, so you can feel how the road surface and tyres are interacting with each other. This will help you to gauge the level of grip available and how much performance you can demand of your tyres.

Every time we ride we are gathering data from the road beneath; from experience on different bikes, road surfaces, different tyres with different levels of wear and in different seasons, hot and cold, wet and dry. All of this information is the databank which we call upon to determine how much grip we have at our disposal, and which informs our decision-making every time we ride. The more we ride, the more experience we gather and the better we will be able to assess and deal with riding situations we might encounter.

When the bike is upright, none of the tyres' available grip is being used for cornering, so we can use it all to accelerate or brake. Under these conditions – providing the suspension is up to the task – the tyre will hold traction even under full acceleration (wheelie) or full braking (stoppie).

Tyres grip better when loaded under acceleration and braking, as a greater force is applied through them as the motorcycle's weight is shifted backwards or forwards ($F=\mu W$: the grip Force equals the tyre's coefficient of friction times the weight acting downward through the tyre).

At the other end of the spectrum, when the bike is fully leaned over at 60 degrees in a race corner, 95 percent of its grip might be used for cornering duties, which leaves only five percent of additional grip for either accelerating or decelerating. When you're leaned over this much, you need to be extremely gentle with the throttle or brakes to avoid a skid and potential crash. Traction control and cornering ABS systems use a lean angle sensor to limit the amount of throttle and brakes you can apply when leaned over.

If you want to use more throttle when leaned over without skidding or spinning up the tyre, you need to reduce the amount of grip being used for cornering, which essentially means standing the bike up.

If you enter a corner at high speed and at a high lean angle, and you encounter an obstacle mid-corner, you have a number of options available to avoid it:

1. You can lean the bike further over to tighten your turn, and ride to the inside of the obstacle.
2. You can use the brakes to scrub off speed while maintaining the same lean angle to tighten your turn, and ride to the inside of the obstacle (useful if you can't lean the bike over any further without grinding metal into the road)
3. You can stand the bike up and use the brakes progressively to change your line and avoid the obstacle.

If these options are not available to you, either because you lack the skill or the experience to lean over any further or hit the brakes mid corner, then your remaining options are to pick the bike up and run off the road into the bushes, or onto the other side of the carriageway into on-coming traffic, or you can grab a handful of front brake and deliberately low-side the bike.

Let's say you have assessed the corner ahead, and you know that you need to be travelling at a certain speed and lean angle to make it round the corner on the line you have chosen. As you enter the corner, you see an obstacle on your chosen line, it could be a dead badger, or a wet manhole cover. As you won't get the same traction (and hence turn rate) on either of these as on hot-rolled-asphalt, you are going to have to adjust your lean angle, your speed, or possibly both.

You might choose a line that avoids the hazard altogether, or in the case of a traction hazard like a wet manhole cover, you might choose to ride over it in a more upright position (which reduces the risk of a skid), and once back on a surface with good grip, lean the bike over more aggressively to make your turn.

If you have entered the corner at a 'fully committed' pace – about as leaned over as you feel comfortable – and you encounter a hazard, you have no wiggle room left. It's badger time!

Riding on the limit is less serious on a racetrack, in fact it's the whole point of going on a track day. More on that in chapter 23. On track you have no oncoming traffic to spook you, and the controlled conditions (no grit, sand, wet leaves, diesel, squashed badgers etc.), and the same corners lap after lap, not to mention riding in a group of similarly experienced riders. This gives you the perfect practice pad for testing your limits of lean, and getting your knee down. Learn to push your lean angle and trail braking limits on track, and you'll have them up your sleeve for your road riding.

Slow In Fast Out

By approaching corners with a 'slow in-fast out' mentality, you make sure you enter at a speed at which you can make the turn comfortably, before accelerating to drive off the corner when you can see where you want to go, and the road is clear ahead.

Precisely how much grip you have available for accelerating and braking whilst cornering is something you will come to learn as your experience grows on track and on road. Modern sports bikes with traction control and cornering ABS can remove this guesswork, giving the rider a feel for what can and can't be done whilst leaned over testing the limits of traction without the risk of a crash.

Using the Brakes when Cornering

When you start out, aim to do the majority of your braking before you tip the bike into the corner. This is good advice, especially in the beginning, because it removes one of the variables in what can quickly become a complicated and overwhelming experience to the beginner.

There's a lots to think about when cornering a motorcycle; reading the road ahead to make sure your speed is right, actively steering the bike by pushing and pulling the handlebars (counter-steering), applying the throttle to arrest the fall of the bike and stabilise it mid corner and then opening it further to pick the bike up and drive off the corner, whilst still actively steering the bike.

If you get your braking done first, and get in the right gear, you need only concern yourself with the steering and the throttle, which are enough to get your head around in the beginning. Braking before entry also ensures that you are not too fast mid corner, and in a better position to deal with unexpected hazards.

The front brake is the most powerful tool on a motorcycle, and it performs the lion's share of stopping duties. When it's applied, the weight of the machine is pressed forward onto the front tyre, increasing the force acting through the front tyre's contact patch into the road and therefore increasing its grip ($F = \mu W$).

As your experience grows, you will find yourself staying on the brakes as you peel into the corner. You may even find yourself using front and rear brakes mid corner to fine-tune your speed. It requires a delicate touch to pull it off, but providing you apply the brakes progressively and use them lightly at high lean angles, you can brake fairly deep into a corner. Just remember to get on and come off the brakes very gently. What matters is a smooth transition which won't upset the bike's suspension. Watch the telemetry loggers in MotoGP if you want to see how late the brakes are released whilst cornering, and how progressively they are applied and released.

The rear brake is also useful when cornering. It can be used in situations where the front brake could easily cause a skid, e.g. where you are leaned over too far, or where steering geometry would cause a front-end slide, such as during slow speed cornering in car parks, when performing full lock turns and other manoeuvres with high steering angle.

The Eyes Have It

In life, we tend to go where we are looking. When you started to ride a bicycle – you can ride a bicycle can't you? – you probably fixated on something like a tree, and ended up riding directly into it. We must bear this in mind when cornering, and look where you want to go rather than at obstacles.

When cornering, you should be looking as far ahead down the road as possible, to gather as much information as possible about the road ahead and constantly update your riding plan to suit the changing conditions. You look into the empty space ahead rather than at things you are trying to avoid, otherwise you may well find yourself hitting them.

A good exercise when looking forward is to try to increase your peripheral vision. Once you practice doing this, you will have a far greater awareness of the road ahead, almost as if you are seeing it in 3D widescreen. In practice, your attention can only really be focused in one place at a time, but by improving your peripheral vision you can train your eyes and mind to take in more of what is going on without taking your sight off the road ahead.

Here's little exercise to demonstrate. Look at something directly in from of you. It might be this book, or a door handle, the curtains, a pot plant. Now with your gaze fixed on that object, draw your attention to other things in the room that you can see in the corners of your eyes. Don't take your eyes off the object in front of you, just allow your perception to focus on the clock on the wall, the floor, the book you're reading, the windows etc. Let your attention wander into your peripheral vision, even through your eyes are looking straight ahead.

Now focus back on the original thing you were looking at again, and sense the increased awareness of the room in front of you. It feels as though you are now seeing in 3D, whereas before you were seeing in 2D. Nothing has changed, but your increased focus on your surroundings has broadened your awareness.

If you can apply this widescreen vision to your riding, you can keep your eyes on the road ahead whilst also being aware of things happening in your peripheral vision. If they are important, look at them directly, if they aren't' then dismiss them and keep looking ahead and scanning your peripheral vision for hazards.

As you identify upcoming hazards, adjust your line, speed, and turn-in point to avoid any nasty surprises. The better you can see the road ahead, including using the other side of the road if it is safe to do so, the sooner you can identify when the corner opens up, and when you can start to roll on the throttle and drive off the corner.

Blipping the Throttle

As you change down, selecting the correct gear for the corner, practice blipping the throttle before you releasing the clutch. This matches the speed of the engine to the next gear, and keeps the transmission and chassis disturbance to a minimum. Blipping is the motorcyclist's equivalent of heel-and-toe to a car driver. You apply the front brake using your index and middle fingers, while blipping the throttle with the other two fingers and thumb of your right hand as you change down the gears sequentially. It will feel strange at first, but you'll soon get the hang of it.

There's no point blipping the throttle on down shifts if you can't brake smoothly at the same time. If your front end is bouncing up and down like a pogo stick, then the exercise isn't helping to stabilise the bike, it's only making things worse. Buy yourself a slipper clutch or an auto-blipper instead.

Lean the Bike Over

Once you are at the correct speed and in the right gear to negotiate your corner at a lean angle which is comfortable for you, lean the bike with positive inputs through both bars to steer your bike on your chosen line as you look ahead through the corner, anticipating where you are going and constantly updating your riding plan to suit any obstacles you come across.

Roll On the Throttle

It is essential once you have reached your maximum lean angle to arrest the fall of the bike by cracking open the throttle, once a small amount of throttle is applied, this stabilises the bike mid corner by shifting some of the bike's weight rearward. Once the corner exit is in view, gentle acceleration is used to pick the bike up from fully leaned over, to start the drive out of the corner.

The sooner you get on the throttle, the more comfortable the bike will be. If you enter a corner too fast for either you or your bike, you will get on the throttle late, which will impact your corner speed, and your corner exit speed. It messes up your corner.

Faster Cornering

What really separates the men from the boys is cornering speed. To go round corners faster than the next man, you need to steer faster than the next man; the time it takes for you to go from fully upright to the maximum lean angle required to make your turn should be as quick as possible.

The best line around any corner can be drawn on the ground. If you want to follow that racing line with your tyres, you will need to steer more quickly as your speed increases. If you can only steer slowly (and if you aren't actively counter steering, then you will be steering slowly) you can only ever take corners at low speed. If you try to take a corner at high speed and you can only steer slowly, you will run off the road.

If you go to a novice track day you will see plenty of people who are fast enough in a straight line but when it comes to the corners, they have to slow right down. They can't steer their bikes accurately or effectively to carry that same speed through the turn, or are unwilling or uneasy about chucking their bikes on their sides at speed. It takes commitment to corner fast, and it's something which is best worked up to gradually. The consequences of getting it wrong are high – like ending up in a ditch; so if you're following a faster rider who can turn quicker than you, don't get pulled into cornering faster than your ability.

Some people think that instead of steering quickly, they can get away with steering early. This never really works and will subject you to a higher than necessary lean angle, and put you on the wrong line exiting the corner. If you want to lean over as little as possible, learn to steer your bike quickly; pump those bars with a direct and powerful input.

Another factor which comes into play is getting on the throttle. On the track, for example, you want to be on the power as soon as possible, so that you can stabilise your bike, and start driving off the corner. The sooner you get the bike turned on its side, the sooner you can get on the throttle and drive off the corner.

The difference between an amateur rider and a professional in terms of steering is significant; the amateur rider might take a whole second to make his steering input from upright to fully leaned over, while the professional might take half a second. During the half second that the amateur is still steering his bike to the correct lean angle, the professional is already carving his arc at maximum turn rate, and is probably already on the throttle accelerating for the corner exit.

As he can get his bike turned faster, the professional can also travel deeper into the corner, braking later before he has to make the turn. If the amateur rider attempted to enter the corner at the same speed and make his turn at the same location, he would run off the track into the gravel.

To steer the bike faster, you need to push the bars with more force. To lean the bike further over you need to increase the duration of your steering input, and be ready with the throttle to arrest the fall.

While we're on the subject of steering, it is worth mentioning your grip on the bars, your positioning on the seat, and your weight on the footpegs.

The Grip of Death

The bike's front suspension works best when left to its own devices. If you relax and keep your hands loose on the bars, you won't impede the efforts of suspension and steering to work as the designers intended. If the front tyre moves over a particularly disruptive series of bumps on the road surface, the front tyre and suspension will both compress to take up the bumps, but when they have no more travel available (effectively becoming solid), the front wheel will shake from side to side and the handlebars with it.

This is a function of motorcycle dynamics, and the reason that steering dampers are fitted to motorcycles with steep steering head angles and stiff front forks. Your job as the rider is to get out of the way and let the suspension and steering work. If you are gripping the bars tightly, the steering and suspension cannot move as intended.

If you feel tense, or if your shoulders and arms feel sore after a ride, remind yourself to consciously loosen your arms, especially before entering a corner. If you go into a corner too fast and you inevitably panic, your arms will lock up and you will probably end up running straight on, as you won't be able to steer or brake affectively. Always ride within your abilities to keep this 'death grip' panic response at bay, and you will find the whole biking experience more enjoyable, and more satisfying.

If you find yourself experiencing the death grip, and live to tell the tale, make a note immediately afterwards that you were pushing well outside of your comfort zone, either because you were following another more experienced rider, or you weren't paying attention to the road ahead so were travelling too fast, or you were riding past the limit of your ability. Make a conscious decision to be more deliberate next time, and chalk it up to good experience.

Another reason to adopt a relaxed grip at the bars is about feedback. If you hold on for dear life, you are more tense, and therefore less likely to gather information from the road, or operate controls with precision. The more relaxed you are, the more you will enjoy your ride, and the more your bike can do what it was designed to. It is far more capable than you are, and you are the weak link in the chain, so try to ride with as light a touch as possible. Of course you must give positive inputs and steer the bike where you want, but as with riding a horse, your inputs should be deliberate and precise when steering, but otherwise light, sensing for feedback.

Bodyweight

Your bodyweight and positioning play a significant role when cornering. You turn a bike by leaning its weight to the inside of the turn. As the rider you make up a large proportion of the overall weight of your vehicle, and as you move your body to the inside of the corner, as racers do when hanging off, you assist the bike to turn.

While it's nice to lean a bike over, the aim of a motorcycle racer is to get the maximum amount of turn for the minimum amount of lean angle. If there's lean angle in reserve, this grip can be used for braking or accelerating, or kept as a margin of safety. This is why racers hang off the inside of the turn.

But you needn't be hanging off the side of your bike to feel the benefits of weight transfer. When riding along in a straight line, stand up on the footpegs, and place all of your bodyweight on the left footpeg. The bike will track to the left. Now do the same on the right footpeg and the bike will track to the right. Shift your body position over the left-hand side of the bike and the same thing happens. Part of the effect of hanging off is to place the weight of the rider through the inside footpeg.

If you have a pillion on the back who happens to be sightseeing, looking over your left shoulder to see the road ahead, then you'll find yourself having to make steering adjustments to continue on your chosen course.

Remind your pillion that when cornering, they should not try to lean either way, just sit on the back as stationary as possible, and if looking ahead while cornering, always over your inside shoulder. If you find them leaning to the outside of the turn, you will need to lean the bike over further than you anticipated to make the corner, which can be disconcerting!

As we discussed in chapter 13, tyre grip has a theoretical maximum value which translates directly to a maximum theoretical lean angle. Once this maximum lean angle is reached, the only way to go faster round a corner is to hang off.

Reading the Corners Ahead

When you're riding down a straight section of road with no hedgerows or houses blocking your view, you have good visibility and can assess the risks which lie ahead.

Road signs and the road paint markings on major roads should alert you to the presence of junctions and other hazards. By scanning the environment, you can keep an eye out for cars turning onto or off the main road. Where there are houses present, there are also likely to be cars either coming onto the carriageway, or slowing down to leave it. The more minor the road, the more likely it is that people are going to pull out onto it, or slow down to leave it. Minor roads are typically used by people who live in the direct vicinity.

If houses adjoin the road, keep your speed appropriate to the conditions, and consider riding with your lights on or using your horn so people have a better chance to see and hear you coming.

Chevrons, warning signs and road markings (SLOW) may be used to mark the sharp corners on major roads, but you're unlikely to find them on minor and unclassified roads. Use road signs as indicators to tell you what bends are coming up on the road ahead, and if you have multiple signs on a post, read them from the top down.

There are plenty of other cues you can use when riding to determine what is around the next corner. Riding at night in the countryside can be hazardous from the perspective of poor visibility, but it can be useful in other regards; the lights of oncoming traffic, or the red tail lights of the car or bike in front can give an indication of the tightness of oncoming bends and whether the road ahead is clear. If the lights suddenly disappear to the left, you might expect a sharp left-hander. Use these cues to your advantage, but remember sometimes the light plays tricks on our eyes, especially when we're tired.

Following a line of electricity or telegraph poles is not such a clever idea as these don't automatically follow the road, and often head off into the fields, but streetlights and hedgerows are more reliable indicators of any upcoming corners as they will more typically line the road ahead.

Road Surface

The road surfaces that you will encounter on your travels will vary significantly. In the UK, the roads are in reasonable condition, with neglected resurfacing which leads to potholes. As you grow your experience, you will be able to identify at a glance the type of road surface, and therefore level of grip available to you, and you will learn to spot a pothole from a distance.

On the approach to roundabouts and junctions, and on some bends, you may find Shell Grip. This is a very tractable road surface applied to the road with an adhesive, much like coarse sandpaper, which provides significant grip in virtually any atmospheric conditions. Shell Grip is applied to help in low grip conditions. It is occasionally coloured red or cream for better visual identification.

Unfortunately it also requires more maintenance than normal surfacing. Being so grippy, it can be worn off by the fixed axles of trucks, and in heavy braking zones, leading to a patchy surface with varying grip levels. On balance, however, I think it is generally a welcome sight.

Toe the Line

One excellent way to anticipate the road ahead is from the road markings themselves. All over the world there are thousands of professional engineers whose day-to-day work involves the design of new roads and the improvement of existing ones, from the approach angles, bend radii, carriageway dimensions, white line markings, and position of warning signs.

Roads are not just thrown together, they have undergone a significant amount of professional design and development and are designed with safety in mind. Use road markings and signage to your advantage.

The number of lines, their length, and whether they are broken or solid can all indicate potential hazards. A single broken white line typically marks the centre-line of the road. If the lines lengthen and the gaps get shorter, this indicates that there is a hazard approaching.

Double white lines, where the line nearest to you is broken, indicates you may overtake if it is safe to do so. If you see a broken line on your side appearing as you exit a corner, it usually means that the road ahead is about to open up, and your visibility will improve, so you can prepare for an overtake.

A double (in some countries single) solid white line indicates that you should not ordinarily cross to the other side of the road. Possible exceptions might be turning into a side road, or overtaking a stationary or very slow moving vehicle (compared to the legal limit, not compared to how fast you're travelling!).

Typically double white lines are on roads where there is insufficient room to overtake safely, or where there are lots of hazards (driveways, junctions, poor visibility etc.). If you are going to overtake on a double white line while riding a motorcycle, be aware that the police will not look upon such behaviour favourably. Also bear in mind people coming the other way will not expect to see anyone on their side of the road, and may be travelling faster than normal as a result.

Pushing the Envelope

When bikers start out, they frequently misread the tightening of a corner and end up standing the bike up and running off the road. Don't worry about it, it happens to everyone at some point. If you come away unscathed, then consider yourself lucky and learn from the episode.

The one thing that frightens new and inexperienced riders into bottling it on a corner, is when a corner tightens up (decreasing radius), and the perceived lack of skill or belief to make it round.

The best thing to do to improve your cornering confidence is to book yourself on a track day. The lean angles and corner speeds available on a closed circuit will far exceed anything you will ordinarily use on the road.

Once you have pushed the envelope on a closed circuit and you are comfortable leaning your bike over to 'track' lean angles, your road riding will feel much safer and much more satisfying.

Vanishing Point

The 'vanishing point' technique is a simple way for you to consciously assess the tightness of the corner, and therefore what you need to do to successfully get around it. The vanishing point is simply the point at which the road vanishes from your view.

If when negotiating a corner, the vanishing point moves further to the inside of the corner or towards you, then the corner is tightening up and you will need to slow down or prepare to lean the bike further over. If the vanishing point straightens up or moves away from you, the corner is opening up. If it stays in the same place then the corner is a constant radius turn.

The vanishing point can and will change mid-corner, and some particularly tricky corners can suck you in, and then have a decreasing radius at the end, just when you might expect to be powering out of them. They are not helpful, but they do still exist, so when riding on unfamiliar roads, especially minor ones which don't have the benefit of the oversight of professional highways engineers, leave a little something in reserve, just in case.

Advanced riding courses teach us to ride to the road ahead, and that means that we only ride as fast as we can see. In this way we can take evasive action if we find a tractor round the next blind corner. Use the vanishing point technique, and adjust your speed and lean angle accordingly.

Road Camber

One of the factors that you should be constantly assessing is the camber of the road. Car drivers may have little interest in signs which read 'negative camber', but they should be significant to motorcyclists, as the camber of the road affects the overall lean angle of any corner.

Road drainage is an integral part of highway design. Roads are drained by gravity, and the surface has a fall (camber) to direct the water into the drainage systems they incorporate. Roads are normally crowned in the centre, falling away to either side, or have a camber to the inside of the turn.

When cornering, a positive camber helps you out, requiring less lean angle (in relation to the road) to negotiate the turn at any given speed.

A negative camber or 'off-camber' turn works against you, and will dictate a higher effective lean angle to get round at the speed you're travelling. This may not be an issue if you have some cornering ability or grip to spare, or if you have time to adjust your line mid-corner.

If you're on a major road with a negative camber and someone has come a cropper before you (usually the more accidents, the more signs are put up), there may be a warning indicating 'negative-camber' or 'adverse camber'.

If the road falls away, like a French mini-roundabout, you're going to need to lean the bike over much further that you thought to make it round safely. You will usually be aware that you have negotiated a negative-camber corner after the fact. Where you thought you were headed, and where you actually went were not the same.

The significance of adverse camber will depend on which side of the road you ordinarily ride. Most roads have a crown in the middle and drain to the edges. In this sense 'adverse camber' only relates to a situation where the camber is different from what you might ordinarily expect.

In the UK we drive on the left, so left-hand bends have a beneficial camber, and right-handers an adverse camber. An 'adverse camber' sign will usually be given as a warning on left-hand bends where the rider might reasonably expect a positive camber, or where a right hander has a particularly adverse camber.

Don't expect warnings on minor roads, and keep your eyes peeled for elevation changes, however small. Roundabouts, slip roads and major junctions will all be profiled and drained differently, so you will need to check the camber and adjust your riding accordingly. If you do go abroad and find yourself riding on the other side of the road, the road camber effect on bends will be reversed.

Putting it all Together

To summarise all of the information in this chapter, let's look at two scenarios and discuss what is happening in each.

Entering a Flat Hairpin Turn with Good Visibility In and Out

Depending on your forward visibility of the road ahead, you can choose to use more of the road for cornering than just your own lane. The former may improve your visibility through the corner.

Look where you want to go, scanning through the corner as you approach it. Slow the bike to an appropriate speed using a combination of brakes and engine braking as you change down until you are in the correct gear for the corner, with the engine in its power band. Keep your eyes on the camber of the road and any potential hazards or obstacles ahead.

Choose your turn-in point, and steer the bike by pushing the inside handlebar while simultaneously pulling the outside. With the bike slowing off the throttle, the combination of deceleration, braking and steering input will easily steer the bike to the chosen lean angle.

Once the bike has reached its maximum lean angle, stop your steering input and barely crack the throttle open gently to steady the bike and arrest the fall. You are not accelerating, just applying maintenance throttle.

As you look through the turn at where you want to go, you can use the throttle and bars to steer the bike precisely. When you see the corner opening up, start to apply more throttle, and gradually pick the bike up accelerate away.

Entering a Decreasing-Radius Turn

As you enter the corner, choose your turn-in point, and ride as above, until you reach the point where you apply 'maintenance throttle' to stabilise the bike at maximum lean. Adjust your line as required by counter steering.

Looking through the turn at the 'vanishing point' of the corner. It becomes clear that the vanishing point is moving to the inside of the turn and towards you; this means that the corner is tightening up.

You roll off the throttle and lean the bike further over further whilst moving your bodyweight further to the inside of the turn, with a gentle dab on the rear brake to tighten the line further. The lean angle feels a little more than you would normally use, but it still feels within your capabilities. You look ahead through the corner where you are headed.

18. OVERTAKING

If you ride motorcycles you will do a lot of overtaking, so this is something that you want to get really good at. The good news is that motorcycles have a very slim profile and an excellent power-to-weight ratio which allows them to overtake with ease.

Overtaking is about safely and successfully negotiating a slower moving hazard, without disrupting the flow of the traffic. As with any hazard, the usual steps apply. Gather the correct Information, be in the correct Position, Speed and Gear, before Accelerating past.

To overtake you will need to move onto the other side of the road, into the path of oncoming traffic, so you want to minimise the time you spend there, and you will be increasing your speed, so you want to avoid any circumstances where other road users could impede your progress.

First you need to find an appropriate stretch of road. This means a clear road, with no driveways or junctions, and no oncoming traffic. Ideally the road will be wide and unobscured on both sides so you can see past the vehicle in front and plan your overtaking manoeuvre.

Before you commit, use your judgement. Clearly your idea of what constitutes a good overtake will improve each every time you ride, but even a newbie can spot a dodgy manoeuvre. It's mostly common sense. Learn to use your gut feeling, and to act on it. You should at all times remain feeling satisfied. If you feel less than satisfied, you need to be patient and plan and wait for a better opportunity.

If there's a possibility the person in front might turn off the road, or may themselves be looking to overtake, then hang back and wait to confirm your suspicions. If the car in front is slowing down, ask yourself if it is waiting for another vehicle to pull out, or is it about to pull into a junction or driveway? Learn to read cars' behaviour and body language.

Given a clear stretch of road, you want the vehicle ahead to have no option but to carry on at its current course and speed. As you add more elements to the frame, you increase the inherent risk: junctions, parking areas, driveways, side roads all introduce the possibility of vehicles pulling out into your path.

Even the most modest motorcycle can overtake cars with ease. Seeing as you are holding most of the cards, why not be really particular about when you overtake, only accepting the very best conditions. Don't overtake on the approach to junctions, in hidden dips or where there are potential hazards ahead. If you are following a large vehicle which is obscuring your view ahead, wait until you have a clear view. An opportunity to overtake will present itself soon enough.

Use your sixth sense to sniff out anything you don't like. If you feel unhappy about anything, hang back and wait until you understand the picture better, so that you can commit with confidence. Motorcycles have a surplus of power and a narrow streamlined form, so overtaking on a motorcycle should never be unduly risky.

Position

Before overtaking, position yourself at a safe distance behind your target so that you can see over or around it. Don't ride right up the backside of the vehicle: your visibility of the road ahead will be obscured, and your ability to gather information impaired.

When a safe opportunity presents itself, you should be in the right position, speed and gear to make your move swiftly. Have a quick safety check in your mirror, indicate and pull out onto the other side of the road to get a better look.

If you've assessed the situation correctly, everything should be ready for you to make your move, but this is the final check to make sure you haven't missed anything. If you are still happy, then wind on the power and overtake, of course watching that you don't reach excessive speed, for there may be a corner coming up.

If you're not happy with the situation, or you spot a hazard you weren't expecting, abort the manoeuvre, and gently pull back into where you were, behind the obstacle, and wait for a better opportunity.

If you are overtaking a vehicle from a long way back, if you are about to make your move and you want to let him know that you are passing, consider using your lights or your horn to signal your intentions.

Back of the Line

Motorcycles have such a surplus of power that they are often seen overtaking from the back of a long line of cars. This isn't in itself a bad thing, especially when none of the other drivers is interested in passing.

Before you commit yourself, study the rolling queue. How fast are they going? Do they look as though they want to overtake, or are they happy sitting in the long line of traffic? If the vehicle is a truck and the road busy, most cars will wait. If the obstacle is a slow-moving tractor, you'd be mad to attempt to overtake the lot in one go, as other drivers are likely to pull out themselves.

If one car is driving closely behind another, it is probably impatient to pass, and may pull out into your path. Treat the cars as you would a stationary line, give them a wide berth in case any of them does something unexpected, and give yourself space to make your manoeuvre safely.

High performance car drivers will always be eager to overtake, so pay them more attention. The same is true for ordinary cars which have been made to look sporting with aftermarket body kits, wheels and tin can exhausts.

The car drivers may assume that because they are at the front of the line, that they get to pass first, but many bikers operate in a different league of performance; where overtaking six cars is as easy as overtaking one. If you're not sure the guy in front has seen you, give him a flash of your lights or use your horn to let him know you're coming by, or overtake the cars gradually rather than in one fell swoop.

If you're behind another biker who is making good progress, but you still want to overtake him, hang behind and wait until he has seen you before attempting an overtaking manoeuvre. He may move over to give you more space to perform your overtake, and you don't want to surprise him; bikers are not used to being overtaken so it can come as quite a shock.

19. URBAN RIDING

The city is the undisputed domain of the two-wheeler. Push-bikes may be faster from A to B over short distances, but for journeys over half an hour, the motorcycle is king.

Motorcycles are small, and have the manoeuvrability to navigate through the gridlocked traffic, in between wing mirrors. Queuing in long lines at traffic lights becomes a thing of the past, and once you've started to move about the city on two wheels, you really can't go back to driving around in a car without wanting to pull your hair out, or that of your fellow gridlocked drivers. Sure, that guy might be driving a Ferrari, but if he's stuck in traffic with all the other cars doing three mph, what difference does it make?

Filtering

If you ride in any kind of reasonably busy urban environment, you will be faced with the question of filtering or 'lane splitting'; riding in the gaps between the lanes of traffic to make progress when the traffic flow backs up.

Most of the benefit of filtering is gained jumping the queue up to traffic lights, on the busy approach to roundabouts and, and on busy stretches of road , single lane or two or even three lanes abreast, where the traffic density has created waves of stop start driving.

Biking the Interstices

When you filter, you will naturally find yourself in the 'spaces in between' the rest of the road users. This vantage point brings you benefits in manoeuvrability, but brings with it added risk.

Outside of the normal lane, you are riding over cats-eyes, raised white lines, road kill, patches of grit, and those joins between lane surfacing which have typically been eroded by frost. All of these will affect the direction of your bike, and need to be taken into account.

When you are filtering on a two-lane highway, you have the hazard of oncoming vehicles to contend with. It's OK if they are moving slowly, not so good when they are moving more quickly or in poor visibility, as they just won't expect you to be there.

Filtering is about feel more than anything else. There is no hard and fast advice that works for everyone. Principally, as with all things motorcycle, you should be aiming to ride at a speed that is comfortable for you.

You might think that you're riding slowly and that even a 50cc scooter with L-plates is doing a better job of filtering, but it really doesn't matter, as long as you stay within your comfort zone, you are in a good place. Plenty of people who ride place little value on their lives, so if their riding behaviour is not acceptable for you, ride at a pace that you are comfortable with.

The more you practice, the more your filtering skills will improve, and with them your comfort level and your confidence to navigate busy traffic. You want to be aiming for a feeling of satisfaction as you effortlessly glide by, thanking and waving at road users who let you pass, and being patient with those who haven't seen you or can't move over because of their size. It's not their job to accommodate you, but if they do, bless them for their courtesy.

The Gaps

Your biggest hazard when filtering isn't the cars; it's the gaps in between them. Even though they're not going anywhere fast, many cars drivers seem to think that jumping from lane to lane in the traffic flow will make for better progress. Clearly they haven't heard about motorcycles, which is probably the reason they are so frustrated in the first place.

Filtering past two cars side by side is a pretty safe bet; although the faster they are travelling the quicker that gap could narrow. When they are stationary, cars cannot move laterally, but when they are doing 40mph, it doesn't take much turn of the steering wheel to move into your path; he reaches for the radio controls, she is putting on her make-up, he is reaching for his phone and their cars seem to have a mind of their own.

If a car moves to one side, don't assume that they have seen you and are moving over to let you by. They may just be reaching to skip a music track, or texting at the wheel.

As a filtering bike, you will recognise the extremities of your machine; the height of the mirrors of your bike, and those of the different types of van and pickup truck.

You will learn to sense vehicles which are about to move, and you can give a cautionary 'toot' on your (now beefed up) horn if you can't see round an obstacle and you want to make your presence known.

In the Flow

In the beginning, filtering is a pretty daunting prospect, but when you get the hang of it, get the measure of other road users, and develop a system which works for you, you will find it just as satisfying as any other biking activity.

You'll get into a rhythm with the other road users, and you'll be gliding through the traffic effortlessly, anticipating their moves and not expecting anything of them.

You will flow effortlessly in between the cars and trucks, keeping your finger on the pulse of how you feel and trying to maintain your sense of appreciation and satisfaction, and your reactions and instincts will be sharp.

You will appreciate how much more progress you're making than the drivers around you; enjoying your motorcycle's responsiveness; your dexterity and agility to control it; and the pleasing vibes, noises and smells from the mechanical harmony beneath you.

Every trip becomes a game, an opportunity to fine-tune your riding skills, to ride smoother, to really get into the flow. There may be people around you who are riding faster, filtering faster, or performing more risky manoeuvres than you, but you are quite happy in your own rhythm, in your comfort zone. You let them go their own way, and you go yours.

The Law of Diminishing Returns

As traffic speeds rise, the benefits of filtering fall, while the risks increase. Most of the benefit of being on two wheels comes from filtering past stationary cars to the front of the line at junctions. Once the traffic is moving above about 30mph, you're not making a great deal more progress than the cars.

To put it into context: A journey of 15 miles, with 7 minutes riding at 60mph, 10 minutes of filtering through stationary traffic and 10 minutes of filtering through traffic moving at 30mph, the rider who decides to not filter at 30mph will get to his destination two-and-a-half minutes after the rider who does.

It could take you that long to get out of your biking gear (on a good day!). To cite "The Tortoise and the Hare" analogy; when you start out has a great deal more impact on journey time, than how fast you ride. Just ask yourself, is it really worth it?

Raised White Lines and Rutted Roads

Motorbikes steer because of the camber of the road and the angle the tyres make with it. Riding along upright and changing the road camber will steer the bike.

If you're travelling in a lane that is used predominantly by heavy goods vehicles or buses, you may find yourself riding in ruts caused by their wheels wearing into the soft course. These will affect the direction your bike is travelling.

Raised white lines painted on the road will have a similar effect, albeit in reverse to a rut; steering your bike even though it is upright.

These 'peaks' and 'troughs' aren't normally a big deal, but when you are filtering in heavy traffic, especially when you are dealing with millimetre-precise manoeuvring and there are wing mirrors at close proximity, they can throw you off course.

Stay alert to unintended lateral movement of your bike when filtering in major cities and over raised white lines, and get ready to use your shifting weight and your steering input to adjust your line.

Positioning

When riding in the city, put yourself in a position that gives you the best advantage. This usually means towards the centre-line of the road, approximately in line with the driver's-side tyre of the vehicle in front.

A prominent position such as this has many benefits; it provides you excellent visibility of the road ahead, but it also allows other road users to see you more clearly. If the vehicle in front slows down, and you want to continue past, you have an escape route to the side of the car, and can quickly and easily turn your following position into a filtering position with minimal disruption.

If you ride directly behind the centre of the car in front, you need to watch your distance, and if the traffic suddenly stops and you want to keep making progress, you have to move further over before you can start to filter. There may also be another motorcycle in the 'filtering lane', so you will need to take my eyes off the road ahead to check over your shoulder, which increases the chance that you hit the vehicle in front.

When moving about in the city, make extensive use of the shoulder-check or 'lifesaver' whenever you are moving into your blind spot. The chances are that at some point there will be someone there. Get into the habit of doing a 'lifesaver' before changing lane, before filtering, and before pulling away from the lights, to check for other two-wheelers including bicycles which are also looking to steal a march on the cars.

Speed Limits

The official line is to follow the speed limits. The alternative line, where you may have broken the rules but are still alive to face the repercussions, says keep up with the flow of the traffic and move at a speed which feels comfortable to you.

I often see bikers (usually recently qualified) driving along in the gutter at 30mph whilst being overtaken by 20-ton trucks. It makes me shudder. What's more important, obeying the law, or staying alive? You can't come back from the grave to tell the police that you were 'in the right', diligently obeying the law like a good citizen, and that the other motorist was speeding.

Get out there into the road space and mark your territory. Hold a dominant position in the centre of your lane, or nearer the centre-line of the road, and ride at a speed and a pace that suits your skills and keeps you safe.

By putting your lights on and keeping your speed reasonable (i.e. neither too fast nor too slow), you give other road users a fighting chance of seeing you coming. You might be a finely tuned high-performance rider, adept at high-speed riding manoeuvres, but you share the road with a normal-distribution of other road users, and the fifth percentile are not merely not as good as you, but cannot see much beyond the end of their bonnets.

Obstacles

My number one tip for riding in cities is to handle any large moving 'obstacles' with complete suspicion. If you can't see what is on the other side of it, assume that it's something bad, and approach with caution.

Bikers who have learned this lesson the hard way, usually have a coming together with a car pulling out of a junction, performing a U-turn or pulling out into the flow of traffic. The emerging driver cannot see the motorcyclist as the vehicle blocked his view.

If the obstacle is obscuring your forward visibility; look for an opportunity to get past it as quickly and as safely as you can, so you can see down the road and be seen by other motorists.

If you cannot get past safely, hang back a reasonable distance so that other road users can see you and you're not obscured by the obstacle. Buses stop frequently, so you can pass them at the next stop, and you will eventually come to a traffic light and have the opportunity to pass, so remember to be patient.

Typical urban 'obstacles' include buses, lorries, trucks, minibuses, limos, SUV's with blacked out windows, rubbish trucks, delivery lorries; any object moving or stationary which is big enough to obscure your view of the road ahead, or their view of you. If it's going to be stopping regularly, get past it as quickly and safely as you can.

If you're behind an obstacle which is turning off the road, hang back deliberately to improve your visibility, and others' visibility of you. Slow yourself right down. Take your time, and give a toot of your horn to alert other road users of your presence; there could be pedestrians stepping out to cross the road, cars pulling out from junctions, taxis doing U-turns. If you're' not sure that you've been spotted, move further over away from the car about to pull across your path, to give yourself additional breathing space in case they haven't seen you.

Traffic Lights

When waiting at the lights, avoid being directly in front of large trucks with reduced visibility, keep your eyes peeled on those changing traffic lights and get out of the junction as soon as they turn.

If you are approaching traffic lights, filtering through traffic, assess whether you can get well out ahead of the vehicle at the front. There's little point squeezing past into 'pole position' only to get squashed because you can't be seen.

If you misjudge a safe route to the front of the line, and end up in a vulnerable place, get attention by using your horn. The majority of fatalities on pedal cycles are when unnoticed riders are squashed by trucks as they pull away from traffic lights. Get off the line ASAP.

If it feels bad to be occupying a traffic light with a truck, provided you can still see the lights ahead, pull forward a bit further even if you're over the stop line, or in the bicycle zone (if there is one), and turn to look the truck driver in the eyes to check he's seen you. Never mind the law, stay safe.

Pedestrians

Pedestrians also need a careful eye when riding in urban environments. In major cities, many urbanites do not routinely drive, as they have no need to do so. They may have limited awareness of the traffic flow and how it works, and be poor at judging the speeds of approaching vehicles.

Pedestrians will naturally want to cross the road, and will jump out from gaps between cars and buses when you're least expecting them. If you can't see past a line of buses at a bus stop, toot your horn to let any pedestrians know you're there, before they pop out and show themselves to you.

Cyclists

Cyclists and motorcycles are two-wheeled brothers, and the crossover between the disciplines is greater than many believe, except of course we bikers don't have to pedal. Cyclists have good road sense, or they don't tend to last long in cities. They can be a bit loose with the law, so watch for cyclists running red lights, jumping pedestrian crossings and the like. Motorcycles and bicycles are also allowed to share certain bus lanes in major cities so treat cyclists with respect and give them as much space as you would a fellow biker.

Couriers

Couriers are experienced riders who cover tens of thousands of miles a year around town. The good ones are extremely adept at filtering and know the roads, traffic lights, junctions and short cuts. As a general rule, go as fast as you feel comfortable, moving to the side from time to time to check your mirrors and let any eager couriers past. If a courier is on a charge, don't try to keep up with him unless you're a competent urban rider.

20. COMMUTING

I'm a big fan of commuting by motorcycle. It is generally more environmentally friendly, (even a 1000cc sports bike will return 40-50mpg), you will spend less time sat in traffic jams, and have a lot more fun than if you were in a car.

Aside from being highly efficient, commuting is a satisfying and invaluable way to build experience and keep your riding skills fresh, all year round.

If you only ride in the warm months of the year, and given the climate in the winter who can blame you, your skills are going to be rusty when things warm up in spring. But if you also ride in the autumn and winter, you will be right up to speed for the warm weather and sunshine. Meanwhile Mr. Fairweather-Biker will take a month of riding to blow away the winter cobwebs.

As I write this, I have just finished a freelance post in London, spending eight of the last ten months commuting from Oxford into Central London every day by motorcycle. In total I have racked up 20,000 miles in less than a year. Come rain, shine or stormy weather, I rode into town to get to work.

There were no mishaps in all of that time, and despite the distance involved, I really looked forward to my daily commute. The fact that I was riding a Suzuki GSX-R1000 for most of it certainly helped.

It might seem a daunting prospect, but with the right gear and the right attitude, you can make light work of commuting by motorcycle. The best attitude is to be relaxed about yourself and your fellow commuters.

There's no rush, at least certainly not for you, because you are in control of your destiny; you're going to get there much quicker than the car drivers around you. Relax and enjoy the progress you're making while others are going nowhere. If you get a bee in your bonnet and start to take the whole thing too seriously, you will lose your cool, and you may as well have been driving a car. Riding a bike gives you the freedom to feel good even in gridlocked traffic. Don't squander that freedom lightly.

Whether you like it or not, as a two wheeled commuter, your natural domain is outside of the main flow of traffic; filtering in-between them. In order to take advantage of your smaller size, you will have learned where your mirrors, handlebars and elbows end, and to spot opening and closing gaps in the traffic. Stay calm and happy in the knowledge that you're making good progress, regardless of the traffic conditions.

Commuting adds a bit of daily motorbike excitement to your life, and gives you an excuse to ride. To put it into context; if you commute 30 miles each way, you will be clocking up around 14,000 miles a year just doing what you need to do to get to your workplace. This is what an average weekend rider might cover in four years.

If you commute, you will be on your way to becoming an accomplished and far safer rider quicker than those who ride only when the sun shines. You will be used to riding in the wet, riding in the dark, and your eyes will be finely tuned to the natural hazards on the roads.

Your hazard perception, depth perception and peripheral vision all improve the more road miles you get under your belt. You will be a faster, smoother and more comfortable rider than someone who has only ridden about 20,000 miles in their entire life, and it will show.

Most importantly of all, you will know your bike, your tyres and your own capabilities inside and out. After a few hundred hours in the saddle, you'll reach a point where you just 'click' with your bike. It suddenly dawns on you that your bike feels more like an extension of you, than some strange machine that you're sitting on. When this point comes, you will know that you have gelled with your machine, and your feeling of satisfaction and appreciation for your bike will be bordering on full blown love.

Just a brief glance through the classified ads shows hundreds of bikes with barely any miles on the clock. Some will cover less than 1,000 miles a year. While this is great for those who like buying second-hand but nearly new machines, it seems a shame to buy a motorcycle and not let it fulfill its reason for being.

It would be like having a big pile of money, and keeping it stored away in a vault your whole life rather than getting out there and spending it. Most motorbikes were designed to be ridden to the red-line, and they cannot do it without our help.

If you actually ride your motorbikes – rather than being a motorcycle curator who cleans polishes and services in anticipation of the next owner – they will depreciate in value and won't be worth as much when you do eventually come to sell them; they will have a few more stone chips than usual and the fasteners will be a little more corroded.

In return, you will have experienced your bike to its fullest, and the satisfaction you will have achieved from your experience with a bike that you really enjoyed will be worth far more to you than a few hundred or even a few thousand pounds in lost resale value.

Until you have really had a relationship with your bike, and dug deep into its performance envelope, for better and occasionally for worse, you will not know what you are looking for in your next one.

It's not a Racetrack

Riding to work every day of the week is great fun, and when you really get into the groove, it's tempting to do super-high speeds on roads you know well. Not everyone will be travelling as fast as you are. Keep your commuting speed to a comfortable level so that you blend in with the flow of the other road users. If you're tearing down the road, and the rest of the traffic is virtually at a standstill, the car drivers may not be expecting your arrival, and the coming together of two objects at very different velocities is troublemaking.

Enjoy Yourself

The most important thing to do when commuting daily is to get yourself into the right frame of mind, and do what is necessary to keep yourself in that frame of mind throughout your journey. You want to be having fun, enjoying your ride in the moment, not dwelling on what you're going to do when you get to work or thinking about what happened yesterday. Keep your focus in the present, giving your full attention to the task at hand.

Get yourself in a good physical state: a good night's sleep, properly fed and watered. If you are tired or dehydrated (or hung-over) give yourself a break and ease off the throttle. If low blood sugar turns you into the incredible hulk, then either train yourself off your dependence on high sugar foods, or have some of them handy to top up your levels. Take nothing which adversely affects your mental frame of mind.

Set your mental frame of mind before you set off, and leave with plenty of time. If pressure starts to rise up inside you, remind yourself that the most important thing is that you stay feeling good, and not necessarily that you get to work on time. Your boss would far rather you turn up late than have to explain to your family that their daddy isn't coming home tonight.

Your privileged position allows you to move effortlessly through traffic jams, and to overtake with ease, so there's no need to entertain feelings of frustration. If a car driver, or heaven forbid another biker – yes, it does happen – acts irrationally, be grateful that you're still in one piece, say nothing more of it and go on your way.

Don't get sucked into another person's bad day. Bless them, hold on to your power and go on your happy way. Control your frame, don't get sucked into another's. When you start to get frustrated or angry, that's when you'll start to bump into your fellow angry road users. Your good judgement evaporates, and this is when accidents, incidents and run-ins with the police inevitably happen.

If necessary, give yourself permission to be late for your appointment, be as nice to yourself as you would be to others, allow those over-zealous kamikaze riders to pass you by, and remind yourself that you want to get to work in a good frame of mind. Ride your own ride, and focus on yourself, but move over when it is safe to do so to let others past.

Remember that *you* are in charge. Ride at your own pace. You will get there when you get there, there's no shame in riding sensibly, and there are no prizes for ending up squashed under a truck.

You are extremely lucky you get to ride a bike to work, to make the beginning and end of your day a fun and stress-free activity. Don't transpose old car frustrations onto two wheels. Don't drive aggressively, point the finger and shake your head at every car driver who doesn't treat you like royalty. If you do, you're missing the point.

Elevate yourself above the throng. Let them be, and accept that they don't need to do anything differently for you to get exactly where you want to go, and for you to feel good throughout your journey.

When you get good at this, you will be gliding through the traffic so gracefully, so effortlessly that most other road users will barely even notice your presence. You will come to see that those really good rides had their beginnings in the cool, calm, centred and deliberate attitude that you held when you climbed aboard. A feeling of invincibility, strength and purpose, mixed with your appreciation of your bike, other road users, and the sheer fun of riding, create the perfect biking experience.

21. GROUP RIDING

When you get your first motorbike and head out onto the roads, you will discover that you are now part of a biking fraternity, one where brothers acknowledge each other's presence with a nod or a tilt of their head as they pass you by. Motorbikes bring people together, and they foster such passion in their owners, that sharing this enthusiasm with other like-minded individuals comes naturally.

Whether you are going for a weekend away in the mountains or a long-distance camping trip to see a World Superbike or MotoGP race, going with a group of friends can be a really fun way to get out and about and enjoy the hobby you love.

When any group gets together, particularly young men, peer pressure invariably comes into play. Add to the mix powerful machines that make a loud noise when you twist the throttle, and bucket loads of testosterone and adrenaline, and something oddly primal happens; ordinarily sensible people end up behaving like little boys.

I'm not a big fan of riding in large groups. For me riding is about personal connection and affirmation of how good life can be if we focus on things that we love. The more opinions I have to take into account, the less in control I am of my own destiny, and that goes against the reason I ride in the first place; power, control and choice.

Someone has to lead, but I'd like that someone to be me. I also see my time in the saddle as precious time where I get to be alone, and enjoy the activity I love. It's nice to ride with one other closely matched rider who can keep up, that way we can share notes and appreciate our mutual experience afterwards. But a group of four or more, there's too much baggage for me to be dealing with.

I'm a loner at heart, and I enjoy spending time with myself. I wasn't always this way, but after a particularly enlightening solo trip to Scotland, I have always appreciated riding on my own more than with others. It is the definition of ultimate freedom. Pack a small rucksack with underwear, toothbrush, earplugs and credit card and take off for the weekend with no fixed destination, riding to wherever the mood takes you. Adventure!

Cornering

It is easy to get lazy when following another rider. You can get sucked into entering a corner too fast for either your ability or your bike's. If you're reading the rider in front, you're not reading the road. He might be an ex-racer with 40 years of biking experience against your five.

Don't take anyone else's cornering line for gospel; read the road yourself, and make your own judgement calls. That way you won't find yourself standing the bike up mid-corner and running off into the bushes.

If you are riding close behind someone, try to stagger your riding so that you are not directly behind. If they hit the brakes you don't want to run into the back of them. If they are on the left of the lane, you can ride on the right and vice-versa.

If there are more than two of you, adopt a formation to take up less space on the road (not a long snake) Bear in mind that this formation may put you in a road position that you don't normally find yourself in, and you will need to anticipate this and make allowances for when cornering.

Go your Own Way

If you're not a big fan of travelling in a group, or if you enjoy motorbikes as a release from the busy social aspects of life, you can experience your own ride at your own pace, and still have fun with others when you get to your destination.

One way of doing this is to pre-arrange a meeting point, and set off from your different locations to get there. That way you can have a ride out with others, and still travel on a route and at a pace that suits you. Unless you are all closely matched in ability, it is highly likely that some of you will be pulling others along. This can cause a bit of tension, where one rider is being pushed into riding faster than he likes, while another feels that slower riders are holding him up.

22. ALL WEATHER BIKING

There's something hugely satisfying about riding in the wet and the cold when most bikers wouldn't dare. It might seem like a crazy idea, but as the daylight hours wane and the chill in the air has you reaching for your overcoat, there's still plenty of fun to be had out on two wheels. If anything, the adventure becomes greater in poor weather.

Properly kitted out in modern riding gear, you can ride comfortably in all but the most inhospitable weather, and you'll feel much more awake and alert than those in their warm sleepy cars.

As you come to a stop and smell the sweet aroma of wet motorcycle vapours rising from your exhaust header pipes, you'll smile to yourself in satisfaction that you took on the elements and won.

In the winter months, there are fewer riders on the roads, the smells and sights of the seasons are there for you to take in, and the sunrises and sunsets are legendary. As long as you wrap up warmly, a ride on a fresh winter's morning can be among the most beautiful you will ever experience.

Get yourself some modern sport touring tyres, some decent warm clothing and gloves, and a neck warmer. When you get back from a winter morning blast, your eyes streaming from the cold and with a big smile on your face, you will feel invigorated as you step back into your centrally heated home. You may very well be the only person out and about, and you will feel like you're living in a time gone by, before every household had three cars.

If you ride all year round, you will also be riding a lot in the dark, which improves your anticipation and your night vision. You will get better at spotting hazards and riding to the limits of the road.

I actively look for excuses to ride in the winter. My bikes get a good coating of ACF-50, and a hose down with cold water after every ride to get the salt off, and I ride in everything but ice and snow. Get yourself the right gear, and even a wet traffic jam can be fun; the car drivers may be dry, but they're not going anywhere, whereas you'll be making excellent progress.

Gear

You can wear leathers in the winter, but you're much better off with a waterproof, windproof breathable suit, which will keep you warm and toasty in the cold and wet. Leathers may keep you dry for a period, but the textile suit will dry out much faster. If you use your motorcycle gear on a daily basis, you will want it to be drying overnight to avoid the 'wet swimming costume' experience the following day.

A pair of warm waterproof winter gloves with plenty of feel is essential to operate the controls and get good feedback at the same time. If your gloves don't breathe well enough, your hands will get cold from their own moisture; in this regard, it pays to go for the best gloves you can afford. A thin but warm lining will keep your hands warm and cosy.

Heated waistcoats can be a godsend in cold weather, keeping you warm and snuggly even at subzero temperatures. If your body's core is kept warm, it doesn't cut the blood supply to the extremities; often your hands are cold not because your hands are cold, but because your core body temperature has dropped and your body is preserving its heat by cutting off the supply to your hands and feet. You may also notice on a long ride that the 'warm hug' of a heated jacket can soothe away many aches and pains.

Depending on what you ride, your feet may be exposed, or tucked away in the fairing and heated by the engine or low-level exhaust, or they may be hanging out in the breeze. Get yourself some waterproof breathable boots, a pair of thick socks, and a neck warmer to keep the cold drafts off your carotid artery and jugular vein.

Tyres

If you routinely ride in the wet and cold, consider getting some appropriate tyres for your bike, a modern sport-touring tyre will do the job nicely. Look for something with high silica content. If you ride on track-biased rubber, these are unlikely to come up to optimum temperature in the winter months. The roads are too cold and speeds too low to generate sufficient heat.

They're not cheap, but sport-touring tyres will give you excellent feel and a nice progressive turn in, perfect for cold wet roads. Personally, I have used Dunlop, Michelin, Pirelli and Metzeler sport-touring tyres and found them all to be excellent and confidence-inspiring in wintry conditions. The bonus is that when summertime comes, you can still use them for normal road riding, and even the occasional track day.

The Benefit of Reduced Grip

In summer you have plenty of grip available, really much more than you need or could sensibly use in most road riding situations. Unless you ride a particularly powerful bike, you are unlikely to overcome the grip of your rear tyre on the road at normal speeds in the warm, dry summer months. The same goes for the front brake.

Abundant grip is a good thing, after all, it's what keeps us shiny side up. What you don't necessarily have is an understanding of how much, or how little grip is at your disposal in any moment. You only know that you have enough. But when you start to ride in the autumn and winter months, you will develop a far greater feel for traction conditions.

It pays to have a communicative bike when riding in the wet, with a front end that is telling you what is going on, but the real skill is learning to listen, or more accurately to feel what the bike is doing beneath you. When you lean a motorcycle over to steer it left or right, you get feedback between the angle of lean and the direction of the bike. The difference between these two is a measure of slip, and indicates the level of grip available.

Even in dry conditions there is a certain amount of slip. Did you know that a tyre grips maximally when braking and accelerating at around 10-percent slip? When braking hard the front tyre is moving 10-percent slower than the road, and when accelerating the rear tyre is moving 10-percent faster.

If you feel like the bike is moving around, you will have less confidence than if it felt stuck to the road with glue. In wet conditions the tyre doesn't achieve the same level of traction on the road (although it is not far off dry grip), and so it feels more reluctant to turn, and tracks a wider arc.

You may find yourself tensing up when riding in low grip conditions, which hinders your steering further. The high lean angles achieved readily in the dry are much more daunting in the wet, but with sensitivity, you can ride nearly as fast in the wet as in the dry.

While a reduction in grip doesn't sound like a good thing, it holds many benefits to you as a rider. It forces you to improve throttle control, make more effective use of your weight in cornering, and gives an understanding of what is possible from gradually pushing the limits of traction. Enhancing your ability to feel how much grip is available, identify hazards such as manhole covers and diesel slicks, and your deftness with the controls will help make you a more progressive rider with an improved ability to read the road.

Tentative riding in reduced grip conditions, especially on more powerful bikes, teaches machine control that you just don't get in the warm and the dry, simply because you never have to be that delicate with the controls.

Riding in low grip conditions can also highlight suspension deficiencies. The better your suspension, the more it will communicate with you in low grip conditions.

Start off riding gently, gauge your level of grip and use your right hand appropriately. If you got away with being ham-fisted in the summer, you will learn to improve your throttle response in the winter. You will also be surprised by how much grip is available when you load up the tyres gradually by progressively squeezing on the front brake and progressively rolling on the throttle.

Autumn Leaves

Autumn is a beautiful time of year, the nights draw in, our appreciation of pubs, open fires, and centrally heated houses is renewed, but those beautiful turning leaves can be quite a hazard to motorcyclists. If you live in a city, the silent army of leaf sweepers will keep your streets clean and grippy, but if you live in the countryside, watch your step when the leaves start falling. They can be as lethal as black ice, and about as hard to spot.

Riding in the Cold

In the winter, things slow down. The air is denser and the motorcycle can fill its lungs with fresh cool air. You will feel as though you have the roads to yourself. It is reminiscent of mountain skiing. The sun is shining and the scenery beautiful. Stop for a warming drink before heading back out for another run.

If you're inappropriately dressed, the fun can quickly turn into misery. You will start to lose valuable blood to your hands, which are not only the means of controlling your bike, but also how you gather feedback. Your body will also tense up, and this tension hinders steering and suspension functions. Wear thermal clothing in multiple layers; ride a bike with a fairing; wear a heated jacket, stop regularly … but keep yourself warm and you can have just as exciting a ride in the winter as in the summer.

Riding in the Ice & Snow

If it has been snowing or there is ice about, I recommend you take the car. Major roads are normally treated, so not a problem; but minor roads without any kind of surface treatment are lethal and, unless you are riding a bike with snow tyres, you are going to have serious traction issues.

The biggest concern is braking. The brakes on any bike are powerful enough to rapidly overwhelm surface grip in the snow. If you have been skiing or have grown up with ice and snow and know how it works, tread carefully, otherwise I would avoid it. Use this as an excuse to work from home, or stay in the hotel another night and put your feet up until the blizzard has passed.

Riding through a Storm

If you've never ridden in strong winds, head down to the south-eastern corner of France and experience Le Mistral. It is quite a force and can make even large bikes feel unstable and precarious. You find yourself riding along at a lean angle of 20 degrees in a straight line.

In situations like this, the faster your bike is travelling the more the gyroscopic effect of the wheels helps to stabilise you in the gusts. If you are stuck behind a lorry doing 40mph, the best thing you can do to improve your confidence is to get past it and get your speed up.

If a side wind is blowing you off course, shift your body weight towards the direction of the wind, and position your bike towards that side of the road. This will give you a little extra leeway should a sudden gust hit. While increased speed does improve stability, it also increases the distance you can veer off course, so experiment with a speed which keeps you the most stable.

Riding into a headwind, or riding at speed, is less concerning but still rather hazardous. Bridges over large rivers with high winds can be lethal and are frequently closed to motorcycles and high sided vehicles in bad weather.

When a rider is blown about by the wind, his body acts rather like a sail and his arms like ropes attached to the handlebars. In windy conditions, check your body tension, and try to keep your hands and arms as relaxed as possible. This usually means you will need to adopt a more crouched position to take the load off the controls.

I wouldn't recommend you ride through a storm on purpose, but you may get caught out and have to deal with one. In a deluge keep an eye out for standing water. Motorcycle tyres are far less likely to aquaplane than car tyres due to their pointier profile, but if your tyre tread is low, or your tyres are at low pressures or squared off, you may have issues with standing water, so ride with caution. If you hit standing water and aquaplane, relax at the controls, let the suspension do its thing, and hope that you're going fast enough that your wheels' inertia will keep you upright until you're back on dry land again.

23. RIDING ON TRACK

If any machine belongs on a racetrack, it's a sports-bike, especially modern European and Japanese supersport bikes of the 600cc+ clip-on variety.

If you own a supersport bike then you need to know that the bike you ride was designed for road racing. To really see what it can do, you need to stretch its legs on a racetrack.

Track days are great because they allow you to focus on machine control, accelerating, braking and cornering. You need not worry about oncoming traffic, and if you get it wrong you won't hit a tree, but a big pile of gravel instead. Hooray!

Most importantly, when you test the cornering ability of your bike on track, you should exceed any lean angle you might reasonably expect to use on the road, which will add huge confidence to your road riding.

There are a number of organisations in the track day business, some are track owners, others are events companies that rent track, marshals and emergency support services.

Some track days are aimed at road-legal vehicles, others look more like club race practice sessions, with slicks and tyre warmers everywhere.

If you're a novice rider consider a road-legal track day as your first; it is less intimidating, and the riders want to ride home so tend to be less 'committed' in their approach.

If you're considering doing a track day, here's a list of things you'll need before attending:

- ✓ leathers: one-piece, or two piece with joining zip
- ✓ back protector (not compulsory but recommended)
- ✓ motorcycle in tip top condition (you can hire bikes at some track days)

- ✓ motorcycle licence
- ✓ full face helmet (ACU approved)
- ✓ protective leather gloves
- ✓ strong protective boots
- ✓ tools to tweak suspension
- ✓ exhaust baffle (track days have dB limits)
- ✓ a relaxed and open-minded attitude to learn as much as you can
- ✓ a drink and a snack
- ✓ a sense of fun (try to not take yourself or anyone else too seriously)

Tip-top Condition

If you are going to test the limits of your bike's performance, you want those limits to be as high as possible. Everything on your bike should be in full working order, including you.

Don't make the mistake of thinking those old squared off road tyres that have been on your bike for the last three years are going to be up to the job of a track day.

When you go on track you are going to have the opportunity to really test your bike and your own riding ability to the limit. You will doubtless be venturing into new territories of grip, lean angle, acceleration and braking performance, so the last thing you want is for your motorcycle or its crappy hardened tyres to be the weak link in the chain. As the tyres are the only thing keeping your bike upright at extreme lean angles, if you do ride on shoddy tyres and crash, the damage is going to cost a great deal more than a decent set of sticky tyres.

If you're riding something a bit less racy then by all means stick with your road tyres, but if you're on a supersport bike, consider getting some of the latest fast road tyres as a minimum. They will make a huge difference to your track experience, and can still be used on the road for the rest of the summer.

Check that your brake pads, chain and sprockets, and suspension are all in good working order before putting them on the track. Clean and adjust, and give your forks some fresh oil.

Your State of Mind

When you do your first track day you will be understandably nervous. The machine you're riding is worth thousands, your clothing and protective equipment a significant amount and you may or may not choose to take out insurance (track day insurance is available but for obvious reasons it's not cheap, and your standard insurance policy will not cover track day mishaps).

While you're not going out on track with the intention of hurting yourself, there is no doubt that a lot is at stake should you get it wrong. The first thing you should remember is that many of the people on the track day will be in the same position as you, that is they are looking to improve their riding skills, and many of them will be novices.

They may appear, by the clothes they are wearing and the bikes they are riding, to be experts, but don't be put off; they probably look better than they really are. Money spent does not equal ability.

It's also comforting to know that the organisers of track days make their living running these events so it is in their interest to run a tight ship. They are (at least in the UK) very good at it, and keep rowdy behaviour mostly under control. Here are some pointers to get you started and feeling comfortable on track:

1. **The instructors are there for your benefit.** Most track days have marshals who are racers or ex-racers, and who know the tracks well. They are available for tuition, typically at no extra cost. Speak to the marshals at the beginning of the day, and get them to follow you round and observe your riding and show you the racing lines. Don't wait until the end of the sessions.

2. **Get the line right and then increase your speed.** The beauty of riding around a race-track is the continuity of corners. This is great if you know the track, but if you don't you're going to have to learn it. Make sure that you take your time to learn the corners and the braking points, and increase your speed gradually throughout the day. Don't go for outright speed from the outset, let your tyres warm up over the first lap or two. Concentrate on getting your lines right and the speed and lean angles (and knee down if that happens) will come in due course. If you go out there trying to get your knee down to start with, you won't be going fast enough, and you will mess up your lines and cause a hazard for other riders. Getting your knee down is a consequence of riding fast, not the other way around. Try different lines and gradually get the measure of the track.

3. **Easy on the throttle.** When you're riding on the road you can get away with being ham-fisted with the throttle. The bike spends most of its time upright where large sudden throttle openings are fine. When the bike is leaned over – and you'll be leaning it over much more than normal on track – the tyres' grip can easily be overwhelmed by the application of too much throttle, resulting in a slide and a potential high-side. As we have discussed, the further over you lean the bike, the smaller and more gradually the throttle needs to be applied to avoid a skid. This doesn't mean that your revs have to be low, it's the size of throttle opening and the

resultant acceleration which matters. At higher engine speeds, the throttle will be more sensitive to your inputs, so begin by using a higher gear when cornering. It can feel odd in the beginning to have an engine which is running at very high revs but with a small throttle opening. Most of the time you hear an engine at high revs, it is in conjunction with a pinned open throttle, and the revs are rising rapidly. The grip which will overwhelm your rear tyre is about your rate of acceleration, which is about your throttle opening, not your engine speed.

4. **Hang off (a little).** If you are going to scrape your knee on the floor, a track day is the place to do it. In your daily road riding, it's unlikely that you will be able to go fast enough, and see far enough ahead to safely and comfortably get your knee down. You might be lucky enough to live in the middle of nowhere and have your own Shell Grip-covered roundabout to play with, but for the rest of us, big lean angles are most easily mastered on track. When you first start hanging off, it may feel uncomfortable, but it will become more familiar with practice. Weight the inside foot peg and grip the outside of the fuel tank with your other thigh and knee, and aim to get your bum-crack on the inside edge of the seat. As far as your upper body is concerned, a starting point is to get your head in line with the inside handlebar, as far forward as feels comfortable. As you lean the bike over, hold your knee out and skim your knee slider on the ground. Knee down comes naturally with increasing speed. Focus on going fast, not on getting your knee down.

5. **Get on the throttle early.** As you brake for your turn-in point and get the bike over on its side, when you reach your desired lean angle, very gently crack open the throttle to settle the bike. As you hit the apex you will need to reduce your rate of turn and start to pick the bike up. As you stand the bike more upright, less tyre grip is being used for cornering so it follows that more can be used to accelerate. Gradually wind the throttle on as you exit the corner and stand the bike upright. Riding the same track lap after lap after lap will give you a feel for how much throttle you can use when leaned over. Start out gently, and build your throttle openings up gradually, feeling how much grip you have available. This will depend of course on a number of factors: the track surface and temperature, tyre condition and tyre temperature. A track-day tyre should give you plenty of warning before it lets go completely, and if things start to move around, dial your throttle hand back a few turns.

6. **Don't turn too early**. One mistake many novice riders make on track is turning too early. Turning too early puts the rider on a poor line into and out of the corner. On the track, turning later means braking later. It also requires faster turning, so you'll need to steer the bike more quickly to get it turned, the deeper into a corner you go. As your speeds increase you will find yourself trail braking into the corner. The later you turn the better your line across the apex. If you are racing, then different rules apply, you will need to make a decision between the fast line and the defensive line.

7. **Use your legs**. When you ride on track you will be accelerating and braking hard all day. This can puts an enormous strain on your arms. Your arms and your hands are the means by which you get feedback from the bike, and apply your throttle, braking and steering inputs. Anything you can do to make life easier on your arms will help you over the course of the day. When braking for a corner and even while cornering use your legs to grip the tank. This leaves your arms free to operate the controls and feel what's going on under the bike. It also helps you to consciously relax your arms. Try to think of yourself as a jockey. You are riding the machine, but you want to stay out of the way and let the bike do its thing. Your legs have very strong muscles and will not tire as fast as your upper body.

8. **Look where you want to go**. Do you remember when you learned to ride a bicycle and on your first few attempts you managed to ride into a: tree-wall-dustbin-your dad's car (delete as appropriate). You got fixated on that object and as a result you ended up riding into it. We tend to go wherever our eyes are looking. When you are riding on track, keep your vision ahead of where you are, particularly when cornering, and you will be able to plan better. Try to keep your eyes on the track, regardless of what's happening in front of you. If you're focused on the person in front of you and he slides off in a flurry of sparks, you'd better get your eyes off him and onto the track, unless you want to join him for an early bath!

9. **Keep your fluids topped up**. I'm not talking about your motorbike running out of petrol. Riding on track is an extremely physical activity. Make sure throughout the day that you keep your body adequately hydrated. Try to keep your blood sugar levels up and if you drink tea and coffee, try to have a 'water chaser' after

each to keep your body hydrated. A good rule is to drink a 500ml bottle of water after every session. That way you'll know that you are hydrated enough. Dehydration can severely affect your performance. Riding on track is strenuous work, especially in the heat of summer whilst wearing a leather suit.

10. **Drop the Pressure**. When you ride on the road your tyres get off lightly. You rarely corner fast enough to get your tyres really hot. When you ride on track however your tyres get a real workout. To prevent them from over inflating, drop the pressure before you start the day. Ask the track day organisers or tyre experts present for advice and get them adjusted.

11. **Relax and Enjoy Yourself**. The most important thing you can do is have a relaxed fun attitude to the day. Putting too much pressure on yourself is going to take away from that fun. There is no rush. There will be plenty more opportunities to improve your riding and have fun on track. The most important thing is that you and your bike go home happy and in one piece.

12. **Find a Group which Works for You**. It won't come as a surprise when I say that male egos are fully on display at track days. Unfortunately this can manifest itself as aggressive and inappropriate riding. If you don't like the feel of a particular group, try to move to another one. If you feel that you have a difficult or dangerous rider in your group, give him a wide berth, and let the marshals know he's causing friction.

If you're getting your lines right and you've done a few track days, I would always recommend the Intermediate group over the Novice. The novices take strange lines and have a tendency to get under your feet, which can be dangerous. Ride with people who are at your level and things will work more smoothly.

Some track day operators are now introducing a wonderful idea where each bike has a transponder attached which measures its lap times. Riders are then moved into the most appropriate rider groups based upon how fast they circulate throughout the day. No more slick-tyres and tyre warmers in the 'novice' group then!

Other track day operators run 'road-bike only' track days which takes the pressure off even further. Bikes must have licence number plates and road tyres and drive to and from the circuit. Track bikes are not permitted. This is useful as often track-bike riders have less concern about binning it than someone who needs their bike to ride to work, and so tend to ride more aggressively.

There are a number of different tracks around the world and they vary in layout, elevation, and speed. Do your research, play them on a computer to get a feel for the track, and then go and ride them for real! Riding on track is seriously good fun, and will improve your road riding skills hugely. I cannot recommend it enough.

24. THE PILLION

As a biker, whether you like it or not, you are a local ambassador for your sport. Your skills and behaviour as a rider will attract all sorts of attention, both male and female, and you will be keen to show other people what all the fuss is about.

When you take a pillion, you have in your hands the care and well-being of another person, and while you probably want to show them 'what it can do', remember that your passenger may have never experienced motorbikes before. Even if they are a seasoned driver, they will not be accustomed to the brutal acceleration we bikers take for granted.

Go easy on them, and give them a bit of a taste of your bike's performance, but not so much that you scare them. You wouldn't want to put them off either biking, or you. If they climb off the back with a smile, having experienced a taste of the thrill and excitement of motorcycling, you will have succeeded. If you take it easy, and follow some basic ground rules, you'll have a lot of fun and share an exciting experience together. If you're trying to impress a woman, your attitude and leadership aboard are what will stir her loins, not having a near death experience.

Your passenger and their movement have a huge effect on the bike's handling, so go easy if you're not used to carrying a pillion, as it takes a while to get used to. Adding another 50kg to a 250kg package increases its weight by 20 percent. Clearly this large, dynamic weight will affect the way the bike handles. It will turn in more slowly, accelerate slower, and require longer distances to stop comfortably. If you are taking a novice pillion and they are holding onto your waist, you will also have their weight to contend with as you try to operate the controls.

I always do a quick toolbox talk before taking a pillion out. I tell them only to get on and off the bike when directed by me, I ask them to keep their feet on the footpegs at all times and I give them a means of telling me if they want me to slow down or stop, like a tap on the shoulder or a gentle squeeze.

I ask my pillion to lean with me and the bike as we corner, following the line of my body as the bike leans into the turn. It is surprising how many pillions think that they have to lean to the outside of the turn, which can be quite a surprise when you realise that your bike isn't steering round the corner as you thought it might.

The pillion, as extra weight over the back wheel, allows the use of more rear brake without locking up the rear tyre. The bike is also more likely to power-wheelie when accelerating hard in first gear, if you and your passenger like that kind of thing! Instead of chopping the throttle and coming down with a clunk, apply a gentle dab of the rear brake to bring the front down smoothly.

If you routinely ride with a pillion passenger, think about getting a grab rail for them to hold on to. A grab rail will leave you free to ride without having to deal with the weight of your pillion under acceleration and braking. It shouldn't be seen as an opportunity to ride as fast as you normally do. It's much easier to stay on a bike by holding something in front of you than holding something behind. If they're struggling with the rear grab handle, they might put one arm around your waist for accelerating, and use the rear grab rail when braking, taking the strain off your arms.

Try to be as smooth with the throttle and brakes as possible. You know when you're going to accelerate and brake, but your pillion doesn't. Try to make your gearchanges almost imperceptible. If your passenger is bashing heads with you, you could do with improving your throttle control. Anything you can do to make your passenger feel relaxed will improve the overall experience; a calm passenger is a bit like a sack of potatoes on the back, they just sit there merrily. An edgy passenger is a fidgeting, moving package, which adds to the nervousness of the whole experience.

You can buy special seat coverings from a company called Triboseat, a rubberized mesh which is strung over the rear pillion seat and provides friction that helps the pillion stay put, reducing the force required to hold on. This makes both of your lives easier. You don't have to contend with pushing and pulling on your waist, and your pillion can use their weight to do the heavy lifting (remember $F=\mu W$). Provided the coefficient of friction μ is sticky enough, the pillion's weight W will create a significant friction force at the seat surface.

Also available are pillion grab handles which are worn around the waist of the rider, and provide easy to reach handles for the pillion to hold on to. This sounds good in practice but I'm not sure I'd like to have to contend with the full weight of my passenger pulling on my body while accelerating and braking. I suppose it is a useful feedback to keep your riding speeds down. You may be able to easily manage the accelerating and braking forces of your own body, but what about if you suddenly have an additional 30-50kg either pulling you back or pushing you forward.

25. TOURING

Twenty years from now you will be more
disappointed by the things that you didn't do than by
the ones you did do, so throw off the bowlines, sail
away from safe harbour, catch the trade winds in
your sails. Explore. Dream. Discover.

\-   *Mark Twain*

If you've never taken your bike on a long trip, you're missing out on real adventure. There's something wonderful about the feeling of covering vast distances on such a small machine with the bare minimum of provisions. When you break down life to its basic constituent parts, you realise how little you need to feel satisfied, and how the clutter in your life slows you down.

You can end up hundreds, or even thousands of miles away from the safety and security of home, and yet feel buoyed by your own ability to navigate the world, and the kindness of the people you meet along the way.

The weather, the foreign sights, sounds and smells, the local people, the exotic food, the entertainment, and of course, the empty roads are all out there waiting for you to enjoy them. The majority of the world's population live in cities, and while they are busy fighting over postage stamp sized plots of urban land, the bulk of the planet is still largely a great big open space.

Motorcycle touring can take many forms; from travelling out on a warm weekend to a nearby county, to heading away for six months with a tent, a sleeping bag and no plans other than a return date. Everything is up to you;

the bike you ride, how far you go, how long you take, and what you do when you get there.

Some people like to stop along the way and do some sightseeing. Others like to spend as much time as possible in the saddle, riding day after day. All I can encourage you to do is get out on your bike and experience some relative wilderness. It offers a release from modern life, and a taste of the calm and serenity of nature.

To Plan or Not to Plan

So what's this trip going to look like? Well, you could take a week off work, giving yourself nowhere to be, and nothing to do and make it up as you go along. Alternatively you could pre-book your trip. Each style has its own merits, but when taking to the road, I find it nice to relax into a sense that life will show me the way.

If your daily life is strictly controlled and regimented, let your touring holiday be an exercise in letting go for a week. See what happens. Try to be more trusting of the world, and its people, and a bit more free and easy with your decision-making. If you fancy staying somewhere another night, do it. If you meet a nice girl and want to hang around for another day, do it. If you don't like a place, move on somewhere else. It's your life, and your choice.

For your first trip, booking ahead for at least a few initial dates will give you something to aim for, and stop you from worrying too much about where you're going to be sleeping tonight. That way you can enjoy the ride and the scenery along the way. If you are travelling in peak season, then booking is recommended as there will be lots of demand and not much supply.

True Satisfaction

At the end of a day's riding, having covered 250-300 miles, when you climb off your bike, take your boots off and lie down on the cool clean sheets of your hotel bed, and take a hot shower before heading out for a few cold beers, life doesn't get much better than that.

You take a trip out to explore the local town, to meet the people, sample the hospitality of the locals and a little nightlife. Life on the open road is good, it is fresh and new, and without the baggage of daily life. The usual reminders of reality are absent, and being free of your daily clutter and habitual thoughts gives a feeling of soaring.

At home, you may be buried by a mountain of stuff which you thought you wanted, but when you're on the open road living out of a bag with nothing but a credit card and a toothbrush, life seems altogether simpler. You feel lighter and freer. You realise how little you actually need to enjoy life.

My advice is pack as little as possible. You will always pack too much, unless you're going for a week and there's no laundry en-route to wash your underpants; in which case focus on underwear and dark coloured T-shirts. Pack a light comfy pair of shoes to give your feet a rest from your riding boots, and a pair of jeans for casual wear and hot weather riding, otherwise try to use warm clothes which won't take up too much precious space.

The Lone Ranger

Touring on your own is a special brand of travelling, but it is not for the faint-hearted. If you do travel abroad on your own, you will definitely come back a different person. Solo touring is an experience of more trust, and more serenity than usual. The great thing about travelling alone is that you go at your own pace. Nothing is rushed. You decide when to stay and when to move on.

Travelling alone also makes you more open. When you travel in a pair or as a group, you may be less likely to meet and befriend strangers. You also don't have anyone to distract you from your own peace and quiet. It's just you. Befriend yourself. I promise you that you will like yourself more than you think.

Some people use their machine as the excuse for not having been touring. The reality is you don't need the latest BMW R1200GS. You can tour on almost anything from a Honda Melody step-through (though it's best to avoid motorways), to the latest superbike. Even modern large capacity scooters make excellent touring machines. Drop the excuses and hit the road.

One of the major reasons I love to ride is escapism. If you're after the perfect tool to escape your daily life on, and you keep finding excuses to visit your 'man cave' at the bottom of the garden to enjoy a bit of solitude, solo touring will be right up your street.

After a day in the saddle, I like my creature comforts, so I tend to stay in B&B's and hotels. There's no denying camping is cheaper, especially in Scandinavia (camping in Scandinavia anyone?) but this is supposed to be a holiday after all, so save up a bit longer, and economise in other ways; skip breakfast or lunch, drink lots of water instead. Spend your money of petrol, hotels, beer and a nice evening meal. If your hotel has a complimentary continental breakfast, knock yourself up a ham and cheese roll and have it at lunch.

Packing List

Besides your usual riding paraphernalia, a typical packing list might include the following:

✓ Your Passport (make sure it's in date with at least three months

    left)
- ✓ Insurance green card from your insurer (if you're going abroad)
- ✓ Credit Cards (as many as you have)
- ✓ Puncture Repair kit plus mini compressed-gas bottles
- ✓ Underwear (pants, socks, dark T-shirts)
- ✓ One pair of dark jeans
- ✓ One pair smartish comfortable shoes (as light and small as possible and good enough for eating out and clubbing)
- ✓ Micro-fleece + neck warmer
- ✓ Wraparound sunglasses
- ✓ Map – preferably with the best routes on it, GPS, or mapping app on your phone
- ✓ Chain lube (a little bottle of engine oil is good)
- ✓ Spare ignition key and immobiliser fob (keep these in a separate place or give to your buddy to look after if travelling in a pair)
- ✓ Spare battery for your immobiliser fob (ideally change it before you go)
- ✓ Bungee cords and cargo net (in case you buy a cuckoo clock)
- ✓ Black gaffer tape and cable ties for emergency repairs
- ✓ Heated jacket (ideal for long days in the saddle even in summer)
- ✓ iPod (ideally with sound isolating ear phones to block out wind noise)
- ✓ Ear Plugs - essential to keep noise fatigue at bay
- ✓ Phone & charger to stay in touch
- ✓ Camera or video camera to record your travels
- ✓ A basic itinerary. And remember to tell your loved ones where you're going, and when you're planning to return.

Luggage

If you can put the majority of your luggage on the bike, whether in a tank bag, tail pack or hard luggage, you will appreciate having no rucksack to tire your shoulders. If you do need to wear a rucksack, buy one with a chest strap to distribute the load across your shoulders.

Packing lightly yields later rewards. Even if you've got the space to fill, you're still going to have to cart your stuff around when you get to your destination; and the more load you are carrying, the more it will affect your bike's handling.

Hard luggage is available for most sport touring and touring bikes. They're secure and waterproof but add significant weight to the bike.

Even for supersport bikes, there are luggage systems worth checking out, but they tend to be soft luggage. A fixed weight carried high up and far back can cause weaving ... a dangerous and uncontrollable oscillation of the bike about its centre. This is probably why hard luggage is not sold for supersport bikes. Soft luggage may not be as convenient, or waterproof, but it is much lighter and will not affect your handling.

When it comes to planning a journey, try to keep things flexible around major dates like ferry tickets or Eurotunnel crossings. For mainland Europe from the UK, Dover to Calais – either train or ferry – will give the most flexibility. You can often just turn up and get on, due to frequent crossings.

Add up fuel costs, time in the saddle and hotel costs when working out whether another overseas route might be cheaper e.g. Harwich-Esbjerg, Portsmouth-Caen, or even Plymouth-Santander. They can save you a day's riding, a hotel, motorway tolls, fuel and tyre wear.

A night on a ferry might cost you the price of a cabin, but if you look at it as a combination of a hotel and travelling expenses, an overnight ferry can kill two birds with one stone (e.g. the Oslo to Copenhagen overnight ferry knocks out some serious miles of your return leg to the UK from Norway).

If you have to be back home in two weeks, explore as far as you can without putting yourself under too much time pressure. Change your plans to suit the weather, and ride the roads that you think are going to be good (the meandering ones in and around the mountain ranges are a good place to start).

Major roads in France, Germany and Spain are all pretty good, minor roads are typically not so great, but they are on a par with the UK's neglected tarmac. Too much B and C road riding will get tiresome on a sports bike; so if you have hard suspension, try to stick to major roads if you're aiming to cover 250+ miles in a day.

Service your Bike

Before you go on a long trip, give your bike a thorough going over, consider servicing it to make sure that everything is in good condition, and check that the tyres will last the distance. If you're in any doubt, replace them.

Make sure your basics are in order; spark plugs are in good condition, brake pads have plenty of life left, oil and filter have been changed recently. Check throttle and clutch cables to make sure they are all in good condition and lubricated.

Thoroughly check all essential bolts for tightness; axle pinch bolts, rear axle, caliper mounting bolts, side-stand bolts etc. If when checking them with a torque wrench, you find they have come loose, consider applying some thread-lock before tightening again. Having a rear brake caliper bolt fall out in the middle of nowhere is not the end of the world, but it is not ideal either.

This bike is going to be your companion for the next several days and several thousand miles, and the last thing you want is for something to go wrong when you're in the middle of Sweden only to find the nearest dealer is 500 miles away and he's closed on a Monday.

Sometimes we take for granted the UK's dealer network, and visiting a country with one tenth of the population but five times the size means bike dealers are fewer and farther in between. On a trip to Sweden, a good friend and I were trying to diagnose his poor running bike. We couldn't find a local bike shop, let alone a Honda dealer, which was open on the weekend. The nearest thing was a garden centre selling everything from ironmongery to ride-on mowers. I had a rear brake caliper mounting bolt fall out, and had to improvise with a chopstick and some cables ties until I could get back to the UK. Don't plan for emergencies (if you do, you may find your planning pays off), but do check that you and your bike are up to the task before heading off.

If you are strapping on soft luggage, protect your bike's bodywork with several layers of black gaffer tape, or a soft mat. Touring bikes are better than race-bikes in this regard because they are designed to carry luggage. The continual rubbing motion of a bungee can wear through glossy paintwork in no time, so protect vulnerable areas where bungee cords or hooks run.

Donde Vas?

Given a seemingly endless choice of places to go, where do you start? Well, firstly, you don't have to go abroad. If you live in the UK, Wales and Scotland provide some fabulous roads, and with fewer people than England they're generally much emptier. The main benefit is you don't need to hop on a ferry to get there.

When riding at home, you are aware of the traffic laws and comfortable with the roads and the driving standards of the locals. You will have access to local currency, (hopefully) speak the language, and can get back home easily. If you go abroad, all of this will be new to some extent.

When looking overseas, in places like France, Germany and Spain, I like to explore the foothills to the mountains and the mountainous regions themselves, as the roads there are more interesting. In France, the Massif Centrale, Pyrenees, and Alps and surrounding foothills are awesome scenically and the roads are usually in good condition. The weather is also usually good in the Mediterranean. If I'm looking for inspiration, I get out the relief map and head for the bumpy bits.

26. THE ZEN RIDER

Engage your emotions at work. Your instincts and
your emotions are there to help you

-   Sir Richard Branson

The majority of 'how-to' guides are based around aiming for a particular outcome. This one is no different. I have only my experience, gathered over many years, to offer. These are things that you can practice and apply to your riding in order to stay safe and have more fun out on the road.

If you want to play a sport, you must first understand the rules and then play by them. The same goes for travelling about on the roads at speed; you need to understand the rules of the road so that you can get satisfaction from playing the game.

What most onlookers miss however, is the personal element to the activity. The majority of plane crashes are caused by pilot error. The same is true of motorcycles. This is a good thing, really! If you realise that you are in charge, then it takes away the randomness of life, and your sense of vulnerability.

I believe very strongly in training. Good skills will get you far, but what really matters much more than good technique is the attitude of the individual, the frame of mind from which they make their decisions.

An action-based approach to riding falls apart because there are too many variables to consider and try to accommodate. Trying to teach someone to be successful by telling them what to do is a waste of time. Life cannot be reduced to an instruction manual, if it were there would only be one book on every subject; the bible of riding motorcycles, and everyone could just follow the word.

But as we know life doesn't happen life that. Life is truly a personal experience, something each of us is acutely aware of, and we wouldn't have it any other way. An individual's journey is totally unique to him. He must carve out his own life in the manner of his choosing, by deciding what he wants and then going after it. The sooner this realisation dawns the sooner satisfaction will follow. It might happen when you're ten, it might happen when you're 70. It comes to us all eventually.

A how to guide cannot be an endless list of dos and don'ts. How could you ever possibly learn all of the eventualities? By the time you had finished analysing the hazards, calculated and practiced your evasive manoeuvres, and calculated your odds of survival, you would most likely have talked yourself out of learning to ride altogether.

'Sir, the possibility of successfully navigating an asteroid field is approximately three thousand seven hundred and twenty to one!'

'Never tell me the odds.'

-   C3PO and Han Solo

Riding can be a fun, cheeky, slightly rebellious activity, or you can play it strictly by the book. The character of the person behind the handlebars sets the tone. This is your life, and your call. You can push the envelope if you choose. You have free will. Your palm is on the throttle, and your fingers are on the brake lever, and you get to choose how fast you go, and what is appropriate for you.

If you believe that your life is not your own, and you have placed your safety and well-being into the hands of others (the government, law makers, other motorists); if you're looking outside of yourself to try to control the conditions of the world, we still have much work to do.

You cannot stop other people from doing what they are doing, and you cannot get the government to legislate on your behalf either. But what you can do is give yourself the best possible chance of identifying trouble, and steering clear of it, or even better not getting into that trouble in the first place.

Pushing the Envelope

At various points in your biking career, you will move beyond your comfort zone. You will enter unchartered, uncomfortable territory. At this point you can choose to rein in your aspirations, or you can choose to keep pushing on. Most people like a bit of drama in their life, and they are usually prepared to put up with the consequences.

A bystander watching the Isle of Man TT races might feel incredible fear for the riders who are participating in the racing, consider they have lost their minds, or have no sense of self preservation. But a quick conversation with the racers tells a different story.

A veteran TT rider with numerous podiums under his belt feels at home lapping the island at 120mph average speed. That's not to say he doesn't have to focus to do what he does, but he certainly isn't trembling with fear. He may be apprehensive and excited to be starting the race, and like a performance athlete, is visualising the course, the movements required, and weighing up how hard he can push, depending on how good he is feeling. He is up to speed with what he is doing, and if he can get in the zone, he'll have a good day at the races.

Winning in life is about psychology, knowing that you can – or perhaps not knowing that you can't (young upstarts!). You need to have the ability, but plenty of people have ability, what you need is desire, and belief that you can achieve what you are seeking. If you want something, and you move towards it while steadily remaining in a state of satisfaction, you will progress, day by day, moment by moment towards your goal.

Once the TT is underway, that rider knows he has a job to do, and he knows that total focus is necessary to win. Once the flag drops, he gets on with the task he has been trained to do. He pushes as hard as he feels comfortable. It is a tough race physically, but the real work is mental. It's about focus.

Road racers don't win on day one. It's a progressive journey, building up skills from a young age, racing at smaller tracks, honing machine control and anticipation skills, then learning the 37.73-mile Isle of Man TT track corner by corner again and again until it is second nature.

The speeds gradually rise, and the confidence with it. Eventually these speeds feel comfortable, normal even. The thrill is in the focus, rather than the fight-or-flight adrenaline rush of impending death. Just as the tennis world number one gets a thrill placing a tennis ball exactly where he intends to, a motorcycle racer gets an equal thrill placing a motorcycle exactly where he wants at 190mph.

The TT racer is operating at a much higher level than most motorcyclists, but that doesn't make him crazy. The rider who feels fear but who pushes forward into a place that doesn't feel good is asking for trouble, and he can feel it in the pit of his stomach. It doesn't matter whether you are a road rider, a road racer, a World Superbike Champion or a Motocross rider. If you put yourself out there all alone, you are asking for a pasting, and you'll probably get one. You know what I'm talking about.

When you start to ride, your friends and family may view your choice with concern. Smile and nod, but hold fast to your own vision of where you are heading and what you want to achieve in life.

What anyone else thinks about what you want has little bearing on your life, unless you take their opinions into consideration. If you focus on what you want, you will get there. If you focus on what they want then you mess up your own focus, and your own path to what you want, and you get a version of what they want for you. They're well-meaning of course, but it's really none of their business what you do with your life.

Own it

If we take responsibility for ourselves and expect others to do the same, rather than playing the blame game like little children, we find ourselves in a much better space to negotiate life. I am a big advocate of getting clued up, after all I went to the effort of writing this book, but I am much more interested in you developing a sense that you can guide yourself to whatever you need to be successful, rather than listening to what I have to say. I don't know what you want, or what you've lived, and I don't know how good you are. You know how good you are, and how you can find your way to each and every thing that you want. Follow your own guidance, not mine, not your parents' and not your lover's.

Be the kind of rider you want to be. Make your own luck out on the roads. Be a self-empowered rider, a happy person who appreciates life, loves riding, someone who makes good decisions; a winner. Let the grumpy chuntering ones have something to grumble about.

Death is a part of life on the roads, but that doesn't mean that it needs to happen to you before you've had your fun. We are all going to die one day, but 'accidents' are never really that. They are the culmination of a multitude of factors, originating in the psyche of the person riding, and every resulting bad decision up to the final one which caused the event.

If we take responsibility for our actions and their consequences, at least we are in charge of creating our own success. Would you rather be in charge or your own life even if you weren't making a good job of it, or have someone else in charge of your life doing what they thought was best for you?

If we accept that we have the power to direct our own lives, then we are in charge. The alternative is living an uncertain and random life where we are at the mercy of others' intentions, wishes and impulses. Of course we get it wrong, and the successful biker owns the bad as well as the good, but the fact remains crashes are caused by poor rider judgement.

My accidents and incidents have always happened when I was in a bad mood, in a mental fuzz, or lost my temper and was unable to think clearly. I may have woken up feeling terrible and just hit the ground running, or had a bad day at the office and not taken the time to calm myself down before climbing aboard. Turning the key and riding off in a frustrated, slightly manic frame of mind is never likely to end well.

When I'm calm and centred, I can feel that all is going to be well on my ride, and it is. I know that I am in a much better frame of mind to deal with the road conditions, and with anything other drivers can throw at me. I have the clarity of mind to predict situations, to anticipate hazards, as all of my senses are working to their fullest. I'm firing on all cylinders, and so is my bike.

When I am in a bad mood, my judgement is impaired, and I am bound to make poor decisions. Decisions which have resulted in motorcycles being stolen, or road accidents involving other vehicles.

If you could take one thing away from this book let it be this: *Only ride when you are in a good mood.* If you can't get into a good mood, don't ride, or do whatever it takes to get back into a good frame of mind.

You know how to cheer yourself up, talk to your children or your sweetheart, watch some comedy, stop listening to the news and avoid politics. There are simple easy things that you can do to feel good every day, so stop making excuses and just do them.

Ditch friends that you've outgrown and grow the balls to tell those who ride like an accident waiting to happen that you'd rather not. Lead yourself away from trouble towards satisfaction, and make no apologies for yourself.

Nobody is ever going to fully get you. You're too unique. Stop trying to get them to understand you, and just be your brilliant self and make a success of your life on the terms that please you.

If you follow this simple advice, you will find yourself protected out of the roads, not by some kind of guardian angel, but by your own good sense of what to do in any given moment, based upon your own good judgement.

As you stay in a place of satisfaction, by avoiding dissatisfying things, and doing satisfying ones, you will recognise you have a heightened sense of awareness of the world around you. People who complain in life generally get more to complain about, whereas people who appreciate life live wonderful lives. How many grumpy millionaires have you met? They're not satisfied because they're rich, they're rich because they found a way to be satisfied where they were and they moved into greater and greater satisfaction little by little, day by day, until they became the person they are today.

If I get exasperated by another's actions, and feel the need to chase them down to give them a piece of my mind, as I feel the tension rising, I try to remind myself what is important. I've been there before, and done that, and it didn't end well. I learn from my mistakes and aim to keep myself in as good a mood as I can whilst riding.

I don't find myself getting frustrated as often nowadays, but I do still get bummed out about life and other drivers, but I try not to act on those impulses anymore. If the situation has come to a fight, and you're dealing with an unreasonable person, you cannot reason with them. They are by definition unreasonable.

There's no shame in walking away from a fight. There's nothing to be gained by getting into a road rage incident with anyone, it will not end in a civilised discussion, and it will just give you something to rant about, to continue to fight about another day. If it doesn't feel satisfying, leave it alone.

Story of a Motorcycle Theft

On the day my motorcycle was stolen, I awoke in a not-very-good mood, and didn't take the time before setting off to get myself into a better headspace. I didn't meditate, I just hit the ground running. I was on the verge of a bad mood, and anything could set me off.

As I filtered down the long lines of traffic on the A40 into London, a particularly bold rider came past me, so close that he actually knocked my mirror forwards. Now I expect some bad behaviour from car drivers, but from one of my own brothers? That was completely disrespectful and rude! I was outraged, and attempted to chase him down to give him a piece of my mind. I didn't manage to catch up with 'kamikaze rider', but by the time I got to work, I was properly fuming; there may have been actual steam coming out of my ears.

It was then that I realised that I'd left my car park pass at home, so had no access to the secure motorcycle parking. At this stage I should have put two and two together and just gone back home, but instead I persevered. Feeling angry, I parked up my motorcycle in a street bay, and not having taken a lock, I just had to leave it there in the street.

Returning to the parking bay after work, my bike was gone. All of my actions, from getting up in the morning and forgetting my pass, to parking in this particular bay had all been poorly made, and had led to this eventual outcome. I wasn't in a clear-minded state where I could even make good judgements, and I had let someone else's erratic behaviour pull me into a state of mind I didn't want. And so I suffered the consequences.

Looking back, it could just as easily have been an accident that came my way that day, but I guess I wasn't' feeling that bad. Just frustrated and outraged and disrespected, which perfectly matched the feeling I felt when my beloved motorcycle was stolen, and the police couldn't seem to care less.

What I should have done was not get sucked into someone else's angry morning. I didn't appreciate the riding, but apart from having my personal space invaded, and my wing mirror knocked, there was no harm done. I could have pulled back, and carried on my way as happily as possible. When I got to work, I would have been in a better frame of mind to find a more appropriate parking solution for my bike, having left my pass behind;

perhaps waiting for someone else to appear so that they could let me in, or finding a secure manned car park nearby, or finding a chain in a nearby motorcycle shop. All of these options were not open to the angry, annoyed person who cannot think clearly. We live and learn.

So I try not to ride in a bad mood. If I do have to ride when I'm feeling rotten, I aim to relax rather than take it out on the bike or other road users. I focus on riding as smoothly as I can, or I focus on the controls, or I look for something to appreciate in the scenery or the weather or a nice car on the road. I try to focus on anything to distract me from the things that are bothering me, and before long I forget what it is I was worrying about.

Biker Boyz

A successful motorcycle career, whether racer, Sunday rider or commuter, begins and ends with your attitude. How do you see yourself as a biker? Are you a safety conscious 'by-the-book' type rider? Do you read Motorcycle Road Craft every night before you drift off under your Kawasaki Green duvet cover? Do you stick to the speed limits, or are you a 'superfast nutter', 'one of the boyz' or do you have a piss pot lid and a pair of ape hangers fitted to your Harley?

If you have built up some kind of persona, if you are using motorcycling as a mask or public image or a reason to 'belong'; don't get carried away with who you think you are. Once we label ourselves as a 'type', we can often forfeit the opportunity to act genuinely. But we always have a choice to do the right thing. Don't get carried away with yourself, and who you think other people think you are, and you are more likely to stay out of trouble.

Mental Warm-up

Before you climb aboard your magnificent motorcycle, warm yourself up mentally for the task ahead. Spend the time that your bike is warming up to appreciate your machine, to appreciate the roads, and the fact that you can go anywhere in the UK on this tiny collection of metal, plastic and rubber.

Appreciate your own nimble reactions and the wonderful riding skills that you have learned over the years, to pilot this powerful and potent machine so well. Appreciate that you can still go down to a local bike dealership and buy a machine as fun as this for a few thousand pounds. These are good times. Set off for your ride with a sense of appreciation, and you will have a much more enjoyable time.

Don't use motorcycling to make you feel good. Feel good, and then experience motorcycling. The same goes for food, sex, work, alcohol, basically anything else you might be using to medicate away a feeling of dissatisfaction.

A couple of minutes of appreciation will put you in the perfect mood to have a great ride. When you feel good, you flow in and out of traffic smoothly and effortlessly. You are totally at one with your machine rarely feeling a sense of fear or concern. You give other road users the benefit of the doubt, and you usually find yourself in a place where you can anticipate their actions anyway.

Try to avoid a 'high horse' attitude; pointing out crappy driving. Rather than trying to re-educate the rest of the world (which could take a while) instead put your full commitment into improving your own riding skills. You will become more aware of your own shortcomings (let he who is without sin cast the first stone), and probably less tolerant of poor driving standards too. Even your own.

Your skills and experience will grow with each ride, and you will soon bring yourself to a place where you feel like a solid, comfortable and relaxed rider. You will feel confident and sure of your growing talent and ability, and you will feel that you can handle any issue you may encounter on the roads. You might be inspired to take a training course, or attend a track day or cornering masterclass, or you might come across a book, article or video which reveals some useful insights to questions that you have been asking.

Staying out of Trouble

While I'll admit riding a litre bike on the road is going to have you travelling around extremely quickly, there's really no reason to attract the unwanted attention of the police or anyone else for that matter.

Modern motorbikes are designed to go fast, and it feels right to ride them that way. But there is a time and a place. Speed is sometimes appropriate and sometimes inappropriate, and you generally know which is which, so I don't need to tell you about that. Develop and learn to rely upon your own judgement.

All bikers hold something that most car drivers lack; an acute sense of self-preservation. When I suggest that friends take up motorcycling and they reply, 'I'd love to, but I would just kill myself', they clearly don't understand what it is like to ride a motorcycle. Bikers are both powerful and vulnerable, and those who are able to balance these two emotions keep themselves out of trouble.

Successful bikers are constantly aware of the risks involved, but are more capable of filtering the information they receive, and can call upon a vast bank of riding experience to inform their decision-making. Unlike cars, motorcycles provide immense feedback so the rider knows exactly where he is and what he is doing. We each find a comfortable place where we can have our thrills and still feel in control.

Fit for Purpose

For high performing athletes to be operating at the top of their game 'in the zone', they need to have certain things going for them. Physical fitness is a given, as are a good diet and adequate hydration, but the captain of the ship must also be in his right mind for the operation to be a success.

Athletes use positive thinking and visualisation to achieve their goals. Jorge Lorenzo meditates to put himself into a centred place so he can focus on his racing. If you're worrying about what might go wrong when you ride, you're clearly doing the opposite.

Your mind is always the weak link. That's right, you are actually the main source of danger to yourself. Not the car drivers, not the police, and not blind nonagenarian motorists in Land Rovers who should have been taken off the roads years ago. Let them all go on their merry ways, and you go on yours, taking responsibility for your life. Once you make the decision that you are in charge, you will find yourself in a lot less trouble.

So to sum up this chapter:

-   Learning to ride is a life-long pursuit. What's the rush? Expand your ability gradually, focus on what you want to achieve and you will get there. Aim to stay as satisfied as you can in every moment, and yours will be a really fun journey.

-   Ride only when you feel in a good mood, and while riding, do what you need to do in order to stay feeling good. If you are due to go for a ride and you feel annoyed, try to get yourself in a better mood before heading off; watch some comedy, spend some time with your children or pets, mow the lawn, listen to some music.

-   Ride for your own pleasure, and not to impress anyone else. If you don't like your riding partners or you feel their behaviour is inappropriate, deliberately take a wrong turn and get yourself 'lost'. Find some new friends, or experience the bliss of riding on your own.

-   When riding, learn to use your gut instinct more to guide your actions. If your gut is screaming DANGER! Don't move forward, wait for a better opportunity.

-   Have fun! This is all a bit serious, but if you can make it your priority to have fun, everything else generally takes care of itself.

27. FUTURE MOTO

Since the invention of the compact internal-combustion engine gave power to the bicycle and the motor-cycle was born, motorbikes have not really changed a great deal. They are still articulated two wheeled vehicles, driven from the rear, and lean towards the inside of the turn to get around corners.

I suppose once something like this is invented, the concept can only be refined, until a new fundamental basis is created. For example, to reduce the risk of a front wheel skid, some manufacturers have created motorcycles with two front wheels, while others have stuck to a single front wheel but employ clever electronics which restrict the accelerating and braking forces applied based upon what the bike is doing in any moment - the information being gathered on multiple axes via Inertia Measurement Units (IMU) and wheel sensors.

Those refinements to the basic technology have been gradual and superb, and bikes now go much faster, accelerate and brake more rapidly and corner better than ever. Here are a few tech items which will become more commonly used over the next decade:

Supercharging

Modern high capacity normally aspirated car engines are one by one being replaced by supercharged and turbocharged designs. Cubic centimetres are literally being blown out of the marketplace in the name of emissions reduction. While emissions regulations are less stringent for motorcycles, we may still see turbocharging and supercharging making a comeback.

Take Kawasaki's flagship bike, the Supercharged H2R. The supercharger is preferential to the turbocharger in a motorcycle as it is mechanically driven off the engine and so delivers a more linear boost pressure.

The issue with turbocharging motorcycles is that turbos lack the responsiveness and instant drive of a normally aspirated engine which is so essential to achieve fine throttle control. Turbocharged and supercharged systems also add bulk and weight, and most motorcycles are already full, so adding anything else creates a packaging problem. Given the strides made in automotive turbocharging, where the best engines lack any noticeable delay in throttle response, perhaps we will see a return to turbocharging on two wheels.

Active Suspension

Active suspension has made its way onto BMW's class leading litre bikes; first the HP4, and then the S1000RR, and its naked brother S1000R. Many other manufacturers have followed suit, and the top of the range sports bikes have adaptive Öhlins forks and rear shock. This system adjusts damping rates on the move to suit road conditions and riding style. The rider sets the suspension mode and the bike uses different parameters to adjust the damping to suit.

The system can provide soft and supple damping when cruising along upright at a constant speed, but when you crank it over and start to become more aggressive with the throttle, it recognises your change of intentions, and tightens the damping to suit. The system can work out whether the bike is braking or accelerating, the angle of lean, and the road surface smoothness, and it adjusts the damping accordingly.

Cornering ABS

The majority of modern motorbikes incorporate ABS as a safety feature. German automotive firm Bosch has developed a 'Cornering ABS' system in conjunction with KTM which is now sold to many motorcycle manufacturers and is available on a variety of bikes.

Cornering ABS adjusts the braking force if the brakes are applied while cornering. It can also apply rear brake to counteract the tendency of a bike to stand up if the front brake is used mid-corner. By braking the rear the suspension geometry remains the same and the bike can steer its course.

Hitting the brakes mid corner used to spell disaster, but with cornering ABS you can hit the brakes mid-turn and the bike will comfortably come to a stop, without standing up, and without crashing. Are we heading towards a truly un-crashable bike? Maybe, but we still have the rider to contend with.

Dual-Clutch-Gearbox (DCT)

I love manual transmissions in cars and motorbikes. They give a far greater sense of control of the machine, through both acceleration and engine braking, and they are much more involving than an automatic transmission. The manual gearbox is a wonderful piece of mechanical engineering, but it has evolved into the DCT, Dual Clutch Transmission.

The DCT is essentially two transmissions in one, which seamlessly swap duties as you change gear. The Dual Clutch Transmission has two clutches, one for odd gears first, third and fifth (and reverse), the other for second, fourth and sixth. The first DCT appeared in 2003 in the VW Golf R32.

In 2009 the brand new Honda VFR1200F was launched with an optional DCT. The second refinement of the six speed DCT appeared in the NC700, where it is perfect. The NC700 engine is half of a Honda Jazz engine; hence it revs to only 6500 rpm. The bike was designed as an economical workhorse; a twist-and-go motorcycle with a storage compartment much like a scooter. The parallel-twin engine has a 270-degree crank offset to emulate a 90-degree V-twin, giving the engine a bit more character. Seventy mpg is easily achievable.

Many modern sports bikes are being fitted with quick-shifters and auto-blippers for seamless, clutchless up- and downshifts. While these are great, I expect that in the future, the motorcycle gear-lever will work both as manual and automatic, in conjunction with a dual clutch transmission. If you want to work the gears, you can via the normal method. If you don't, you can just put it in one of the many driving modes (eco, sport, race) and let the bike change gear for you.

Electric Vehicles

The TT-Zero race at the Isle of Man hints at a very real future which will be with us in no time at all; electric motorcycles. Electric Vehicles (EVs) are currently hampered by heavy battery technology, but as charge density improves, and with it power to weight ratio, electric technology will take off in a big way.

Alternative fuels such as hydrogen have their supporters. I can see their appeal in an internal combustion engine layout, as the technology can be retrofitted to petrol engines. Others cite hydrogen fuel cells as the future, giving us a comfortable intermediate step between liquid fuels and electric power.

Given the rate at which auto manufacturers are embracing EVs, and at which battery technology is improving, I have no doubt that electric vehicles will be dominant in the future. As EVs gain popularity and sales, manufacturers will increase R&D budgets. When the money really starts to flow, we will see the electric vehicle technology development accelerate.

Modern electric cars and scooters are expensive to buy, but cheap to run. The main barrier to uptake is vehicle range (battery life). They can only manage around 60-100 miles per charge depending on usage. Scooters and town cars will be a popular first choice for EV technology, but as energy storage technology, wireless charging and wireless power transmission are developed, EV technology will extend to much larger vehicles.

Wireless charging is one concept which fascinates me. Imagine that the roads were like giant Scalextric tracks, with inductive charging loops in the road surface, and that the vehicles travelling down them were being powered (or recharged) wirelessly from the road. If we can receive data energy wirelessly, why can't we transmit power in the same way? Have a look at Drayson Racing Technologies and the work they have been doing with Qualcomm. It is fascinating stuff.

Manufacturers will focus on saving weight to extend battery life. Forward-looking auto makers Nissan, Toyota, Renault and BMW have all heavily invested in electric-vehicle technology. BMW realises the key element is improving range, most easily gained by reducing vehicle weight.

Rather than bolting an electric motor and battery pack into a steel shell designed for an internal combustion engine, BMW has developed the i3 and i8, dedicated electric hybrid vehicles which make extensive use of carbon-fibre-reinforced plastic (CFRP) in their construction. BMW have also released an electric scooter, the C-Evolution, which borrows technology directly from the i3; it holds three of the i3 battery modules in an alloy casing which also serves as the chassis.

BMW is investing heavily in R&D to reduce production costs of CFRP for the mass market. Carbon-fibre will certainly be used in larger quantities in the future, but expect to see materials like Graphene developed and used for its light weight and high strength.

Removing the Chains

As much as I appreciate motorcycles, there are some elements which seem prehistoric. Chains and sprockets are surely the most outdated technology to still appear on a motorcycle, and I'm surprised we haven't come up with a better power transmission system by now. I can see why they prevail in racing – a simple change of chain and sprockets alters the final-drive gearing with ease.

Chains are noisy, cause vibration and poor drive. They need constant adjustment and lubrication, and seem out of place on a machine with traction control and ABS. I appreciate that shaft drives may not be preferred, but can't a new technology be developed which improves on these things? Perhaps a diesel-electric drive, where a small, heavily turbocharged diesel engine provides electric current to the drive motor mounted on the rear hub. In this case the chain has been replaced by an electric cable.

Climate Clothing

I am looking forward to the emergence of the climatically controlled jacket, it will be waterproof and windproof, but it will also offer heating and cooling. The suit is maintained at the desired temperature via a miniature heat pump powered by the motorcycle's battery, and delivered either via a fan blowing warm or cool air into the jacket, or by means of a coolant running through tubing in the jacket body.

Helmet Visor Auto-wiper

Another invention yet to make the bike show stands is the motorcycle helmet with integral windscreen wiper. I cannot express how much I am looking forward to this solution. Riding along in drizzle, or a wet slippery road surface one handed is not my idea of safety, so the sooner the 'left-hand wipe' is eliminated the better.

Speed Limits

As the world embraces the improvements in cost, safety and speed of automated transportation (driverless cars), it would be wonderful to see road safety campaigners curb their impulse to control and restrict others' behaviour. Motorcycling is about the thrill of riding, and it's fun to go fast. We should be allowed to do so as long as we cause no harm.

I have confidence in humanity. People are waking up to their own power. They want to be able to make decisions for themselves about what they do and how they live. They are not interested in being told what is best for them by others, who think they know better. People want to be free to choose for themselves, and once technology affords a more pure form of democracy to give the decision-making directly to the people, not only will they be properly engaged in the process, but they will become far more informed on the subjects.

Then we will start to see more freedom at the level of the individual. Of course the Highway Code will still apply – we need a set of rules to play the game – and inflicting harm on another will carry a heavy punishment, but victimless crimes such as speeding will be recognised for what they are: nothing more than revenue-raising measures which antagonise the public and destroy confidence in the police.

The relationship between the state and the individual will be refreshed as follows: As an individual living your specific life, you and you alone know what it deemed good and proper behaviour. Therefore the state places in your hands the trust of the wider society, to act in a socially responsible way, in the manner befitting a mature adult human being. Should you by dereliction of these duties, harm another, you will pay for that harm.

This simple shift in attitude will bring about, after an initial free-for-all, more responsible driving behaviour, and the appropriate use of speed. Those who fear motorcycles can opt out and choose the safety and security of the driverless car, while the rest of us can go on our merry ways, forging our own paths with satisfaction, each step along the way.

28. RECOMMENDED READING

The following are some recommended resources / reference material for further study:

Riding Technique / Rule

- The Highway Code (sounds basic but a huge amount of information in there)
- Sport Riding Techniques - Nick Ienatsch
- Twist of the Wrist 2 - Keith Code
- Motorcycle Roadcraft: The Police Rider's Handbook (2013)

Motorcycle Culture

- Hogs, Blogs, Leathers and Lattes: The Sociology of Modern American Motorcycling – William E Thompson

Suspension Setup

- Sportbike Suspension Tuning - Andrew Trevitt
- Race Tech's Motorcycle Suspension Bible - Paul Thede & Lee Parks

Technology

- Neil Spalding - MotoGP Technology
- Sportbike Performance Handbook - Kevin Cameron

Riding Courses

- Ady Smith Offroad and Supermoto Schools
- California Superbike School
- BikeSafe London
- IAM Roadsmart